OCT 12

The Collected Shorter Plays

WORKS BY SAMUEL BECKETT PUBLISHED BY GROVE PRESS

Collected Poems in English and French

The Collected Shorter Plays
(All That Fall, Act Without Words I,
Act Without Words II, Krapp's Last Tape,
Rough for Theatre I, Rough for Theatre II,
Embers, Rough for Radio I, Rough for
Radio II, Words and Music, Cascando,
Play, Film, The Old Tune, Come and Go,
Eh Joe, Breath, Not I, That Time, Footfalls,
Ghost Trio, . . . but the clouds . . . , A Piece
of Monologue, Rockaby, Ohio Impromptu,
Quad, Catastrophe, Nacht and Träume,
What Where)

The Complete Short Prose: 1929–1989,
edited by S. E. Gontarski
(Assumption, Sedendo et Quiescendo,
Text, A Case in a Thousand, First Love, The
Expelled, The Calmative, The End, Texts for
Nothing 1–13, From an Abandoned Work,
The Image, All Strange Away, Imagination
Dead Imagine, Enough, Ping, Lessness,
The Lost Ones, Fizzles 1–8, Heard in the
Dark 1, Heard in the Dark 2, One Evening,
As the story was told, The Cliff, neither,
Stirrings Still, Variations on a "Still" Point,
Faux Départs, The Capital of the Ruins)

Disjecta: Miscellaneous Writings and
a Dramatic Fragment

Endgame and Act Without Words

First Love and Other Shorts

Grove Centenary Editions
Volume I: Novels
(Murphy, Watt, Mercier and Camier)
Volume II: Novels
(Molloy, Malone Dies, The Unnamable,
How It Is)
Volume III: Dramatic Works
Volume IV: Poems, Short Fiction, Criticism

Happy Days

Happy Days: Production Notebooks

How It Is

I Can't Go On, I'll Go On:
A Samuel Beckett Reader

Krapp's Last Tape
(All That Fall, Embers, Act Without Words I,
Act Without Words II)

Mercier and Camier

Molloy

More Pricks Than Kicks
(Dante and the Lobster, Fingal, Ding-Dong,
A Wet Night, Love and Lethe, Walking Out,
What a Misfortune, The Smeraldina's Billet
Doux, Yellow, Draff)

Murphy

Nohow On
(Company, Ill Seen Ill Said, Worstward Ho)

Proust

The Shorter Plays: Theatrical Notebooks,
edited by S. E. Gontarski
(Play, Come and Go, Eh Joe, Footfalls, That
Time, What Where, Not I)

Stories and Texts for Nothing
(The Expelled, The Calmative, The End,
Texts for Nothing 1–13)

Three Novels
(Molloy, Malone Dies, The Unnamable)

Waiting for Godot

Waiting for Godot: A Bilingual Edition

Waiting for Godot: Theatrical Notebooks

Watt

Samuel Beckett

The Collected
Shorter Plays

Grove Press
New York

Printed in the United States of America

Design and textual supervision by Laura Lindgren

ISBN: 978-0-8021-4438-6

Library of Congress Catalog Card Number 60-8388

Grove Press
an imprint of Grove/Atlantic, Inc.
841 Broadway
New York, NY 10003

DISTRIBUTED BY PUBLISHERS GROUP WEST
WWW.GROVEATLANTIC.COM

10 11 12 13 14   10 9 8 7 6 5 4 3 2 1

All That Fall 1

Act Without Words I 35

Act Without Words II 41

Krapp's Last Tape 47

Rough for Theatre I 59

Rough for Theatre II 69

Embers 85

Rough for Radio I 103

Rough for Radio II 111

Words and Music 125

Cascando 135

Play 147

Film 163

The Old Tune 177

Come and Go 193

Eh Joe 199

Breath 209

Not I 213

That Time 225

Footfalls 235

Ghost Trio 243

... but the clouds ... 253

A Piece of Monologue 261

Rockaby 269

Ohio Impromptu 281

Quad 287

Catastrophe 293

Nacht und Träume 301

What Where 305

Notes 315

The Collected
Shorter Plays

ALL THAT FALL

A play for radio

Mrs. Rooney (Maddy), a lady in her seventies
Christy, a carter
Mr. Tyler, a retired bill-broker
Mr. Slocum, Clerk of the Racecourse
Tommy, a porter
Mr. Barrell, a station-master
Miss Fitt, a lady in her thirties
A Female Voice
Dolly, a small girl
Mr. Rooney (Dan), husband of Mrs. Rooney, blind
Jerry, a small boy

Rural sounds. Sheep, bird, cow, cock, severally, then together.

Silence.

Mrs. Rooney advances along country road towards railway station. Sound of her dragging feet.

Music faint from house by way. "Death and the Maiden."

The steps slow down, stop.

MRS. ROONEY   Poor woman. All alone in that ruinous old house.
              [*Music louder. Silence but for music playing. The steps resume. Music dies. Mrs. Rooney murmurs, melody. Her murmur dies.*
              Sound of approaching cartwheels. The cart stops.
              The steps slow down, stop.]
              Is that you, Christy?

CHRISTY   It is, Ma'am.

MRS. ROONEY   I thought the hinny was familiar. How is your poor wife?

CHRISTY   No better, Ma'am.

MRS. ROONEY   Your daughter then?

CHRISTY   No worse, Ma'am.
          [*Silence.*]

MRS. ROONEY   Why do you halt? [*Pause.*] But why do I halt? [*Silence.*]

CHRISTY   Nice day for the races, Ma'am.

MRS. ROONEY   No doubt it is. [*Pause.*] But will it hold up? [*Pause. With emotion.*] Will it hold up?
[*Silence.*]

CHRISTY   I suppose you wouldn't—

MRS. ROONEY   Hist! [*Pause.*] Surely to goodness that cannot be the up mail I hear already.
[*Silence. The hinny neighs. Silence.*]

CHRISTY   Damn the mail.

MRS. ROONEY   Oh thank God for that! I could have sworn I heard it, thundering up the track in the far distance. [*Pause.*] So hinnies whinny. Well, it is not surprising.

CHRISTY   I suppose you wouldn't be in need of a small load of dung?

MRS. ROONEY   Dung? What class of dung?

CHRISTY   Stydung.

MRS. ROONEY   Stydung . . . I like your frankness, Christy. [*Pause.*] I'll ask the master. [*Pause.*] Christy.

CHRISTY   Yes, Ma'am.

MRS. ROONEY   Do you find anything . . . bizarre about my way of speaking? [*Pause.*] I do not mean the voice. [*Pause.*] No, I mean the words. [*Pause. More to herself.*] I use none but the simplest words, I hope, and yet I sometimes find my way of speaking very . . . bizarre. [*Pause.*] Mercy! What was that?

CHRISTY   Never mind her, Ma'am, she's very fresh in herself today.
[*Silence.*]

MRS. ROONEY   Dung? What would we want with dung, at our time of life? [*Pause.*] Why are you on your feet down on the road? Why do you not climb up on the crest of your manure and let yourself be carried along? Is it that you have no head for heights?
[*Silence.*]

CHRISTY   [*to the hinny*] Yep! [*Pause. Louder.*] Yep wiyya to hell owwa that!

[*Silence.*]

MRS. ROONEY   She does not move a muscle. [*Pause.*] I too should be
getting along, if I do not wish to arrive late at the
station. [*Pause.*] But a moment ago she neighed and
pawed the ground. And now she refuses to advance.
Give her a good welt on the rump. [*Sound of welt.
Pause.*] Harder! [*Sound of welt. Pause.*] Well! If someone
were to do that for me I should not dally. [*Pause.*] How
she gazes at me to be sure, with her great moist
cleg-tormented eyes! Perhaps if I were to move on,
down the road, out of her field of vision. . . . [*Sound of
welt.*] No, no, enough! Take her by the snaffle and pull
her eyes away from me. Oh this is awful! [*She moves on.
Sound of her dragging feet.*] What have I done to deserve
all this, what, what? [*Dragging feet.*] So long ago. . . . No!
No! [*Dragging feet. Quotes.*] "Sigh out a something
something tale of things, Done long ago and ill done."
[*She halts.*] How can I go on, I cannot. Oh let me just
flop down flat on the road like a big fat jelly out of a
bowl and never move again! A great big slop thick
with grit and dust and flies, they would have to scoop
me up with a shovel. [*Pause.*] Heavens, there is that up
mail again, what will become of me! [*The dragging steps
resume.*] Oh I am just a hysterical old hag I know,
destroyed with sorrow and pining and gentility and
church-going and fat and rheumatism and
childlessness. [*Pause. Brokenly.*] Minnie! Little Minnie!
[*Pause.*] Love, that is all I asked, a little love, daily, twice
daily, fifty years of twice daily love like a Paris horse-
butcher's regular, what normal woman wants
affection? A peck on the jaw at morning, near the ear,
and another at evening, peck, peck, till you grow
whiskers on you. There is that lovely laburnum again.
[*Dragging feet. Sound of bicycle-bell. It is old Mr. Tyler*

coming up behind her on his bicycle, on his way to the station. Squeak of brakes. He slows down and rides abreast of her.]

MR. TYLER   Mrs. Rooney! Pardon me if I do not doff my cap, I'd fall off. Divine day for the meeting.

MRS. ROONEY   Oh, Mr. Tyler, you startled the life out of me stealing up behind me like that like a deer-stalker! Oh!

MR. TYLER   [*playfully*] I rang my bell, Mrs. Rooney, the moment I sighted you I started tinkling my bell, now don't you deny it.

MRS. ROONEY   Your bell is one thing, Mr. Tyler, and you are another. What news of your poor daughter?

MR. TYLER   Fair, fair. They removed everything, you know, the whole . . . er . . . bag of tricks. Now I am grandchildless.
[*Dragging feet.*]

MRS. ROONEY   Gracious how you wobble! Dismount, for mercy's sake, or ride on.

MR. TYLER   Perhaps if I were to lay my hand lightly on your shoulder, Mrs. Rooney, how would that be?
[*Pause.*] Would you permit that?

MRS. ROONEY   No, Mr. Rooney, Mr. Tyler I mean, I am tired of light old hands on my shoulders and other senseless places, sick and tired of them. Heavens, here comes Connolly's van! [*She halts. Sound of motor-van. It approaches, passes with thunderous rattles, recedes.*] Are you all right, Mr. Tyler? [*Pause.*] Where is he? [*Pause.*] Ah there you are! [*The dragging steps resume.*] That was a narrow squeak.

MR. TYLER   I alit in the nick of time.

MRS. ROONEY   It is suicide to be abroad. But what is it to be at home, Mr. Tyler, what is it to be at home? A lingering dissolution. Now we are white with dust from head to foot. I beg your pardon?

MR. TYLER   Nothing, Mrs. Rooney, nothing, I was merely cursing, under my breath, God and man, under my breath, and the wet Saturday afternoon of my conception. My back tyre has gone down again. I pumped it hard as iron before I set out. And now I am on the rim.

MRS. ROONEY   Oh what a shame!

MR. TYLER   Now if it were the front I should not so much mind. But the back. The back! The chain! The oil! The grease! The hub! The brakes! The gear! No! It is too much!
[*Dragging steps.*]

MRS. ROONEY   Are we very late, Mr. Tyler? I have not the courage to look at my watch.

MR. TYLER   [*bitterly*] Late! I on my bicycle as I bowled along was already late. Now therefore we are doubly late, trebly, quadrupedly late. Would I had shot by you, without a word.
[*Dragging feet.*]

MRS. ROONEY   Whom are you meeting, Mr. Tyler?

MR. TYLER   Hardy. [*Pause.*] We used to climb together. [*Pause.*] I saved his life once. [*Pause.*] I have not forgotten it.
[*Dragging feet. They stop.*]

MRS. ROONEY   Let us halt a moment and let this vile dust fall back upon the viler worms.
[*Silence. Rural sounds.*]

MR. TYLER   What sky! What light! Ah in spite of all it is a blessed thing to be alive in such weather, and out of hospital.

MRS. ROONEY   Alive?

MR. TYLER   Well half alive shall we say?

MRS. ROONEY   Speak for yourself, Mr. Tyler. I am not half alive nor anything approaching it. [*Pause.*] What are we standing here for? This dust will not settle in our time. And when it does some great roaring machine will come and whirl it all skyhigh again.

MR. TYLER   Well, shall we be getting along in that case?

MRS. ROONEY   No.

MR. TYLER   Come, Mrs. Rooney—

MRS. ROONEY   Go, Mr. Tyler, go on and leave me, listening to the cooing of the ringdoves. [*Cooing.*] If you see my poor blind Dan tell him I was on my way to meet him when it all came over me again, like a flood. Say to him, Your poor wife, she told me to tell you it all came flooding over her again and . . . [*the voice breaks*] . . . she simply went back home . . . straight back home. . . .

MR. TYLER   Come, Mrs. Rooney, come, the mail has not yet gone up, just take my free arm and we'll be there with time and to spare.

MRS. ROONEY   [*sobbing*] What? What's all this now? [*Calmer.*] Can't you see I'm in trouble? [*With anger.*] Have you no respect for misery? [*Sobbing.*] Minnie! Little Minnie!

MR. TYLER   Come, Mrs. Rooney, come, the mail has not yet gone up, just take my free arm and we'll be there with time and to spare.

MRS. ROONEY   [*brokenly*] In her forties now she'd be, I don't know, fifty, girding up her lovely little loins, getting ready for the change. . . .

MR. TYLER   Come, Mrs. Rooney, come, the mail—

MRS. ROONEY   [*exploding*] Will you get along with you, Mr. Rooney, Mr. Tyler I mean, will you get along with you now and cease molesting me? What kind of a country is this where a woman can't weep her heart out on the highways and byways without being tormented by retired bill-brokers! [*Mr. Tyler prepares to mount his bicycle.*] Heavens you're not going to ride her flat! [*Mr. Tyler mounts.*] You'll tear your tube to ribbons! [*Mr. Tyler rides off. Receding sound of bumping bicycle. Silence. Cooing.*] Venus birds! Billing in the woods all the long summer long. [*Pause.*] Oh cursed corset! If I

could let it out, without indecent exposure. Mr. Tyler!
Mr. Tyler! Come back and unlace me behind the
hedge! [*She laughs wildly, ceases.*] What's wrong with
me, what's wrong with me, never tranquil, seething
out of my dirty old pelt, out of my skull, oh to be in
atoms, in atoms! [*Frenziedly.*] ATOMS! [*Silence. Cooing.
Faintly.*] Jesus! [*Pause.*] Jesus! [*Sound of car coming up
behind her. It slows down and draws up beside her, engine
running. It is Mr. Slocum, the Clerk of the Racecourse.*]

MR. SLOCUM   Is anything wrong, Mrs. Rooney? You are bent all
double. Have you a pain in the stomach?
[*Silence. Mrs. Rooney laughs wildly. Finally.*]

MRS. ROONEY   Well if it isn't my old admirer the Clerk of the Course,
in his limousine.

MR. SLOCUM   May I offer you a lift, Mrs. Rooney? Are you going in my
direction?

MRS. ROONEY   I am, Mr. Slocum, we all are. [*Pause.*] How is your poor
mother?

MR. SLOCUM   Thank you, she is fairly comfortable. We manage to keep
her out of pain. That is the great thing, Mrs. Rooney,
is it not?

MRS. ROONEY   Yes, indeed, Mr. Slocum, that is the great thing, I don't
know how you do it. [*Pause. She slaps her cheek violently.*]
Ah these wasps!

MR. SLOCUM   [*coolly*] May I then offer you a seat, Madam?

MRS. ROONEY   [*with exaggerated enthusiasm*] Oh that would be heavenly,
Mr. Slocum, just simply heavenly. [*Dubiously.*] But
would I ever get in, you look very high off the ground
today, these new balloon tyres I presume. [*Sound of
door opening and Mrs. Rooney trying to get in.*] Does this
roof never come off? No? [*Efforts of Mrs. Rooney.*]
No. . . . I'll never do it . . . you'll have to get down,
Mr. Slocum, and help me from the rear. [*Pause.*]
What was that? [*Pause. Aggrieved.*] This is all your

suggestion, Mr. Slocum, not mine. Drive on, Sir, drive on.

MR. SLOCUM   [*switching off engine*] I'm coming, Mrs. Rooney, I'm coming, give me time, I'm as stiff as yourself. [*Sound of Mr. Slocum extracting himself from driver's seat.*]

MRS. ROONEY   Stiff! Well I like that! And me heaving all over back and front. [*To herself.*] The dry old reprobate!

MR. SLOCUM   [*in position behind her*] Now, Mrs. Rooney, how shall we do this?

MRS. ROONEY   As if I were a bale, Mr. Slocum, don't be afraid. [*Pause. Sounds of effort.*] That's the way! [*Effort.*] Lower! [*Effort.*] Wait! [*Pause.*] No, don't let go! [*Pause.*] Suppose I do get up, will I ever get down?

MR. SLOCUM   [*breathing hard*] You'll get down, Mrs. Rooney, you'll get down. We may not get you up, but I warrant you we'll get you down.

[*He resumes his efforts. Sound of these.*]

MRS. ROONEY   Oh! . . . Lower! . . . Don't be afraid! . . . We're past the age when . . . There! . . . Now! . . . Get your shoulder under it. . . . Oh! . . . [*Giggles.*] Oh glory! . . . Up! Up! . . . Ah! . . . I'm in! [*Panting of Mr. Slocum. He slams the door. In a scream.*] My frock! You've nipped my frock! [*Mr. Slocum opens the door. Mrs. Rooney frees her frock. Mr. Slocum slams the door. His violent unintelligible muttering as he walks round to the other door. Tearfully.*] My nice frock! Look what you've done to my nice frock! [*Mr. Slocum gets into his seat, slams driver's door, presses starter. The engine does not start. He releases starter.*] What will Dan say when he sees me?

MR. SLOCUM   Has he then recovered his sight?

MRS. ROONEY   No, I mean when he knows, what will he say when he feels the hole? [*Mr. Slocum presses starter. As before. Silence.*] What are you doing, Mr. Slocum?

MR. SLOCUM   Gazing straight before me, Mrs. Rooney, through the windscreen, into the void.

MRS. ROONEY   Start her up, I beseech you, and let us be off. This is awful!

MR. SLOCUM   [*dreamily*] All morning she went like a dream and now she is dead. That is what you get for a good deed. [*Pause. Hopefully.*] Perhaps if I were to choke her. [*He does so, presses the starter. The engine roars. Roaring to make himself heard.*] She was getting too much air! [*He throttles down, grinds in his first gear, moves off, changes up in a grinding of gears.*]

MRS. ROONEY   [*in anguish*] Mind the hen! [*Scream of brakes. Squawk of hen.*] Oh, mother, you have squashed her, drive on, drive on! [*The car accelerates. Pause.*] What a death! One minute picking happy at the dung, on the road, in the sun, with now and then a dust bath, and then— bang!—all her troubles over. [*Pause.*] All the laying and the hatching. [*Pause.*] Just one great squawk and then . . . peace. [*Pause.*] They would have slit her weasand in any case. [*Pause.*] Here we are, let me down. [*The car slows down, stops, engine running. Mr. Slocum blows his horn. Pause. Louder. Pause.*] What are you up to now, Mr. Slocum? We are at a standstill, all danger is past and you blow your horn. Now if instead of blowing it now you had blown it at that unfortunate—
[*Horn violently. Tommy the porter appears at top of station steps.*]

MR. SLOCUM   [*calling*] Will you come down, Tommy, and help this lady out, she's stuck.
[*Tommy descends the steps.*] Open the door, Tommy, and ease her out. [*Tommy opens the door.*]

TOMMY   Certainly, Sir. Nice day for the races, sir. What would you fancy for—

MRS. ROONEY Don't mind me. Don't take any notice of me. I do not exist. The fact is well known.

MR. SLOCUM Do as you're asked, Tommy, for the love of God.

TOMMY Yessir. Now, Mrs. Rooney.

[*He starts pulling her out.*]

MRS. ROONEY Wait, Tommy, wait now, don't bustle me, just let me wheel round and get my feet to the ground. [*Her efforts to achieve this.*] Now.

TOMMY [*pulling her out*] Mind your feather, Ma'am. [*Sounds of effort.*] Easy now, easy.

MRS. ROONEY Wait, for God's sake, you'll have me beheaded.

TOMMY Crouch down, Mrs. Rooney, crouch down, and get your head in the open.

MRS. ROONEY Crouch down! At my time of life! This is lunacy!

TOMMY Press her down, sir. [*Sounds of combined efforts.*]

MRS. ROONEY Pity!

TOMMY Now! She's coming! Straighten up, Ma'am! There!

[*Mr. Slocum slams the door.*]

MRS. ROONEY Am I out?

[*The voice of Mr. Barrell, the station-master, raised in anger.*]

MR. BARRELL Tommy! Tommy! Where the hell is he? [*Mr. Slocum grinds in his gear.*]

TOMMY [*hurriedly*] You wouldn't have something for the Ladies Plate, sir? I was given Flash Harry.

MR. SLOCUM [*scornfully*] Flash Harry! That carthorse!

MR. BARRELL [*at top of steps, roaring*] Tommy! Blast your bleeding bloody— [*He sees Mrs. Rooney.*] Oh, Mrs. Rooney. . . . [*Mr. Slocum drives away in a grinding of gears.*] Who's that crucifying his gearbox, Tommy?

TOMMY Old Cissy Slocum.

MRS. ROONEY Cissy Slocum! That's a nice way to refer to your betters. Cissy Slocum! And you an orphan!

MR. BARRELL [*angrily to Tommy*] What are you doing stravaging down here on the public road? This is no place for you at all! Nip up there on the platform now and whip out the truck! Won't the twelve thirty be on top of us before we can turn round?

TOMMY   [*bitterly*] And that's the thanks you get for a Christian act.

MR. BARRELL   [*violently*] Get on with you now before I report you! [*Slow feet of Tommy climbing steps.*] Do you want me to come down to you with the shovel? [*The feet quicken, recede, cease.*] Ah God forgive me, it's a hard life. [*Pause.*] Well, Mrs. Rooney, it's nice to see you up and about again. You were laid up there a long time.

MRS. ROONEY   Not long enough, Mr. Barrell. [*Pause.*] Would I were still in bed, Mr. Barrell. [*Pause.*] Would I were lying stretched out in my comfortable bed, Mr. Barrell, just wasting slowly, painlessly away, keeping up my strength with arrowroot and calves-foot jelly, till in the end you wouldn't see me under the blankets any more than a board. [*Pause.*] Oh no coughing or spitting or bleeding or vomiting, just drifting gently down into the higher life, and remembering, remembering . . . [*the voice breaks*] . . . all the silly unhappiness . . . as though . . . it had never happened. . . . What did I do with that handkerchief? [*Sound of handkerchief loudly applied.*] How long have you been master of this station now, Mr. Barrell?

MR. BARRELL   Don't ask me, Mrs. Rooney, don't ask me.

MRS. ROONEY   You stepped into your father's shoes, I believe, when he took them off.

MR. BARRELL   Poor Pappy! [*Reverent pause.*] He didn't live long to enjoy his ease.

MRS. ROONEY   I remember him clearly. A small ferrety purple-faced widower, deaf as a doornail, very testy and snappy. [*Pause.*] I suppose you'll be retiring soon yourself, Mr. Barrell, and growing your roses. [*Pause.*] Did I understand you to say the twelve thirty would soon be upon us?

MR. BARRELL	Those were my words.
MRS. ROONEY	But according to my watch which is more or less right—or was—by the eight o'clock news the time is now coming up to twelve . . . [*pause as she consults her watch*] . . . thirty-six. [*Pause.*] And yet upon the other hand the up mail has not yet gone through. [*Pause.*] Or has it sped by unbeknown to me? [*Pause.*] For there was a moment there, I remember now, I was so plunged in sorrow I wouldn't have heard a steam roller go over me. [*Pause. Mr. Barrell turns to go.*] Don't go, Mr. Barrell! [*Mr. Barrell goes. Loud.*] Mr. Barrell! [*Pause. Louder.*] Mr. Barrell! [*Mr. Barrell comes back.*]
MR. BARRELL	[*testily*] What is it, Mrs. Rooney, I have my work to do. [*Silence. Sound of wind.*]
MRS. ROONEY	The wind is getting up. [*Pause. Wind.*] The best of the day is over. [*Pause. Wind. Dreamily.*] Soon the rain will begin to fall and go on falling, all afternoon. [*Mr. Barrell goes.*] Then at evening the clouds will part, the setting sun will shine an instant, then sink, behind the hills. [*She realizes Mr. Barrell has gone.*] Mr. Barrell! Mr. Barrell! [*Silence.*] I estrange them all. They come towards me, uninvited, bygones bygones, full of kindness, anxious to help . . . [*the voice breaks*] . . . genuinely pleased . . . to see me again . . . looking so well. . . . [*Handkerchief.*] A few simple words . . . from my heart . . . and I am all alone . . . once more. . . . [*Handkerchief. Vehemently.*] I should not be out at all! I should never leave the grounds! [*Pause.*] Oh there is that Fitt woman, I wonder will she bow to me. [*Sound of Miss Fitt approaching, humming a hymn. She starts climbing the steps.*] Miss Fitt! [*Miss Fitt halts, stops humming.*] Am I then invisible, Miss Fitt? Is this cretonne so becoming to me that I merge into the masonry? [*Miss Fitt descends a step.*] That is right,

Miss Fitt, look closely and you will finally distinguish a once female shape.

MISS FITT   Mrs. Rooney! I saw you, but I did not know you.

MRS. ROONEY   Last Sunday we worshipped together. We knelt side by side at the same altar. We drank from the same chalice. Have I so changed since then?

MISS FITT   [*shocked*] Oh but in church, Mrs. Rooney, in church I am alone with my Maker. Are not you? [*Pause.*] Why even the sexton himself, you know, when he takes up the collection, knows it is useless to pause before me. I simply do not see the plate, or bag, whatever it is they use, how could I? [*Pause.*] Why even when all is over and I go out into the sweet fresh air, why even then for the first furlong or so I stumble in a kind of daze as you might say, oblivious to my co-religionists. And they are very kind I must admit—the vast majority—very kind and understanding. They know me now and take no umbrage. There she goes, they say, there goes the dark Miss Fitt, alone with her Maker, take no notice of her. And they step down off the path to avoid my running into them. [*Pause.*] Ah yes, I am distray, very distray, even on week-days. Ask Mother, if you do not believe me. Hetty, she says, when I start eating my doily instead of the thin bread and butter, Hetty, how can you be so distray? [*Sighs.*] I suppose the truth is I am not there, Mrs. Rooney, just not really there at all. I see, hear, smell, and so on, I go through the usual motions, but my heart is not in it, Mrs. Rooney, my heart is in none of it. Left to myself, with no one to check me, I would soon be flown . . . home. [*Pause.*] So if you think I cut you just now, Mrs. Rooney, you do me an injustice. All I saw was a big pale blur, just another big pale blur. [*Pause.*] Is anything amiss, Mrs. Rooney, you do not look normal somehow. So bowed and bent.

MRS. ROONEY   [*ruefully*] Maddy Rooney, née Dunne, the big pale blur. [*Pause.*] You have piercing sight, Miss Fitt, if you only knew it, literally piercing. [*Pause.*]

MISS FITT   Well . . . is there anything I can do, now that I am here?

MRS. ROONEY   If you would help me up the face of this cliff, Miss Fitt, I have little doubt your Maker would requite you, if no one else.

MISS FITT   Now, now, Mrs. Rooney, don't put your teeth in me. Requite! I make these sacrifices for nothing—or not at all. [*Pause. Sound of her descending steps.*] I take it you want to lean on me, Mrs. Rooney.

MRS. ROONEY   I asked Mr. Barrell to give me his arm, just give me his arm. [*Pause.*] He turned on his heel and strode away.

MISS FITT   Is it my arm you want then? [*Pause. Impatiently.*] Is it my arm you want, Mrs. Rooney, or what is it?

MRS. ROONEY   [*exploding*] Your arm! Any arm! A helping hand! For five seconds! Christ what a planet!

MISS FITT   Really. . . . Do you know what it is, Mrs. Rooney, I do not think it is wise of you to be going about at all.

MRS. ROONEY   [*violently*] Come down here, Miss Fitt, and give me your arm, before I scream down the parish! [*Pause. Wind. Sound of Miss Fitt descending last steps.*]

MISS FITT   [*resignedly*] Well, I suppose it is the Protestant thing to do.

MRS. ROONEY   Pismires do it for one another. [*Pause.*] I have seen slugs do it. [*Miss Fitt proffers her arm.*] No, the other side, my dear, if it's all the same to you, I'm left-handed on top of everything else. [*She takes Miss Fitt's right arm.*] Heavens, child, you're just a bag of bones, you need building up. [*Sound of her toiling up steps on Miss Fitt's arm.*] This is worse than the Matterhorn, were you ever up the Matterhorn, Miss Fitt, great honeymoon resort. [*Sound of toiling.*] Why don't they have a handrail? [*Panting.*] Wait till I get some air. [*Pause.*]

Don't let me go! [*Miss Fitt hums her hymn. After a moment Mrs. Rooney joins in with the words.*] . . . the encircling gloo-oom . . . [*Miss Fitt stops humming.*] . . . tum tum me on. [*Forte.*] The night is dark and I am far from ho-ome, tum tum—

MISS FITT   [*hysterically*] Stop it, Mrs. Rooney, stop it, or I'll drop you!

MRS. ROONEY   Wasn't it that they sung on the *Lusitania*? Or Rock of Ages? Most touching it must have been. Or was it the *Titanic*?

[*Attracted by the noise a group, including Mr. Tyler, Mr. Barrell and Tommy, gathers at top of steps.*]

MR. BARRELL   What the— [*Silence.*]

MR. TYLER   Lovely day for the fixture.

[*Loud titter from Tommy cut short by Mr. Barrell with backhanded blow in the stomach. Appropriate noise from Tommy.*]

A FEMALE VOICE   [*shrill*] Oh look, Dolly, look!

DOLLY   What, Mamma?

A FEMALE VOICE   They are stuck! [*Cackling laugh.*] They are stuck!

MRS. ROONEY   Now we are the laughing-stock of the twenty-six counties. Or is it thirty-six?

MR. TYLER   That is a nice way to treat your defenceless subordinates, Mr. Barrell, hitting them without warning in the pit of the stomach.

MISS FITT   Has anyone seen my mother?

MR. BARRELL   Who is that?

TOMMY   The dark Miss Fitt.

MR. BARRELL   Where is her face?

MRS. ROONEY   Now, deary, I am ready if you are. [*They toil up remaining steps.*] Stand back, you cads! [*Shuffle of feet.*]

A FEMALE VOICE   Mind yourself, Dolly!

MRS. ROONEY   Thank you, Miss Fitt, thank you, that will do, just prop me up against the wall like a roll of tarpaulin and that will be all, for the moment. [*Pause.*] I am sorry for all this ramdam, Miss Fitt, had I known you were looking for your mother I should not have importuned you, I know what it is.

MISS FITT   [*in marvelling aside*] Ramdam!

A FEMALE VOICE   Come, Dolly darling, let us take up our stand before the first class smokers. Give me your hand and hold me tight, one can be sucked under.

MR. TYLER   You have lost your mother, Miss Fitt?

MISS FITT   Good morning, Mr. Tyler.

MR. TYLER   Good morning, Miss Fitt.

MR. BARRELL   Good morning, Miss Fitt.

MISS FITT   Good morning, Mr. Barrell.

MR. TYLER   You have lost your mother, Miss Fitt?

MISS FITT   She said she would be on the last train.

MRS. ROONEY   Do not imagine, because I am silent, that I am not present, and alive, to all that is going on.

MR. TYLER   [*to Miss Fitt*] When you say the last train—

MRS. ROONEY   Do not flatter yourselves for one moment, because I hold aloof, that my sufferings have ceased. No. The entire scene, the hills, the plain, the racecourse with its miles and miles of white rails and three red stands, the pretty little wayside station, even you yourselves, yes, I mean it, and over all the clouding blue, I see it all, I stand here and see it all with eyes . . . [*the voice breaks*] . . . through eyes . . . oh if you had my eyes . . . you would understand . . . the things they have seen . . . and not looked away . . . this is nothing . . . nothing . . . what did I do with that handkerchief? [*Pause.*]

MR. TYLER   [*to Miss Fitt*] When you say the last train— [*Mrs. Rooney blows her nose violently and long.*] —when you say the last train, Miss Fitt, I take it you mean the twelve thirty.

MISS FITT   What else could I mean, Mr. Tyler, what else could I *conceivably* mean?

MR. TYLER   Then you have no cause for anxiety, Miss Fitt, for the twelve thirty has not yet arrived. Look. [*Miss Fitt looks.*] No, up the line. [*Miss Fitt looks. Patiently.*] No, Miss Fitt, follow the direction of my index. [*Miss Fitt looks.*] There. You see now. The signal. At the bawdy hour of nine. [*In rueful afterthought.*] Or three alas! [*Mr. Barrell stifles a guffaw.*] Thank you, Mr. Barrell.

MISS FITT   But the time is now getting on for—

MR. TYLER   [*patiently*] We all know, Miss Fitt, we all know only too well what the time is now getting on for, and yet the cruel fact remains that the twelve thirty has not yet arrived.

MISS FITT   Not an accident, I trust! [*Pause.*] Do not tell me she has left the track! [*Pause.*] Oh darling mother! With the fresh sole for lunch!

[*Loud titter from Tommy, checked as before by Mr. Barrell.*]

MR. BARRELL   That's enough old guff out of you. Nip up to the box now and see has Mr. Case anything for me.

[*Tommy goes.*]

MRS. ROONEY   Poor Dan!

MISS FITT   [*in anguish*] What terrible thing has happened?

MR. TYLER   Now now, Miss Fitt, do not—

MRS. ROONEY   [*with vehement sadness*] Poor Dan!

MR. TYLER   Now now, Miss Fitt, do not give way . . . to despair, all will come right . . . in the end. [*Aside to Mr. Barrell.*] What *is* the situation, Mr. Barrell? Not a collision surely?

MRS. ROONEY   [*enthusiastically*] A collision! Oh that would be wonderful!

MISS FITT   [*horrified*] A collision! I knew it!

MR. TYLER   Come, Miss Fitt, let us move a little up the platform.

MRS. ROONEY   Yes, let us all do that. [*Pause.*] No? [*Pause.*] You have changed your mind? [*Pause.*] I quite agree, we are better here, in the shadow of the waiting-room.

MR. BARRELL   Excuse me a moment.

MRS. ROONEY   Before you slink away, Mr. Barrell, please, a statement of some kind, I insist. Even the slowest train on this brief line is not ten minutes and more behind its scheduled time without good cause, one imagines. [*Pause.*] We all know your station is the best kept of the entire network, but there are times when that is not enough, just not enough. [*Pause.*] Now, Mr. Barrell, leave off chewing your whiskers, we are waiting to hear from you—we the unfortunate ticket-holders' nearest if not dearest. [*Pause.*]

MR. TYLER   [*reasonably*] I do think we are owed some kind of explanation, Mr. Barrell, if only to set our minds at rest.

MR. BARRELL   I know nothing. All I know is there has been a hitch. All traffic is retarded.

MRS. ROONEY   [*derisively*] Retarded! A hitch! Ah these celibates! Here we are eating our hearts out with anxiety for our loved ones and he calls that a hitch! Those of us like myself with heart and kidney trouble may collapse at any moment and he calls that a hitch! In our ovens the Saturday roast is burning to a shrivel and he calls that—

MR. TYLER   Here comes Tommy, running! I am glad I have been spared to see this.

TOMMY   [*excitedly, in the distance*] She's coming. [*Pause. Nearer.*] She's at the level-crossing!
[*Immediately exaggerated station sounds. Falling signals. Bells. Whistles. Crescendo of train whistle approaching. Sound of train rushing through station.*]

MRS. ROONEY   [*above rush of train*] The up mail! The up mail! [*The up mail recedes, the down train approaches, enters the station, pulls up with great hissing of steam and clashing of couplings. Noise of passengers descending, doors banging, Mr. Barrell shouting "Boghill! Boghill!," etc. Piercingly.*]

Dan! . . . Are you all right? . . . Where is he? . . . Dan!
Did you see my husband? . . . Dan! . . . [*Noise of station
emptying. Guard's whistle. Train departing, receding.
Silence.*] He isn't on it! The misery I have endured to
get here, and he isn't on it! . . . Mr. Barrell! . . . Was he
not on it? [*Pause.*] Is anything the matter, you look as
if you had seen a ghost. [*Pause.*] Tommy! . . . Did you
see the master?

TOMMY He'll be along, Ma'am, Jerry is minding him.
[*Mr. Rooney suddenly appears on platform, advancing on
small boy Jerry's arm. He is blind, thumps the ground with
his stick and pants incessantly.*]

MRS. ROONEY Oh, Dan! There you are! [*Her dragging feet as she hastens
towards him. She reaches him. They halt.*] Where in the
world were you?

MR. ROONEY [*coolly*] Maddy.

MRS. ROONEY Where were you all this time?

MR. ROONEY In the men's.

MRS. ROONEY Kiss me!

MR. ROONEY Kiss you? In public? On the platform? Before the boy?
Have you taken leave of your senses?

MRS. ROONEY Jerry wouldn't mind. Would you, Jerry?

JERRY No, Ma'am.

MRS. ROONEY How is your poor father?

JERRY They took him away, Ma'am.

MRS. ROONEY Then you are all alone?

JERRY Yes, Ma'am.

MR. ROONEY Why are you here? You did not notify me.

MRS. ROONEY I wanted to give you a surprise. For your birthday.

MR. ROONEY My birthday?

MRS. ROONEY Don't you remember? I wished you your happy returns
in the bathroom.

MR. ROONEY I did not hear you.

MRS. ROONEY But I gave you a tie! You have it on!

[*Pause.*]

MR. ROONEY How old am I now?

MRS. ROONEY Now never mind about that. Come.

MR. ROONEY Why did you not cancel the boy? Now we shall have to give him a penny.

MRS. ROONEY [*miserably*] I forgot! I had such a time getting here! Such horrid nasty people! [*Pause. Pleading.*] Be nice to me, Dan, be nice to me today!

MR. ROONEY Give the boy a penny.

MRS. ROONEY Here are two halfpennies, Jerry. Run along now and buy yourself a nice gobstopper.

JERRY Yes, Ma'am.

MR. ROONEY Come for me on Monday, if I am still alive.

JERRY Yessir.

[*He runs off.*]

MR. ROONEY We could have saved sixpence. We have saved fivepence. [*Pause.*] But at what cost?

[*They move off along platform arm in arm. Dragging feet, panting, thudding stick.*]

MRS. ROONEY Are you not well?

[*They halt, on Mr. Rooney's initiative.*]

MR. ROONEY Once and for all, do not ask me to speak and move at the same time. I shall not say this in this life again.

[*They move off. Dragging feet, etc. They halt at top of steps.*]

MRS. ROONEY Are you not—

MR. ROONEY Let us get this precipice over.

MRS. ROONEY Put your arm around me.

MR. ROONEY Have you been drinking again? [*Pause.*] You are quivering like a blancmange. [*Pause.*] Are you in a condition to lead me? [*Pause.*] We shall fall into the ditch.

MRS. ROONEY Oh, Dan! It will be like old times!

MR. ROONEY Pull yourself together or I shall send Tommy for the cab. Then instead of having saved sixpence, no, fivepence, we shall have lost ... [*calculating mumble*] ... two and three less six one and no plus one one and no plus three one and nine and one ten and three two and one ... [*normal voice*] two and one, we shall be the poorer to the tune of two and one. [*Pause.*] Curse that sun, it has gone in. What is the day doing?

[*Wind.*]

MRS. ROONEY   Shrouding, shrouding, the best of it is past. [*Pause.*] Soon the first great drops will fall splashing in the dust.

MR. ROONEY   And yet the glass was firm. [*Pause.*] Let us hasten home and sit before the fire. We shall draw the blinds. You will read to me. I think Effie is going to commit adultery with the Major. [*Brief drag of feet.*] Wait! [*Feet cease. Stick tapping at steps.*] I have been up and down these steps five thousand times and still I do not know how many there are. When I think there are six there are four or five or seven or eight and when I remember there are five there three or four or six or seven and when finally I realize there are seven there are five or six or eight or nine. Sometimes I wonder if they do not change them in the night. [*Pause. Irritably.*] Well? How many do you make them today?

MRS. ROONEY   Do not ask me to count, Dan, not now.

MR. ROONEY   Not count! One of the few satisfactions in life!

MRS. ROONEY   Not steps, Dan, please, I always get them wrong. Then you might fall on your wound and I would have that on my manure-heap on top of everything else. No, just cling to me and all will be well.

[*Confused noise of their descent. Panting, stumbling, ejaculations, curses. Silence.*]

MR. ROONEY   Well! That is what you call well!

MRS. ROONEY   We are down. And little the worse. [*Silence. A donkey brays. Silence.*] That was a true donkey. Its father and mother were donkeys.

[*Silence.*]

MR. ROONEY   Do you know what it is, I think I shall retire.

MRS. ROONEY   [*appalled*] Retire! And live at home? On your grant!

MR. ROONEY   Never tread these cursed steps again. Trudge this hellish road for the last time. Sit at home on the remnants of my bottom counting the hours—till the next meal. [*Pause.*] The very thought puts life in me! Forward, before it dies!

[*They move on. Dragging feet, panting, thudding stick.*]

MRS. ROONEY   Now mind, here is the path. . . . Up! . . . Well done! Now we are in safety and a straight run home.

MR. ROONEY   [*without halting, between gasps*] A straight . . . run! . . . She calls that . . . a straight . . . run! . . .

MRS. ROONEY   Hush! Do not speak as you go along, you know it is not good for your coronary. [*Dragging steps, etc.*] Just concentrate on putting one foot before the next or whatever the expression is. [*Dragging feet, etc.*] That is the way, now we are doing nicely. [*Dragging feet, etc. They suddenly halt, on Mrs. Rooney's initiative.*] Heavens! I knew there was something! With all the excitement! I forgot!

MR. ROONEY   [*quietly*] Good God!

MRS. ROONEY   But you must know, Dan, of course, you were on it. Whatever happened? Tell me!

MR. ROONEY   I have never known anything to happen.

MRS. ROONEY   But you must—

MR. ROONEY   [*violently*] All this stopping and starting again is devilish, devilish! I get a little way on me and begin to be carried along when suddenly you stop dead! Two hundred pounds of unhealthy fat! What possessed you to come out at all? Let go of me!

MRS. ROONEY   [*in great agitation*] No, I must know, we won't stir from here till you tell me. Fifteen minutes late! On a thirty minute run! It's unheard of!

MR. ROONEY   I know nothing. Let go of me before I shake you off.

MRS. ROONEY   But you must know! You were on it! Was it at the terminus? Did you leave on time? Or was it on the line? [*Pause.*] Did something happen on the line? [*Pause.*] Dan! [*Brokenly.*] Why won't you tell me! [*Silence. They move off. Dragging feet, etc. They halt. Pause.*]

MR. ROONEY   Poor Maddy! [*Pause. Children's cries.*] What was that? [*Pause for Mrs. Rooney to ascertain.*]

MRS. ROONEY   The Lynch twins jeering at us. [*Cries.*]

MR. ROONEY   Will they pelt us with mud today, do you suppose? [*Cries.*]

MRS. ROONEY   Let us turn and face them. [*Cries. They turn. Silence.*] Threaten them with your stick. [*Silence.*] They have run away.
[*Pause.*]

MR. ROONEY   Did you ever wish to kill a child? [*Pause.*] Nip some young doom in the bud. [*Pause.*] Many a time at night, in winter, on the black road home, I nearly attacked the boy. [*Pause.*] Poor Jerry! [*Pause.*] What restrained me then? [*Pause.*] Not fear of man. [*Pause.*] Shall we go on backwards now a little?

MRS. ROONEY   Backwards?

MR. ROONEY   Yes. Or you forwards and I backwards. The perfect pair. Like Dante's damned, with their faces arsy-versy. Our tears will water our bottoms.

MRS. ROONEY   What is the matter, Dan? Are you not well?

MR. ROONEY   Well! Did you ever know me to be well? The day you met me I should have been in bed. The day you proposed to me the doctors gave me up. You knew that, did you not? The night you married me they came for me with an ambulance. You have not forgotten that, I suppose? [*Pause.*] No, I cannot be said to be well. But I am no worse. Indeed I am better than I was. The loss of my sight was a great fillip. If I could go deaf and dumb I think I might pant on to be a hundred. Or have I done so? [*Pause.*] Was I a hundred today? [*Pause.*] Am I a hundred, Maddy?

[*Silence.*]

MRS. ROONEY   All is still. No living soul in sight. There is no one to ask. The world is feeding. The wind—[*brief wind*]—scarcely stirs the leaves and the birds—[*brief chirp*]—are tired singing. The cows— [*brief moo*]—and sheep—[*brief baa*]—ruminate in silence. The dogs—[*brief bark*]—are hushed and the hens—[*brief cackle*]—sprawl torpid in the dust. We are alone. There is no one to ask.

[*Silence*]

MR. ROONEY   [*clearing his throat, narrative tone*] We drew out on the tick of time, I can vouch for that. I was—

MRS. ROONEY   How can you vouch for it?

MR. ROONEY   [*normal tone, angrily*] I can vouch for it, I tell you! Do you want my relation or don't you? [*Pause. Narrative tone.*] On the tick of time. I had the compartment to myself, as usual. At least I hope so, for I made no attempt to restrain myself. My mind— [*Normal tone.*] But why do we not sit down somewhere? Are we afraid we should never rise again?

MRS. ROONEY   Sit down on what?

MR. ROONEY   On a bench, for example.

MRS. ROONEY   There is no bench.

MR. ROONEY   Then on a bank, let us sink down upon a bank.

MRS. ROONEY   There is no bank.

MR. ROONEY   Then we cannot. [*Pause.*] I dream of other roads, in other lands. Of another home, another— [*He hesitates.*] —another home. [*Pause.*] What was I trying to say?

MRS. ROONEY   Something about your mind.

MR. ROONEY   [*startled*] My mind? Are you sure? [*Pause. Incredulous.*] My mind? . . . [*Pause.*] Ah yes. [*Narrative tone.*] Alone in the compartment my mind began to work, as so often after office hours, on the way home, in the train, to the lilt of the bogeys. Your season-ticket, I said, costs you twelve pounds a year and you earn, on an average, seven and six a day, that is to say barely enough to keep you alive and twitching with the help of food, drink, tobacco and periodicals until you finally reach home and fall into bed. Add to this—or subtract from it—rent, stationery, various subscriptions, tramfares to and fro, light and heat, permits and licences, hairtrims and shaves, tips to escorts, upkeep of premises and appearances, and a thousand unspecifiable sundries, and it is clear that by lying at home in bed, day and night, winter and summer, with a change of pyjamas once a fortnight, you would add very considerably to your income. Business, I said— [*A cry. Pause. Again. Normal tone.*] Did I hear a cry?

MRS. ROONEY   Mrs. Tully I fancy. Her poor husband is in constant pain and beats her unmercifully.

[*Silence.*]

MR. ROONEY   That was a short knock. [*Pause.*] What was I trying to get at?

MRS. ROONEY   Business.

MR. ROONEY   Ah yes, business. [*Narrative tone.*] Business, old man, I said, retire from business, it has retired from you. [*Normal tone.*] One has these moments of lucidity.

MRS. ROONEY   I feel very cold and weak.

MR. ROONEY   [*narrative tone*] On the other hand, I said, there are the horrors of home life, the dusting, sweeping, airing, scrubbing, waxing, waning, washing, mangling, drying, mowing, clipping, raking, rolling, scuffling, shovelling, grinding, tearing, pounding, banging and slamming. And the brats, the happy little healthy little howling neighbours' brats. Of all this and much more the week-end, the Saturday intermission and then the

day of rest, have given you some idea. But what must
it be like on a working-day? A Wednesday? A Friday?
What must it be like on a Friday! And I fell to
thinking of my silent, backstreet, basement office,
with its obliterated plate, rest-couch and velvet
hangings, and what it means to be buried there alive,
if only from ten to five, with convenient to the one
hand a bottle of light pale ale and to the other a long
ice-cold fillet of hake. Nothing, I said, not even fully
certified death, can ever take the place of that. It was
then I noticed that we were at a standstill. [*Pause.
Normal tone. Irritably.*] Why are you hanging out of me
like that? Have you swooned away?

MRS. ROONEY   I feel very cold and faint. The wind—[*whistling wind*]—is
whistling through my summer frock as if I had
nothing on over my bloomers. I have had no solid
food since my elevenses.

MR. ROONEY   You have ceased to care. I speak—and you listen to the
wind.

MRS. ROONEY   No, no, I am agog, tell me all, then we shall press on and
never pause, never pause, till we come safe to haven.
[*Pause.*]

MR. ROONEY   Never pause . . . safe to haven. . . . Do you know, Maddy,
sometimes one would think you were struggling with
a dead language.

MRS. ROONEY   Yes indeed, Dan, I know full well what you mean, I often
have that feeling, it is unspeakably excruciating.

MR. ROONEY   I confess I have it sometimes myself, when I happen to
overhear what I am saying.

MRS. ROONEY   Well, you know, it will be dead in time, just like our own
poor dear Gaelic, there is that to be said. [*Urgent baa.*]

MR. ROONEY   [*startled*] Good God!

MRS. ROONEY   Oh the pretty little woolly lamb, crying to suck its
mother! Theirs has not changed, since Arcady.

[*Pause.*]

MR. ROONEY   Where was I in my composition?

MRS. ROONEY   At a standstill.

MR. ROONEY   Ah yes. [*Clears his throat. Narrative tone.*] I concluded
naturally that we had entered a station and would
soon be on our way again, and I sat on, without
misgiving. Not a sound. Things are very dull today, I
said, nobody getting down, nobody getting on. Then
as time flew by and nothing happened I realized my
error. We had not entered a station.

MRS. ROONEY   Did you not spring up and poke your head out of the
window?

MR. ROONEY   What good would that have done me?

MRS. ROONEY   Why to call out to be told what was amiss.

MR. ROONEY   I did not care what was amiss. No, I just sat on, saying, If
this train were never to move again I should not
greatly mind. Then gradually a—how shall I say—a
growing desire to—er—you know—welled up within
me. Nervous probably. In fact now I am sure. You
know, the feeling of being confined.

MRS. ROONEY   Yes yes, I have been through that.

MR. ROONEY   If we sit here much longer, I said, I really do not know
what I shall do. I got up and paced to and fro between
the seats, like a caged beast.

MRS. ROONEY   That is a help sometimes.

MR. ROONEY   After what seemed an eternity we simply moved off. And
the next thing was Barrell bawling the abhorred
name. I got down and Jerry led me to the men's, or Fir
as they call it now, from Vir Viris I suppose, the V
becoming F, in accordance with Grimm's Law. [*Pause.*]
The rest you know. [*Pause.*] You say nothing? [*Pause.*]
Say something. Maddy. Say you believe me.

MRS. ROONEY   I remember once attending a lecture by one of these new
mind doctors. I forget what you call them. He spoke—

MR. ROONEY	A lunatic specialist?
MRS. ROONEY	No no, just the troubled mind. I was hoping he might shed a little light on my lifelong preoccupation with horses' buttocks.
MR. ROONEY	A neurologist.
MRS. ROONEY	No no, just mental distress, the name will come back to me in the night. I remember his telling us the story of a little girl, very strange and unhappy in her ways, and how he treated her unsuccessfully over a period of years and was finally obliged to give up the case. He could find nothing wrong with her, he said. The only thing wrong with her as far as he could see was that she was dying. And she did in fact die, shortly after he had washed his hands of her.
MR. ROONEY	Well? What is there so wonderful about that?
MRS. ROONEY	No, it was just something he said, and the way he said it, that have haunted me ever since.
MR. ROONEY	You lie awake at night, tossing to and fro and brooding on it.
MRS. ROONEY	On it and other . . . wretchedness. [*Pause.*] When he had done with the little girl he stood there motionless for some time, quite two minutes I should say, looking down at his table. Then he suddenly raised his head and exclaimed, as if he had had a revelation, The trouble with her was she had never really been born! [*Pause.*] He spoke throughout without notes. [*Pause.*] I left before the end.
MR. ROONEY	Nothing about your buttocks? [*Mrs. Rooney weeps. In affectionate remonstrance.*] Maddy!
MRS. ROONEY	There is nothing to be done for those people!
MR. ROONEY	For which is there? [*Pause.*] That does not sound right somehow. [*Pause.*] What way am I facing?
MRS. ROONEY	What?
MR. ROONEY	I have forgotten what way I am facing.

MRS. ROONEY   You have turned aside and are bowed down over the ditch.

MR. ROONEY   There is a dead dog down there.

MRS. ROONEY   No no, just the rotting leaves.

MR. ROONEY   In June? Rotting leaves in June?

MRS. ROONEY   Yes, dear, from last year, and from the year before last, and from the year before that again. [*Silence. Rainy wind. They move on. Dragging steps, etc.*] There is that lovely laburnum again. Poor thing, it is losing all its tassels. [*Dragging steps, etc.*] There are the first drops. [*Rain. Dragging steps, etc.*] Golden drizzle. [*Dragging steps, etc.*] Do not mind me, dear, I am just talking to myself. [*Rain heavier. Dragging steps, etc.*] Can hinnies procreate, I wonder? [*They halt.*]

MR. ROONEY   Say that again.

MRS. ROONEY   Come on, dear, don't mind me, we are getting drenched.

MR. ROONEY   [*forcibly*] Can what what?

MRS. ROONEY   Hinnies procreate. [*Silence.*] You know, hinnies, or jinnies, aren't they barren, or sterile, or whatever it is? [*Pause.*] It wasn't an ass's colt at all, you know, I asked the Regius Professor.
[*Pause.*]

MR. ROONEY   He should know.

MRS. ROONEY   Yes, it was a hinny, he rode into Jerusalem or wherever it was on a hinny. [*Pause.*] That must mean something. [*Pause.*] It's like the sparrows, than many of which we are of more value, they weren't sparrows at all.

MR. ROONEY   Than many of which! . . . You exaggerate, Maddy.

MRS. ROONEY   [*with emotion*] They weren't sparrows at all!

MR. ROONEY   Does that put our price up?
[*Silence. They move on. Wind and rain. Dragging feet, etc. They halt.*]

MRS. ROONEY   Do you want some dung? [*Silence. They move on. Wind and rain, etc. They halt.*] Why do you stop? Do you want to say something?

MR. ROONEY   No.

MRS. ROONEY   Then why do you stop?

MR. ROONEY   It is easier.

MRS. ROONEY   Are you very wet?

MR. ROONEY   To the buff.

MRS. ROONEY   The buff?

MR. ROONEY   The buff. From buffalo.

MRS. ROONEY   We shall hang up all our things in the hot-cupboard and get into our dressing-gowns. [*Pause.*] Put your arm round me. [*Pause.*] Be nice to me! [*Pause. Gratefully.*] Ah, Dan! [*They move on. Wind and rain. Dragging feet, etc. Faintly same music as before. They halt. Music clearer. Silence but for music playing. Music dies.*] All day the same old record. All alone in that great empty house. She must be a very old woman now.

MR. ROONEY   [*indistinctly*] Death and the Maiden. [*Silence.*]

MRS. ROONEY   You are crying. [*Pause.*] Are you crying?

MR. ROONEY   [*violently*] Yes! [*They move on. Wind and rain. Dragging feet, etc. They halt. They move on. Wind and rain. Dragging feet, etc. They halt.*] Who is the preacher tomorrow? The incumbent?

MRS. ROONEY   No.

MR. ROONEY   Thank God for that. Who?

MRS. ROONEY   Hardy.

MR. ROONEY   "How to be Happy though Married"?

MRS. ROONEY   No no, he died, you remember. No connexion.

MR. ROONEY   Has he announced his text?

MRS. ROONEY   "The Lord upholdeth all that fall and raiseth up all those that be bowed down." [*Silence. They join in wild laughter. They move on. Wind and rain. Dragging feet, etc.*] Hold me tighter, Dan! [*Pause.*] Oh yes! [*They halt.*]

MR. ROONEY   I hear something behind us. [*Pause.*]

MRS. ROONEY   It looks like Jerry. [*Pause.*] It is Jerry.

[*Sound of Jerry's running steps approaching. He halts beside them, panting.*]

JERRY   [*panting*] You dropped—

MRS. ROONEY   Take your time, my little man, you will burst a blood-vessel.

JERRY   [*panting*] You dropped something, sir. Mr. Barrell told me to run after you.

MRS. ROONEY   Show. [*She takes the object.*] What is it? [*She examines it.*] What is this thing, Dan?

MR. ROONEY   Perhaps it is not mine at all.

JERRY   Mr. Barrell said it was, sir.

MRS. ROONEY   It looks like a kind of ball. And yet it is not a ball.

MR. ROONEY   Give it to me.

MRS. ROONEY   [*giving it*] What *is* it, Dan?

MR. ROONEY   It is a thing I carry about with me.

MRS. ROONEY   Yes, but what—

MR. ROONEY   [*violently*] It is a thing I carry about with me!

[*Silence. Mrs. Rooney looks for a penny.*]

MRS. ROONEY   I have no small money. Have you?

MR. ROONEY   I have none of any kind.

MRS. ROONEY   We are out of change, Jerry. Remind Mr. Rooney on Monday and he will give you a penny for your pains.

JERRY   Yes, Ma'am.

MR. ROONEY   If I am alive.

JERRY   Yessir.

[*Jerry starts running back towards the station.*]

MRS. ROONEY   Jerry! [*Jerry halts.*] Did you hear what the hitch was? [*Pause.*] Did you hear what kept the train so late?

MR. ROONEY   How would he have heard? Come on.

MRS. ROONEY   What was it, Jerry?

JERRY   It was a—

MR. ROONEY   Leave the boy alone, he knows nothing! Come on!

MRS. ROONEY   What was it, Jerry?

JERRY   It was a little child, Ma'am.

[*Mr. Rooney groans.*]

MRS. ROONEY   What do you mean, it was a little child?

JERRY   It was a little child fell out of the carriage, Ma'am. [*Pause.*] On to the line, Ma'am. [*Pause.*] Under the wheels, Ma'am.

[*Silence. Jerry runs off. His steps die away. Tempest of wind and rain. It abates. They move on. Dragging steps, etc. They halt. Tempest of wind and rain.*]

End

ACT WITHOUT WORDS I

A mime for one player

Desert. Dazzling light.

The man is flung backwards on stage from right wing. He falls, gets up immediately, dusts himself, turns aside, reflects.

Whistle from right wing.

He reflects, goes out right.

Immediately flung back on stage he falls, gets up immediately, dusts himself, turns aside, reflects.

Whistle from left wing.

He reflects, goes out left.

Immediately flung back on stage he falls, gets up immediately, dusts himself, turns aside, reflects.

Whistle from left wing.

He reflects, goes towards left wing, hesitates, thinks better of it, halts, turns aside, reflects.

A little tree descends from flies, lands. It has a single bough some three yards from ground and at its summit a meagre tuft of palms casting at its foot a circle of shadow.

He continues to reflect.

Whistle from above.

He turns, sees tree, reflects, goes to it, sits down in its shadow, looks at his hands.

A pair of tailor's scissors descends from flies, comes to rest before tree, a yard from ground.

He continues to look at his hands.

Whistle from above.

He looks up, sees scissors, takes them and starts to trim his nails.

The palms close like a parasol, the shadow disappears.

He drops scissors, reflects.

A tiny carafe, to which is attached a huge label inscribed WATER, descends from flies, comes to rest some three yards from ground.

He continues to reflect.

Whistle from above.

He looks up, sees carafe, reflects, gets up, goes and stands under it, tries in vain to reach it, renounces, turns aside, reflects.

A big cube descends from flies, lands.

He continues to reflect.

Whistle from above.

He turns, sees cube, looks at it, at carafe, reflects, goes to cube, takes it up, carries it over and sets it down under carafe, tests its stability, gets up on it, tries in vain to reach carafe, renounces, gets down, carries cube back to its place, turns aside, reflects.

A second smaller cube descends from flies, lands.

He continues to reflect.

Whistle from above.

He turns, sees second cube, looks at it, at carafe, goes to second cube, takes it up, carries it over and sets it down under carafe, tests its stability, gets up on it, tries in vain to reach carafe, renounces, gets down, takes up second cube to carry it back to its place, hesitates, thinks better of it, sets it down, goes to big cube, takes it up, carries it over and puts it on small one, tests their stability, gets up on them, the cubes collapse, he falls, gets up immediately, brushes himself, reflects.

He takes up small cube, puts it on big one, tests their stability, gets up on them and is about to reach carafe when it is pulled up a little way and comes to rest beyond his reach.

He gets down, reflects, carries cubes back to their place, one by one, turns aside, reflects.

A third still smaller cube descends from flies, lands.

He continues to reflect.

Whistle from above.

He turns, sees third cube, looks at it, reflects, turns aside, reflects.

The third cube is pulled up and disappears in flies.

Beside carafe a rope descends from flies, with knots to facilitate ascent.

He continues to reflect.

Whistle from above.

He turns, sees rope, reflects, goes to it, climbs up it and is about to reach carafe when rope is let out and deposits him back on ground.

He reflects, looks around for scissors, sees them, goes and picks them up, returns to rope and starts to cut it with scissors.

The rope is pulled up, lifts him off ground, he hangs on, succeeds in cutting rope, falls back on ground, drops scissors, gets up again immediately, brushes himself, reflects.

The rope is pulled up quickly and disappears in flies.

With length of rope in his possession he makes a lasso with which he tries to lasso the carafe.

The carafe is pulled up quickly and disappears in flies.

He turns aside, reflects.

He goes with lasso in his hand to tree, looks at bough, turns and looks at cubes, looks again at bough, drops lasso, goes to cubes, takes up small one, carries it over and sets it down under bough, goes back for big one, takes it up and carries it over under bough, makes to put it on small one, hesitates, thinks better of it, sets it down, takes up small one and puts it on big one, tests their stability, turns aside and stoops to pick up lasso.

The bough folds down against trunk.

He straightens up with lasso in his hand, turns and sees what has happened.

He drops lasso, turns aside, reflects.

He carries back cubes to their place, one by one, goes back for lasso, carries it over to the cubes and lays it in a neat coil on small one.

He turns aside, reflects.

Whistle from right wing.

He reflects, goes out right.

Immediately flung back on stage he falls, gets up immediately, brushes himself, turns aside, reflects.

Whistle from left wing.

He does not move.

He looks at his hands, looks round for scissors, sees them, goes and picks them up, starts to trim his nails, stops, reflects, runs his finger along blade of scissors, goes and lays them on small cube, turns aside, opens his collar, frees his neck and fingers it.

The small cube is pulled up and disappears in flies, carrying away rope and scissors.

He turns to take scissors, sees what has happened.

He turns aside, reflects.

He goes and sits down on big cube.

The big cube is pulled from under him. He falls. The big cube is pulled up and disappears in flies.

He remains lying on his side, his face towards auditorium, staring before him.

The carafe descends from flies and comes to rest a few feet from his body.

He does not move.

Whistle from above.

He does not move.

The carafe descends further, dangles and plays about his face.

He does not move.

The carafe is pulled up and disappears in flies.

The bough returns to horizontal, the palms open, the shadow returns.

Whistle from above.

He does not move.

The tree is pulled up and disappears in flies.

He looks at his hands.

Curtain

ACT WITHOUT WORDS II

A mime for two players

This mime should be played on a low and narrow platform at back of stage, violently lit in its entire length, the rest of the stage being in darkness. Frieze effect.

A is slow, awkward (gags dressing and undressing), absent. B brisk, rapid, precise. The two actions therefore, though B has more to do than A, should have approximately the same duration.

ARGUMENT

Beside each other on ground, two yards from right wing, two sacks, A's and B's, A's being to right (as seen from auditorium) of B's, i.e. nearer right wing. On ground beside sack B a little pile of clothes (C) neatly folded (coat and trousers surmounted by boots and hat).

Enter goad right, strictly horizontal. The point stops a foot short of sack A. Pause. The point draws back, pauses, darts forward into sack, withdraws, recoils to a foot short of sack. Pause. The sack does not move. The point draws back again, a little further than before, pauses, darts forward again into sack, withdraws, recoils to a foot short of sack. Pause. The sack moves. Exit goad.

A, wearing shirt, crawls out of sack, halts, broods, prays, broods, gets to his feet, broods, takes a little bottle of pills from his shirt pocket, broods, swallows a pill, puts bottle back, broods, goes to clothes, broods, puts on clothes, broods, takes a large partly eaten carrot from coat pocket, bites off a piece, chews an instant, spits it out with disgust, puts carrot back, broods, picks up two sacks, carries them bowed and staggering halfway to left wing, sets them down, broods, takes off clothes (except shirt), lets them fall in an untidy heap, broods, takes another pill, broods, kneels, prays, crawls into sack and lies still, sack A being now to left of sack B.

Pause.

Enter goad right on wheeled support (one wheel). The point stops a foot short of sack B. Pause. The point draws back, pauses, darts forward into sack, withdraws, recoils to a foot short of sack. Pause. The sack moves. Exit goad.

B, wearing shirt, crawls out of sack, gets to his feet, takes from shirt pocket and consults a large watch, puts watch back, does exercises, consults watch, takes a tooth brush from shirt pocket and brushes teeth vigorously, puts brush back, rubs scalp vigorously, takes a comb from shirt pocket and combs hair, puts comb back, consults watch, goes to clothes, puts them on, consults watch, takes a brush from coat pocket and brushes clothes vigorously, brushes hair vigorously, puts brush back, takes a little mirror from coat pocket and inspects appearance, puts mirror back, takes carrot from coat pocket, bites off a piece, chews and swallows with appetite, puts carrot back, consults watch, takes a map from coat pocket and consults it, puts map back, consults watch, takes a compass from coat pocket and consults it, puts compass back, consults watch, picks up two sacks and carries them bowed and staggering to two yards short of left wing, sets them down, consults watch, takes off clothes (except shirt), folds them in a neat pile, consults watch, does exercises, consults watch, rubs scalp, combs hair, brushes teeth, consults and winds watch, crawls into sack and lies still, sack B being now to left of sack A as originally.

Pause.

Enter goad right on wheeled support (two wheels). The point stops a foot short of sack A. Pause. The point draws back, pauses, darts forward into sack, withdraws, recoils to a foot short of sack. Pause. The sack does not move. The point draws back again, a little further than before, pauses, darts forward again into sack, withdraws, recoils to a foot short of sack. Pause. The sack moves. Exit goad.

A crawls out of sack, halts, broods, prays.

Curtain

POSITION I

```
┌──────────────────────────────────┐
│                      CBA ←┤       │
└──────────────────────────────────┘
```

POSITION II

```
┌──────────────────────────────────┐
│          CAB ←───────            │
│                    ⊙             │
└──────────────────────────────────┘
```

POSITION III

```
┌──────────────────────────────────┐
│ CBA ←──────────────────          │
│        ⊙          ⊙             │
└──────────────────────────────────┘
```

STAGE FRONT

KRAPP'S LAST TAPE

A late evening in the future.

Krapp's den.

Front centre a small table, the two drawers of which open towards the audience.

Sitting at the table, facing front, i.e. across from the drawers, a wearish old man: Krapp.

Rusty black narrow trousers too short for him. Rusty black sleeveless waistcoat, four capacious pockets. Heavy silver watch and chain. Grimy white shirt open at neck, no collar. Surprising pair of dirty white boots, size ten at least, very narrow and pointed.

White face. Purple nose. Disordered grey hair. Unshaven.

Very near-sighted (but unspectacled). Hard of hearing.

Cracked voice. Distinctive intonation.

Laborious walk.

On the table a tape-recorder with microphone and a number of cardboard boxes containing reels of recorded tapes.

Table and immediately adjacent area in strong white light. Rest of stage in darkness.

Krapp remains a moment motionless, heaves a great sigh, looks at his watch, fumbles in his pockets, takes out an envelope, puts it back, fumbles, takes out a small bunch of keys, raises it to his eyes, chooses a key, gets up and moves to front of table. He stoops, unlocks first drawer, peers into it, feels about inside it, takes out a reel of tape, peers at it, puts it back, locks drawer, unlocks second drawer, peers into it, feels about inside it, takes out a large banana, peers at it, locks drawer, puts keys back in his pocket. He turns, advances to edge of stage, halts, strokes banana, peels it, drops skin at his feet, puts end of banana in his mouth and remains motionless, staring vacuously before him. Finally he bites off the end, turns aside and begins pacing to and fro at edge of stage, in the light, i.e. not more than four or five paces either way, meditatively eating banana. He treads on skin, slips, nearly falls, recovers himself, stoops and peers at skin and finally pushes it, still stooping, with his foot over edge of stage into pit. He resumes his pacing, finishes banana, returns to table, sits down, remains a moment motionless, heaves a great sigh, takes keys from his pockets, raises them to his eyes, chooses key, gets up and moves to front of table, unlocks second drawer, takes out a second large banana, peers at it, locks drawer, puts back keys in his pocket, turns, advances to edge of stage, halts, strokes banana, peels it, tosses skin into pit, puts end of banana in his mouth and remains motionless, staring vacuously before him. Finally he has an idea, puts banana in his waistcoat pocket, the end emerging, and goes with all the speed he can muster backstage into darkness. Ten seconds. Loud pop of cork. Fifteen seconds. He comes back into light carrying an old ledger and sits down at table. He lays ledger on table, wipes his mouth, wipes his hands on the front of his waistcoat, brings them smartly together and rubs them.

KRAPP   [*briskly*] Ah! [*He bends over ledger, turns the pages, finds the entry he wants, reads.*] Box . . . thrree . . . spool five. [*He raises his head and stares front. With relish.*] Spool! [*Pause.*] Spooool! [*Happy smile. Pause. He bends over table, starts peering and poking at the boxes.*] Box . . . thrree . . . thrree . . . four . . . two . . . [*with surprise*] nine! good God! . . . seven . . . ah! the little rascal! [*He takes up box, peers at it.*] Box thrree. [*He lays it on table, opens it and peers at spools inside.*] Spool . . . [*he peers at ledger*] . . . five . . . [*he peers at spools*] . . . five . . . five . . . ah! the little scoundrel! [*He takes out a spool, peers at it.*] Spool five. [*He lays it on table, closes box three, puts it back with the others, takes up the spool.*] Box thrree, spool five. [*He bends over the machine, looks up. With relish.*] Spooool! [*Happy smile. He bends, loads spool on machine, rubs his hands.*] Ah! [*He peers at*

ledger, reads entry at foot of page.] Mother at rest at last. . . . Hm. . . .
The black ball. . . . [*He raises his head, stares blankly front. Puzzled.*]
Black ball? . . . [*He peers again at ledger, reads.*] The dark nurse. . . .
[*He raises his head, broods, peers again at ledger, reads.*] Slight
improvement in bowel condition. . . . Hm. . . . Memorable . . .
what? [*He peers closer.*] Equinox, memorable equinox. [*He raises
his head, stares blankly front. Puzzled.*] Memorable equinox? . . .
[*Pause. He shrugs his shoulders, peers again at ledger, reads.*] Farewell
to—[*he turns page*]—love.
[*He raises his head, broods, bends over machine, switches on and
assumes listening posture, i.e. leaning forward, elbows on table, hand
cupping ear towards machine, face front.*]

TAPE   [*strong voice, rather pompous, clearly Krapp's at a much earlier time*]
Thirty-nine today, sound as a— [*Settling himself more comfortably
he knocks one of the boxes off the table, curses, switches off, sweeps
boxes and ledger violently to the ground, winds tape back to
beginning, switches on, resumes posture.*] Thirty-nine today,
sound as a bell, apart from my old weakness, and intellectually
I have now every reason to suspect at the . . . [*hesitates*] . . .
crest of the wave—or thereabouts. Celebrated the awful
occasion, as in recent years, quietly at the Winehouse. Not a
soul. Sat before the fire with closed eyes, separating the grain
from the husks. Jotted down a few notes, on the back of an
envelope. Good to be back in my den, in my old rags. Have
just eaten I regret to say three bananas and only with difficulty
refrained from a fourth. Fatal things for a man with my
condition. [*Vehemently.*] Cut'em out! [*Pause.*] The new light
above my table is a great improvement. With all this darkness
round me I feel less alone. [*Pause.*] In a way. [*Pause.*] I love to
get up and move about in it, then back here to [*hesitates*] . . .
me. [*Pause.*] Krapp.
[*Pause.*]
The grain, now what I wonder do I mean by that, I mean . . .
[*hesitates*] . . . I suppose I mean those things worth having when

all the dust has—when all *my* dust has settled. I close my eyes
and try and imagine them.

[*Pause. Krapp closes his eyes briefly.*]

Extraordinary silence this evening, I strain my ears and do not
hear a sound. Old Miss McGlome always sings at this hour. But
not tonight. Songs of her girlhood, she says. Hard to think of
her as a girl. Wonderful woman though. Connaught, I fancy.
[*Pause.*] Shall I sing when I am her age, if I ever am? No. [*Pause.*]
Did I sing as a boy? No. [*Pause.*] Did I ever sing? No.

[*Pause.*]

Just been listening to an old year, passages at random. I did not
check in the book, but it must be at least ten or twelve years ago.
At that time I think I was still living on and off with Bianca in
Kedar Street. Well out of that, Jesus yes! Hopeless business.
[*Pause.*] Not much about her, apart from a tribute to her eyes.
Very warm. I suddenly saw them again. [*Pause.*] Incomparable!
[*Pause.*] Ah well. . . . [*Pause.*] These old P.M.s are gruesome, but I
often find them—[*Krapp switches off, broods, switches on*]—a help
before embarking on a new . . . [*hesitates*] . . . retrospect. Hard to
believe I was ever that young whelp. The voice! Jesus! And the
aspirations! [*Brief laugh in which Krapp joins.*] And the
resolutions! [*Brief laugh in which Krapp joins.*] To drink less, in
particular. [*Brief laugh of Krapp alone.*] Statistics. Seventeen
hundred hours, out of the preceding eight thousand odd,
consumed on licensed premises alone. More than 20 per cent,
say 40 per cent of his waking life. [*Pause.*] Plans for a less . . .
[*hesitates*] engrossing sexual life. Last illness of his father.
Flagging pursuit of happiness. Unattainable laxation. Sneers at
what he calls his youth and thanks to God that it's over. [*Pause.*]
False ring there. [*Pause.*] Shadows of the opus . . . magnum.
Closing with a—[*brief laugh*]—yelp to Providence. [*Prolonged
laugh in which Krapp joins.*] What remains of all that misery? A
girl in a shabby green coat, on a railway-station platform? No?
[*Pause.*]

When I look—

[*Krapp switches off, broods, looks at his watch, gets up, goes backstage into darkness. Ten seconds. Pop of cork. Ten seconds. Second cork. Ten seconds. Third cork. Ten seconds. Brief burst of quavering song.*]

KRAPP   [*sings*] Now the day is over,

        Night is drawing nigh-igh,

        Shadows—

[*Fit of coughing. He comes back into light, sits down, wipes his mouth, switches on, resumes his listening posture.*]

TAPE   —back on the year that is gone, with what I hope is perhaps a glint of the old eye to come, there is of course the house on the canal where mother lay a-dying, in the late autumn, after her long viduity [*Krapp gives a start*] and the—[*Krapp switches off, winds back tape a little, bends his ear closer to machine, switches on*]— a-dying, in the late autumn, after her long viduity, and the— [*Krapp switches off, raises his head, stares blankly before him. His lips move in the syllables of "viduity." No sound. He gets up, goes backstage into darkness, comes back with an enormous dictionary, lays it on table, sits down and looks up the word.*]

KRAPP   [*reading from dictionary*] State—or condition—of being—or remaining—a widow—or widower. [*Looks up. Puzzled.*] Being—or remaining? . . . [*Pause. He peers again at dictionary. Reading.*] "Deep weeds of viduity." . . . Also of an animal, especially a bird . . . the vidua or weaver-bird. . . . Black plumage of male. . . . [*He looks up. With relish.*] The vidua-bird!

[*Pause. He closes dictionary, switches on, resumes listening posture.*]

TAPE   —bench by the weir from where I could see her window. There I sat, in the biting wind, wishing she were gone. [*Pause.*] Hardly a soul, just a few regulars, nursemaids, infants, old men, dogs. I got to know them quite well—oh by appearance of course I mean! One dark young beauty I recollect particularly, all white and starch, incomparable bosom, with a big black hooded perambulator, most funereal thing. Whenever I looked in her direction she had her eyes on me. And yet when I was bold

enough to speak to her—not having been introduced—she
threatened to call a policeman. As if I had designs on her virtue!
[*Laugh. Pause.*] The face she had! The eyes! Like ... [*hesitates*] ...
chrysolite! [*Pause.*] Ah well. ... [*Pause.*] I was there when—[*Krapp
switches off, broods, switches on again*]—the blind went down, one
of those dirty brown roller affairs, throwing a ball for a little
white dog as chance would have it. I happened to look up and
there it was. All over and done with, at last. I sat on for a few
moments with the ball in my hand and the dog yelping and
pawing at me. [*Pause.*] Moments. Her moments, my moments.
[*Pause.*] The dog's moments. [*Pause.*] In the end I held it out to
him and he took it in his mouth, gently, gently. A small, old,
black, hard, solid rubber ball. [*Pause.*] I shall feel it, in my hand,
until my dying day. [*Pause.*] I might have kept it. [*Pause.*] But I
gave it to the dog.

[*Pause.*]

Ah well. ...

[*Pause.*]

Spiritually a year of profound gloom and indigence until that
memorable night in March, at the end of the jetty, in the
howling wind, never to be forgotten, when suddenly I saw the
whole thing. The vision at last. This I fancy is what I have
chiefly to record this evening, against the day when my work
will be done and perhaps no place left in my memory, warm or
cold, for the miracle that ... [*hesitates*] ... for the fire that set it
alight. What I suddenly saw then was this, that the belief I had
been going on all my life, namely—[*Krapp switches off impatiently,
winds tape forward, switches on again*]—great granite rocks the
foam flying up in the light of the lighthouse and the wind-
gauge spinning like a propeller, clear to me at last that the dark
I have always struggled to keep under is in reality my most—
[*Krapp curses, switches off, winds tape forward, switches on again*]—
unshatterable association until my dissolution of storm and
night with the light of the understanding and the fire—[*Krapp

curses louder, switches off, winds tape forward, switches on
again]—my face in her breasts and my hand on her. We lay there
without moving. But under us all moved, and moved us, gently,
up and down, and from side to side.
[*Pause.*]
Past midnight. Never knew such silence. The earth might be
uninhabited.
[*Pause.*] Here I end—
[*Krapp switches off, winds tape back, switches on again.*]
—upper lake, with the punt, bathed off the bank, then pushed
out into the stream and drifted. She lay stretched out on the
floorboards with her hands under her head and her eyes closed.
Sun blazing down, bit of a breeze, water nice and lively. I
noticed a scratch on her thigh and asked her how she came by
it. Picking gooseberries, she said. I said again I thought it was
hopeless and no good going on and she agreed, without
opening her eyes. [*Pause.*] I asked her to look at me and after a
few moments—[*pause*]—after a few moments she did, but the
eyes just slits, because of the glare. I bent over her to get them
in the shadow and they opened. [*Pause. Low.*] Let me in. [*Pause.*]
We drifted in among the flags and stuck. The way they went
down, sighing, before the stem! [*Pause.*] I lay down across her
with my face in her breasts and my hand on her. We lay there
without moving. But under us all moved, and moved us, gently,
up and down, and from side to side.
[*Pause.*]
Past midnight. Never knew—
[*Krapp switches off, broods. Finally he fumbles in his pockets,*
encounters the banana, takes it out, peers at it, puts it back, fumbles,
brings out envelope, fumbles, puts back envelope, looks at his watch,
gets up and goes backstage into darkness. Ten seconds. Sound of bottle
against glass, then brief siphon. Ten seconds. Bottle against glass alone.
Ten seconds. He comes back a little unsteadily into light, goes to front
of table, takes out keys, raises them to his eyes, chooses key, unlocks first

drawer, peers into it, feels about inside, takes out reel, peers at it, locks
drawer, puts keys back in his pocket, goes and sits down, takes reel off
machine, lays it on dictionary, loads virgin reel on machine, takes
envelope from his pocket, consults back of it, lays it on table, switches
on, clears his throat and begins to record.]

KRAPP   Just been listening to that stupid bastard I took myself for
thirty years ago, hard to believe I was ever as bad as that. Thank
God that's all done with anyway. [*Pause.*] The eyes she had!
[*Broods, realizes he is recording silence, switches off, broods. Finally.*]
Everything there, everything, all the— [*Realizes this is not being*
recorded, switches on.] Everything there, everything on this old
muckball, all the light and dark and famine and feasting of . . .
[*hesitates*] . . . the ages! [*In a shout.*] Yes! [*Pause.*] Let that go! Jesus!
Take his mind off his homework! Jesus! [*Pause. Weary.*] Ah well,
maybe he was right. [*Pause.*] Maybe he was right. [*Broods.*
Realizes. Switches off. Consults envelope.] Pah! [*Crumples it and*
throws it away. Broods. Switches on.] Nothing to say, not a squeak.
What's a year now? The sour cud and the iron stool. [*Pause.*]
Revelled in the word spool. [*With relish.*] Spooool! Happiest
moment of the past half million. [*Pause.*] Seventeen copies sold,
of which eleven at trade price to free circulating libraries
beyond the seas. Getting known. [*Pause.*] One pound six and
something, eight I have little doubt. [*Pause.*] Crawled out once
or twice, before the summer was cold. Sat shivering in the park,
drowned in dreams and burning to be gone. Not a soul. [*Pause.*]
Last fancies. [*Vehemently.*] Keep 'em under! [*Pause.*] Scalded the
eyes out of me reading *Effie* again, a page a day, with tears again.
Effie. . . . [*Pause.*] Could have been happy with her, up there on
the Baltic, and the pines, and the dunes. [*Pause.*] Could I? [*Pause.*]
And she? [*Pause.*] Pah! [*Pause.*] Fanny came in a couple of times.
Bony old ghost of a whore. Couldn't do much, but I suppose
better than a kick in the crutch. The last time wasn't so bad.
How do you manage it, she said, at your age? I told her I'd been

saving up for her all my life. [*Pause.*] Went to Vespers once, like when I was in short trousers. [*Pause. Sings.*]

> Now the day is over,
> Night is drawing nigh-igh,
> Shadows—[*coughing, then almost inaudible*]—of the evening
> Steal across the sky.

[*Gasping.*] Went to sleep and fell off the pew. [*Pause.*] Sometimes wondered in the night if a last effort mightn't— [*Pause.*] Ah finish your booze now and get to your bed. Go on with this drivel in the morning. Or leave it at that. [*Pause.*] Leave it at that. [*Pause.*] Lie propped up in the dark—and wander. Be again in the dingle on a Christmas Eve, gathering holly, the red-berried. [*Pause.*] Be again on Croghan on a Sunday morning, in the haze, with the bitch, stop and listen to the bells. [*Pause.*] And so on. [*Pause.*] Be again, be again. [*Pause.*] All that old misery. [*Pause.*] Once wasn't enough for you. [*Pause.*] Lie down across her. [*Long pause. He suddenly bends over machine, switches off, wrenches off tape, throws it away, puts on the other, winds it forward to the passage he wants, switches on, listens staring front.*]

TAPE —gooseberries, she said. I said again I thought it was hopeless and no good going on and she agreed, without opening her eyes. [*Pause.*] I asked her to look at me and after a few moments—[*pause*]—after a few moments she did, but the eyes just slits, because of the glare. I bent over to get them in the shadow and they opened. [*Pause. Low.*] Let me in. [*Pause.*] We drifted in among the flags and stuck. The way they went down, sighing, before the stem! [*Pause.*] I lay down across her with my face in her breasts and my hand on her. We lay there without moving. But under us all moved, and moved us, gently, up and down, and from side to side.

[*Pause. Krapp's lips move. No sound.*]

Past midnight. Never knew such silence. The earth might be uninhabited.

[*Pause.*]

Here I end this reel. Box—[*pause*]—three, spool—[*pause*]—five.
[*Pause.*] Perhaps my best years are gone. When there was a
chance of happiness. But I wouldn't want them back. Not with
the fire in me now. No, I wouldn't want them back.

[*Krapp motionless staring before him. The tape runs on in silence.*]

Curtain

ROUGH FOR THEATRE I

Street corner. Ruins.

*A, blind, sitting on a folding-stool, scrapes his fiddle. Beside him the case,
half open, upended, surmounted by alms bowl. He stops playing, turns his head
audience right, listens. Pause.*

A   A penny for a poor old man, a penny for a poor old man. [*Silence. He
resumes playing, stops again, turns his head right, listens. Enter B right, in a
wheelchair which he propels by means of a pole. He halts. Irritated.*] A
penny for a poor old man!
[*Pause.*]

B   Music! [*Pause.*] So it is not a dream. At last! Nor a vision, they are mute
and I am mute before them. [*He advances, halts, looks into bowl.
Without emotion.*] Poor wretch. [*Pause.*] Now I may go back, the
mystery is over. [*He pushes himself backwards, halts.*] Unless we join
together, and live together, till death ensue. [*Pause.*] What would you
say to that, Billy, may I call you Billy, like my son? [*Pause.*] Do you
like company, Billy? [*Pause.*] Do you like tinned food, Billy?

A   What tinned food?

B   Corned beef, Billy, just corned beef. Enough to keep body and soul
together, till summer, with care. [*Pause.*] No? [*Pause.*] A few potatoes
too, a few pounds of potatoes too. [*Pause.*] Do you like potatoes, Billy?
[*Pause.*] We might even let them sprout and then, when the time

came, put them in the ground, we might even try that. [*Pause.*] I would choose the place and you would put them in the ground. [*Pause.*] No? [*Pause.*]

A   How are the trees doing?

B   Hard to say. It's winter, you know.
     [*Pause.*]

A   Is it day or night?

B   Oh . . . [*he looks at the sky*] . . . day, if you like. No sun of course, otherwise you wouldn't have asked. [*Pause.*] Do you follow my reasoning? [*Pause.*] Have you your wits about you, Billy, have you still some of your wits about you?

A   But light?

B   Yes. [*Looks at sky.*] Yes, light, there is no other word for it. [*Pause.*] Shall I describe it to you? [*Pause.*] Shall I try to give you an idea of this light?

A   It seems to me sometimes I spend the night here, playing and listening. I used to feel twilight gather and make myself ready. I put away fiddle and bowl and had only to get to my feet, when she took me by the hand.
     [*Pause.*]

B   She?

A   My woman. [*Pause.*] A woman. [*Pause.*] But now . . .
     [*Pause.*]

B   Now?

A   When I set out I don't know, and when I get here I don't know, and while I am here I don't know, whether it is day or night.

B   You were not always as you are. What befell you? Women? Gambling? God?

A   I was always as I am.

B   Come!

A   [*violently*] I was always as I am, crouched in the dark, scratching an old jangle to the four winds!

B   [*violently*] We had our women, hadn't we? You yours to lead you by the hand and I mine to get me out of the chair in the evening and back into it again in the morning and to push me as far as the corner when I went out of my mind.

A   Cripple? [*Without emotion.*] Poor wretch.

B   Only one problem: the about-turn. I often felt, as I struggled, that it
     would be quicker to go on, right round the world. Till the day I
     realized I could go home backwards. [*Pause.*] For example, I am at A.
     [*He pushes himself forward a little, halts.*] I push on to B. [*He pushes
     himself back a little, halts.*] And I return to A. [*With élan.*] The straight
     line! The vacant space! [*Pause.*] Do I begin to move you?

A   Sometimes I hear steps. Voices. I say to myself, They are coming back,
     some are coming back, to try and settle again, or to look for
     something they had left behind, or to look for someone they had left
     behind.

B   Come back! [*Pause.*] Who would want to come back here? [*Pause.*] And
     you never called out? [*Pause.*] Cried out? [*Pause.*] No?

A   Have you observed nothing?

B   Oh me you know, observe . . . I sit there, in my lair, in my chair, in the
     dark, twenty-three hours out of the twenty-four. [*Violently.*] What
     would you have me observe? [*Pause.*] Do you think we would make a
     match, now you are getting to know me?

A   Corned beef, did you say?

B   Apropos, what have you been living on, all this time? You must be
     famished.

A   There are things lying around.

B   Edible?

A   Sometimes.

B   Why don't you let yourself die?

A   On the whole I have been lucky. The other day I tripped over a sack of
     nuts.

B   No!

A   A little sack, full of nuts, in the middle of the road.

B   Yes, all right, but why don't you let yourself die?

A   I have thought of it.

B   [*irritated*] But you don't do it!

A   I'm not unhappy enough. [*Pause.*] That was always my unhap, unhappy,
     but not unhappy enough.

B   But you must be every day a little more so.

A   [*violently*] I am not unhappy enough!
     [*Pause.*]

B   If you ask me we were made for each other.

A   [*comprehensive gesture*] What does it all look like now?

B   Oh me you know . . . I never go far, just a little up and down before my
     door. I never yet pushed on to here till now.

A   But you look about you?

B   No no.

A   After all those hours of darkness you don't—

B   [*violently*] No! [*Pause.*] Of course if you wish me to look about me I
     shall. And if you care to push me about I shall try to describe the
     scene, as we go along.

A   You mean you would guide me? I wouldn't get lost any more?

B   Exactly. I would say, Easy, Billy, we're heading for a great muckheap,
     turn back and wheel left when I give you the word.

A   You'd do that!

B   [*pressing his advantage*] Easy, Billy, easy, I see a round tin over there in
     the gutter, perhaps it's soup, or baked beans.

A   Baked beans!
     [*Pause.*]

B   Are you beginning to like me? [*Pause.*] Or is it only my imagination?

A   Baked beans! [*He gets up, puts down fiddle and bowl on the stool and gropes
     towards B.*] Where are you?

B   Here, dear fellow. [*A lays hold of the chair and starts pushing it blindly.*] Stop!

A   [*pushing the chair*] It's a gift! A gift!

B   Stop! [*He strikes behind him with the pole. A lets go the chair, recoils. Pause. A
     gropes towards his stool, halts, lost.*] Forgive me! [*Pause.*] Forgive me, Billy!

A   Where am I? [*Pause.*] Where was I?

B   Now I've lost him. He was beginning to like me and I struck him. He'll
     leave me and I'll never see him again. I'll never see anyone again.
     We'll never hear the human voice again.

A   Have you not heard it enough? The same old moans and groans from
     the cradle to the grave.

B   [*groaning*] Do something for me, before you go!

A   There! Do you hear it? [*Pause. Groaning.*] I can't go! [*Pause.*] Do you hear it?

B   You can't go?

A   I can't go without my things.

B   What good are they to you?

A   None.

B   And you can't go without them?

A   No. [*He starts groping again, halts.*] I'll find them in the end. [*Pause.*] Or leave them for ever behind me.
    [*He starts groping again.*]

B   Straighten my rug, I feel the cold air on my foot. [*A halts.*] I'd do it myself, but it would take too long. [*Pause.*] Do that for me, Billy. Then I may go back, settle in the old nook again and say, I have seen man for the last time, I struck him and he succoured me. [*Pause.*] Find a few rags of love in my heart and die reconciled, with my species. [*Pause.*] What has you gaping at me like that? [*Pause.*] Have I said something I shouldn't have? [*Pause.*] What does my soul look like? [*A gropes towards him.*]

A   Make a sound.
    [*B makes one. A gropes towards it, halts.*]

B   Have you no sense of smell either?

A   It's the same stink everywhere. [*He stretches out his hand.*] Am I within reach of your hand?
    [*He stands motionless with outstretched hand.*]

B   Wait, you're not going to do me a service for nothing? [*Pause.*] I mean unconditionally? [*Pause.*] Good God!
    [*Pause. He takes A's hand and draws it towards him.*]

A   Your foot.

B   What?

A   You said your foot.

B   Had I but known! [*Pause.*] Yes, my foot, tuck it in. [*A stoops, groping.*] On your knees, on your knees, you'll be more at your ease. [*He helps him to kneel at the right place.*] There.

A   [*irritated*] Let go my hand! You want me to help you and you hold my hand! [*B lets go his hand. A fumbles in the rug.*] Have you only one leg?

B   Just the one.

A   And the other?

B   It went bad and was removed.
    [*A tucks in the foot.*]

A   Will that do?

B   A little tighter. [*A tucks in tighter.*] What hands you have!
    [*Pause.*]

A   [*groping towards B's torso*] Is all the rest there?

B   You may stand up now and ask me a favour.

A   Is all the rest there?

B   Nothing else has been removed, if that is what you mean.
    [*A's hand, groping higher, reaches the face, stays.*]

A   Is that your face?

B   I confess it is. [*Pause.*] What else could it be? [*A's fingers stray, stay.*] That?
    My wen.

A   Red?

B   Purple. [*A withdraws his hand, remains kneeling.*] What hands you have!
    [*Pause.*]

A   Is it still day?

B   Day? [*Looks at sky.*] If you like. [*Looks.*] There is no other word for it.

A   Will it not soon be evening?
    [*B stoops to A, shakes him.*]

B   Come, Billy, get up, you're beginning to incommode me.

A   Will it not soon be night?
    [*B looks at sky.*]

B   Day . . . night . . . [*Looks.*] It seems to me sometimes the earth must have
    got stuck, one sunless day, in the heart of winter, in the grey of
    evening. [*Stoops to A, shakes him.*] Come on, Billy, up, you're beginning
    to embarrass me.

A   Is there grass anywhere?

B   I see none.

A   [*vehement*] Is there no green anywhere?

B   There's a little moss. [*Pause. A clasps his hands on the rug and rests his head
    on them.*] Good God! Don't tell me you're going to pray?

A   No.

B   Or weep?

A   No. [*Pause.*] I could stay like that for ever, with my head on an old man's knees.

B   Knee. [*Shaking him roughly.*] Get up, can't you!

A   [*settling himself more comfortably*] What peace! [*B pushes him roughly away, A falls to his hands and knees.*] Dora used to say, the days I hadn't earned enough, You and your harp! You'd do better crawling on all fours, with your father's medals pinned to your arse and a money box round your neck. You and your harp! Who do you think you are? And she made me sleep on the floor. [*Pause.*] Who I thought I was . . . [*Pause.*] Ah that . . . I never could . . . [*Pause. He gets up.*] Never could . . . [*He starts groping again for his stool, halts, listens.*] If I listened long enough I'd hear it, a string would give.

B   Your harp? [*Pause.*] What's all this about a harp?

A   I once had a little harp. Be still and let me listen.
     [*Pause.*]

B   How long are you going to stay like that?

A   I can stay for hours listening to all the sounds.
     [*They listen.*]

B   What sounds?

A   I don't know what they are.
     [*They listen.*]

B   I can see it. [*Pause.*] I can—

A   [*imploring*] Will you not be still?

B   No! [*A takes his head in his hands.*] I can see it clearly, over there on the stool. [*Pause.*] What if I took it, Billy, and made off with it? [*Pause.*] Eh Billy, what would you say to that? [*Pause.*] There might be another old man, some day, would come out of his hole and find you playing the mouth-organ. And you'd tell him of the little fiddle you once had. [*Pause.*] Eh Billy? [*Pause.*] Or singing. [*Pause.*] Eh Billy, what would you say to that? [*Pause.*] There croaking to the winter wind [*rime with unkind*], having lost his little mouth-organ. [*He pokes him in the back with the pole.*] Eh Billy? [*A whirls round, seizes the end of the pole and wrenches it from B's grasp.*]

ROUGH FOR THEATRE II

Upstage centre high double window open on bright night sky. Moon invisible.

Downstage audience left, equidistant from wall and axis of window, small table and chair. On table an extinguished reading-lamp and a briefcase crammed with documents.

Downstage right, forming symmetry, identical table and chair. Extinguished lamp only.

Downstage left door.

Standing motionless before left half of window with his back to stage, C. Long pause.

Enter A. He closes door, goes to table on right and sits with his back to right wall. Pause. He switches on lamp, takes out his watch, consults it and lays it on the table. Pause. He switches off. Long pause.

Enter B. He closes door, goes to table on left and sits with his back to left wall. Pause. He switches on lamp, opens briefcase and empties contents on table. He looks round, sees A.

B   Well!

A   Hsst! Switch off. [*B switches off. Long pause. Low.*] What a night! [*Long pause. Musing.*] I still don't understand. [*Pause.*] Why he needs our services. [*Pause.*] A man like him. [*Pause.*] And why we give them free. [*Pause.*] Men like us. [*Pause.*] Mystery. [*Pause.*] Ah well . . . [*Pause. He switches on.*] Shall we go? [*B switches on, rummages in his papers.*]

The crux. [*B rummages.*] We sum up and clear out. [*B rummages.*] Set to go?

B   Rearing.

A   We attend.

B   Let him jump.

A   When?

B   Now.

A   From where?

B   From here will do. Three to three and a half metres per floor, say twenty-five in all.
[*Pause.*]

A   I could have sworn we were only on the sixth. [*Pause.*] He runs no risk?

B   He has only to land on his arse, the way he lived. The spine snaps and the tripes explode.
[*Pause. A gets up, goes to the window, leans out, looks down. He straightens up, looks at the sky. Pause. He goes back to his seat.*]

A   Full moon.

B   Not quite. Tomorrow.
[*A takes a little diary from his pocket.*]

A   What's the date?

B   Twenty-fourth. Twenty-fifth tomorrow.

A   [*turning pages*] Nineteen . . . twenty-two . . . twenty-four. [*Reads.*] "Our Lady of Succour. Full moon." [*He puts back the diary in his pocket.*] We were saying then . . . what was it . . . let him jump. Our conclusion. Right?

B   Work, family, third fatherland, cunt, finances, art and nature, heart and conscience, health, housing conditions, God and man, so many disasters.
[*Pause.*]

A   [*meditative*] Does it follow? [*Pause.*] Does it follow? [*Pause.*] And his sense of humour? Of proportion?

B   Swamped.
[*Pause.*]

A   May we not be mistaken?

B [*indignant*] We have been to the best sources. All weighed and weighed again, checked and verified. Not a word here [*brandishing sheaf of papers*] that is not cast iron. Tied together like a cathedral. [*He flings down the papers on the table. They scatter on the floor.*] Shit!
[*He picks them up. A raises his lamp and shines it about him.*]

A Seen worse dumps. [*Turning towards window.*] Worse outlooks. [*Pause.*] Is that Jupiter we see?
[*Pause.*]

B Where?

A Switch off. [*They switch off.*] It must be.

B [*irritated*] Where?

A [*irritated*] There. [*B cranes.*] There, on the right, in the corner.
[*Pause.*]

B No. It twinkles.

A What is it then?

B [*indifferent*] No idea. Sirius. [*He switches on.*] Well? Do we work or play?
[*A switches on.*] You forget this is not his home. He's only here to take care of the cat. At the end of the month shoosh back to the barge.
[*Pause. Louder.*] You forget this is not his home.

A [*irritated*] I forget, I forget! And he, does he not forget? [*With passion.*] But that's what saves us!

B [*searching through his papers*] Memory . . . memory . . . [*He takes up a sheet.*] I quote: "An elephant's for the eating cares, a sparrow's for the Lydian airs." Testimony of Mr. Swell, organist at Seaton Sluice and lifelong friend.
[*Pause.*]

A [*glum*] Tsstss!

B I quote: "Questioned on this occasion"—open brackets—"(judicial separation)"—close brackets—"regarding the deterioration of our relations, all he could adduce was the five or six miscarriages which clouded"—open brackets—"(oh through no act of mine!)"—close brackets—"the early days of our union and the veto which in consequence I had finally to oppose"—open brackets—"(oh not for want of inclination!)"—close brackets—"to anything remotely

resembling the work of love. But on the subject of our happiness"—
open brackets— "(for it too came our way, unavoidably, and here my
mind goes back to the first vows exchanged at Wootton Bassett
under the bastard acacias, or again to the first fifteen minutes of our
wedding night at Littlestone-on-Sea, or yet again to those first long
studious evenings in our nest on Commercial Road East)"—close
brackets—"on the subject of our happiness not a word, Sir, not one
word." Testimony of Mrs. Aspasia Budd-Croker, button designer in
residence, Commercial Road East.

A [*glum*] Tsstss!

B I quote again: "Of our national epos he remembered only the
calamities, which did not prevent him from winning a minor
scholarship in the subject." Testimony of Mr. Peaberry, market
gardener in the Deeping Fens and lifelong friend. [*Pause.*] "Not a tear
was known to fall in our family, and God knows they did in torrents,
that was not caught up and piously preserved in that inexhaustible
reservoir of sorrow, with the date, the hour and the occasion, and
not a joy, fortunately they were few, that was not on the contrary
irrevocably dissolved, as by a corrosive. In that he took after me."
Testimony of the late Mrs. Darcy-Croker, woman of letters. [*Pause.*]
Care for more?

A Enough.

B I quote: "To hear him talk about his life, after a glass or two, you would
have thought he had never set foot outside hell. He had us in
stitches. I worked it up into a skit that went down well." Testimony
of Mr. Moore, light comedian, c/o Widow Merryweather-Moore, All
Saints on the Wash, and lifelong friend.
[*Pause.*]

A [*stricken*] Tsstss! [*Pause.*] Tsstsstss!

B You see. [*Emphatic.*] This is not his home and he knows it full well.
[*Pause.*]

A Now let's have the positive elements.

B Positive? You mean of a nature to make him think . . . [*hesitates, then
with sudden violence*] . . . that some day things might change? Is that
what you want? [*Pause. Calmer.*] There are none.

A   [*wearily*] Oh yes there are, that's the beauty of it.
       [*Pause. B rummages in his papers.*]
B   [*looking up*] Forgive me, Bertrand. [*Pause. Rummages. Looks up.*] I don't
       know what came over me. [*Pause. Rummages. Looks up.*] A moment of
       consternation. [*Pause. Rummages.*] There is that incident of the
       lottery . . . possibly. Remember?
A   No.
B   [*reading*] "Two hundred lots . . . winner receives high class watch . . .
       solid gold, hallmark nineteen carats, marvel of accuracy, showing
       year, month, date, day, hour, minute and second, super chic,
       unbreakable hair spring, chrono escapement nineteen rubies,
       anti-shock, anti-magnetic, airtight, waterproof, stainless, self-
       winding, centre seconds hand, Swiss parts, de luxe lizard band."
A   What did I tell you? However unhopefully. The mere fact of chancing
       his luck. I knew he had a spark left in him.
B   The trouble is he didn't procure it himself. It was a gift. That you
       forget.
A   [*irritated*] I forget, I forget! And he, does he not— [*Pause.*] At least he
       kept it.
B   If you can call it that.
A   At least he accepted it. [*Pause.*] At least he didn't refuse it.
B   I quote: "The last time I laid eyes on him I was on my way to the Post
       Office to cash an order for back-pay. The area before the building is
       shut off by a row of bollards with chains hung between them. He
       was seated on one of these with his back to the Thompson works. To
       all appearances down and out. He sat doubled in two, his hands on
       his knees, his legs astraddle, his head sunk. For a moment I
       wondered if he was not vomiting. But on drawing nearer I could see
       he was merely scrutinizing, between his feet, a lump of dogshit. I
       moved it slightly with the tip of my umbrella and observed how his
       gaze followed the movement and fastened on the object in its new
       position. This at three o'clock in the afternoon if you please! I
       confess I had not the heart to bid him the time of day, I was over-
       come. I simply slipped into his hip pocket a lottery ticket I had no
       use for, while silently wishing him the best of luck. When two hours

later I emerged from the Post Office, having cashed my order, he was at the same place and in the same attitude. I sometimes wonder if he is still alive." Testimony of Mr. Feckman, certified accountant and friend for better and for worse.

[*Pause.*]

A   Dated when?

B   Recent.

A   It has such a bygone ring. [*Pause.*] Nothing else?

B   Oh ... bits and scraps ... good graces of an heirless aunt ... unfinished—

A   Hairless aunt?

B   ... heirless aunt ... unfinished game of chess with a correspondent in Tasmania ... hope not dead of living to see the extermination of the species ... literary aspirations incompletely stifled ... bottom of a dairy-woman in Waterloo Lane ... you see the kind of thing.

[*Pause.*]

A   We pack up this evening, right?

B   Without fail. Tomorrow we're at Bury St. Edmunds.

A   [*sadly*] We'll leave him none the wiser. We'll leave him now, never to meet again, having added nothing to what he knew already.

B   All these testimonies were new to him. They will have finished him off.

A   Not necessarily. [*Pause.*] Any light on that? [*Papers.*] This is vital. [*Papers.*] Something ... I seem to remember ... something ... he said himself.

B   [*papers*] Under "Confidences" then. [*Brief laugh.*] Slim file. [*Papers.*] Confidences ... confidences ... ah!

A   [*impatient*] Well?

B   [*reading*] "... sick headaches ... eye trouble ... irrational fear of vipers ... ear trouble ..."—nothing for us there—"... fibroid tumours ... pathological horror of songbirds ... throat trouble ... need of affection ..."—we're coming to it—"... inner void ... congenital timidity ... nose trouble ..."—ah! listen to this!— "... morbidly sensitive to the opinion of others ..." [*Looks up.*] What did I tell you?

A   [*glum*] Tsstss!

B   I'll read the whole passage: "... morbidly sensitive to the opinion of others—" [*His lamp goes out.*] Well! The bulb has blown! [*The lamp goes on again.*] No, it hasn't! Must be a faulty connexion. [*Examines lamp, straightens flex.*] The flex was twisted, now all is well. [*Reading.*] "... morbidly sensitive—" [*The lamp goes out.*] Bugger and shit!

A   Try giving her a shake. [*B shakes the lamp. It goes on again.*] See! I picked up that wrinkle in the Band of Hope. [*Pause.*]

B }
    } [*together*]   "... morbidly sensitive—"
A }   Keep your hands off the table.

B   What?

A   Keep your hands off the table. If it's a connexion the least jog can do it.

B   [*having pulled back his chair a little way*] "... morbidly sensitive—" [*The lamp goes out. B bangs on the table with his fist. The lamp goes on again. Pause.*]

A   Mysterious affair, electricity.

B   [*hurriedly*] "... morbidly sensitive to the opinion of others at the time, I mean as often and for as long as they entered my awareness—" What kind of Chinese is that?

A   [*nervously*] Keep going, keep going!

B   "... for as long as they entered my awareness, and that in either case, I mean whether such on the one hand as to give me pleasure or on the contrary on the other to cause me pain, and truth to tell—" Shit! Where's the verb?

A   What verb?

B   The main!

A   I give up.

B   Hold on till I find the verb and to hell with all this drivel in the middle. [*Reading.*] "... were I but ... could I but ..." —Jesus!— "... though it be ... be it but ..."—Christ!—ah! I have it—"... I was unfortunately incapable ..." Done it!

A   How does it run now?

B [*solemnly*] ". . . morbidly sensitive to the opinion of others at the time . . ."—drivel drivel drivel—". . . I was unfortunately incapable—" [*The lamp goes out. Long pause.*]

A Would you care to change seats? [*Pause.*] You see what I mean? [*Pause.*] That you come over here with your papers and I go over there. [*Pause.*] Don't whinge, Morvan, that will get us nowhere.

B It's my nerves. [*Pause.*] Ah if I were only twenty years younger I'd put an end to my sufferings!

A Fie! Never say such horrid things! Even to a well-wisher!

B May I come to you? [*Pause.*] I need animal warmth. [*Pause.*]

A [*coldly*] As you like. [*B gets up and goes towards A.*] With your files if you don't mind. [*B goes back for papers and briefcase, returns towards A, puts them on A's table, remains standing. Pause.*] Do you want me to take you on my knees? [*Pause. B goes back for his chair, returns towards A, stops before A's table with the chair in his arms. Pause.*]

B [*shyly*] May I sit beside you? [*They look at each other.*] No? [*Pause.*] Then opposite. [*He sits down opposite A, looks at him. Pause.*] Do we continue?

A [*forcibly*] Let's get it over and go to bed. [*B rummages in his papers.*]

B I'll take the lamp. [*He draws it towards him.*] Please God it holds out. What would we do in the dark the pair of us? [*Pause.*] Have you matches?

A Never without. [*Pause.*] What we would do? Go and stand by the window in the starlight. [*B's lamp goes on again.*] That is to say you would.

B [*fervently*] Oh no not alone I wouldn't!

A Pass me a sheet. [*B passes him a sheet.*] Switch off. [*B switches off.*] Oh lord, yours is on again.

B This gag has gone on long enough for me.

A Just so. Go and switch it off. [*B goes to his table, switches off his lamp. Pause.*]

B What am I to do now? Switch it on again?

A   Come back.

B   Switch on then till I see where I'm going.

[*A switches on. B goes back and sits down opposite A. A switches off, goes to window with sheet, halts, contemplates the sky.*]

A   And to think all that is nuclear combustion! All that faerie! [*He stoops over sheet and reads haltingly.*] "Aged ten, runs away from home first time, brought back next day, admonished, forgiven." [*Pause.*] "Aged fifteen, runs away from home second time, dragged back a week later, thrashed, forgiven." [*Pause.*] "Aged seventeen, runs away from home third time, slinks back six months later with his tail between his legs, locked up, forgiven." [*Pause.*] "Aged seventeen runs away from home last time, crawls back a year later on his hands and knees, kicked out, forgiven."

[*Pause. He moves up against window to inspect C's face, to do which he has to lean out a little way, with his back to the void.*]

B   Careful!

[*Long pause, all three dead still.*]

A   [*sadly*] Tsstss! [*He resumes his equilibrium.*] Switch on. [*B switches on. A goes back to his table, sits, returns the sheet to B.*] It's heavy going, but we're nearly home.

B   How does he look?

A   Not at his best.

B   Has he still got that little smile on his face?

A   Probably.

B   What do you mean, probably, haven't you just been looking at him?

A   He didn't have it then.

B   [*with satisfaction*] Ah! [*Pause.*] Could never make out what he thought he was doing with that smile on his face. And his eyes? Still goggling?

A   Shut.

B   Shut!

A   Oh it was only so as not to see me. He must have opened them again since. [*Pause. Violently.*] You'd need to stare them in the face day and night! Never take your eyes off them for a week on end! Unbeknownst to them!

[*Pause.*]

B   Looks to me we have him.

A   [*impatiently*] Come on, we're getting nowhere, get on with it.
[*B rummages in his papers, finds the sheet.*]

B   [*reading at top speed*] ". . . morbidly sensitive to the opinion of others at
the time . . ." —drivel drivel drivel— ". . . I was unfortunately
incapable of retaining it for more than ten or fifteen minutes at the
most, that is to say the time required to take it in. From then on it
might as well never have been uttered." [*Pause.*] Tsstss!

A   [*with satisfaction*] You see. [*Pause.*] Where does that come in?

B   In a letter presumably never posted to an anonymous admiratrix.

A   An admiratrix? He had admiratrixes?

B   It begins: "Dear friend and admiratrix . . ." That's all we know.

A   Come, Morvan, calm yourself, letters to admiratrixes, we all know what
they're worth. No need to take everything literally.

B   [*violently, slapping down his hand on the pile of papers*] There's the record,
closed and final. That's what we're going on. Too late now to start
saying that [*slapping to his left*] is right and that [*slapping to his right*]
wrong. You're a pain in the arse.
[*Pause.*]

A   Good. Let us sum up.

B   We do nothing else.

A   A black future, an unpardonable past—so far as he can remember,
inducements to linger on all equally preposterous and the best
advice dead letter. Agreed?

B   An heirless aunt preposterous?

A   [*warmly*] He's not the interested type. [*Sternly.*] One has to consider the
client's temperament. To accumulate documents is not enough.

B   [*vexed, slapping on his papers*] Here, as far as I'm concerned the client is
here and nowhere else.

A   All right. Is there a single reference there to personal gain? That old
aunt, was he ever as much as commonly civil to her? And that
dairy-woman, come to that, in all the years he's been going to her for
his bit of cheddar, was he ever once wanting in respect? [*Pause.*] No,
Morvan, look you—

[*Feeble miaow. Pause. Second miaow, louder.*]

B   That must be the cat.

A   Sounds like it. [*Long pause.*] So, agreed? Black future, unpardonable—

B   As you wish. [*He starts to tidy back the papers in the briefcase. Wearily.*] Let him jump.

A   No further exhibit?

B   Let him jump, let him jump. [*He finishes tidying, gets up with the briefcase in his hand.*] Let's go.
    [*A consults his watch.*]

A   It is now . . . ten . . . twenty-five. We have no train before eleven twenty. Let us kill the time here, talking of this and that.

B   What do you mean, eleven twenty? Ten fifty.
    [*A takes a time-table from his pocket, opens it at relevant page and hands it to B.*]

A   Where it's marked with a cross. [*B consults the time-table, hands it back to A and sits down again. Long pause. A clears his throat. Pause. Impassionately.*] How many unfortunates would be so still today if they had known in time to what extent they were so? [*Pause.*] Remember Smith?

B   Smith? [*Pause.*] Never knew anyone of that name.

A   Yes you did! A big fat redhair. Always to be seen hanging round World's End. Hadn't done a hand's turn for years. Reputed to have lost his genitals in a shooting accident. His own double-barrel that went off between his legs in a moment of abstraction, just as he was getting set to let fly at a quail.

B   Stranger to me.

A   Well to make a long story short he had his head in the oven when they came to tell him his wife had gone under an ambulance. Hell, says he, I can't miss that, and now he has a steady job in Marks and Spencer's. [*Pause.*] How is Mildred?

B   [*disgustedly*] Oh you know— [*Brief burst of birdsong. Pause.*] Good God!

A   Philomel!

B   Oh that put the heart across me!

A   Hsst! [*Low.*] Hark hark! [*Pause. Second brief burst, louder. Pause.*] It's in the room! [*He gets up, moves away on tiptoe.*] Come on, let's have a look.

B   I'm scared!

[*He gets up none the less and follows cautiously in the wake of* A.
A advances on tiptoe upstage right, B tiptoes after.]

A   [*turning*] Hsst! [*They advance, halt in the corner. A strikes a match, holds it
above his head. Pause. Low.*] She's not here. [*He drops the match and
crosses the stage on tiptoe followed on tiptoe by B. They pass before the
window, halt in the corner upstage left. Match as before. Pause.*] Here she is!

B   [*recoiling*] Where?

[*A squats. Pause.*]

A   Lend me a hand.

B   Let her be! [*A straightens up painfully, clutching to his belly a large birdcage
covered with a green silk cloth fringed with beads. He starts to stagger with
it towards the table.*] Give it here.

[*B helps to carry the cage. Holding it between them they advance warily
towards A's table.*]

A   [*breathing hard*] Hold on a second. [*They halt. Pause.*] Let's go. [*They move
on, set down cage gently on the table. A lifts cautiously the cloth on the side
away from the audience, peers. Pause.*] Show a light.

[*B takes up the lamp and shines it inside the cage. They peer, stooped. Long
pause.*]

B   There's one dead.

[*They peer.*]

A   Have you a pencil? [*B hands him a long pencil. A pokes it between the bars of
the cage. Pause.*] Yes. [*He withdraws the pencil, puts it in his pocket.*]

B   Hi!

[*A gives him back his pencil. They peer. A takes B's hand and changes its
position.*]

A   There.

[*They peer.*]

B   Is it the cock or the hen?

A   The hen. See how drab she is.

B   [*revolted*] And he goes on singing! [*Pause.*] There's lovebirds for you!

A   Lovebirds! [*Guffaw.*] Ah Morvan, you'd be the death of me if I were
sufficiently alive! Lovebirds! [*Guffaw.*] Finches, pinhead! Look at that

lovely little green rump! And the blue cap! And the white bars! And the gold breast! [*Didactic.*] Note moreover the characteristic warble, there can be no mistaking it. [*Pause.*] Oh you pretty little pet, oh you bonny wee birdie! [*Pause. Glum.*] And to think all that is organic waste! All that splendour!

[*They peer.*]

B   They have no seed. [*Pause.*] No water. [*Pointing.*] What's that there?

A   That? [*Pause. Slow, toneless.*] An old cuttle-bone.

B   Cuttle-bone?

A   Cuttle-bone.

[*He lets the cloth fall back. Pause.*]

B   Come, Bertrand, don't, there is nothing we can do. [*A takes up the cage and goes with it upstage left. B puts down the lamp and hastens after him.*] Give it here.

A   Leave it, leave it! [*He advances to the corner, followed by B, and puts down the cage where he found it. He straightens up and moves back towards his table, still followed by B. A stops short.*] Will you have done dogging me! Do you want me to jump too? [*Pause. B goes to A's table, takes up briefcase and chair, goes to his table and sits with back to window. He switches on his lamp, switches it off again immediately.*] How end? [*Long pause. A goes to window; strikes a match, holds it high and inspects C's face. The match burns out, he throws it out of window.*] Hi! Take a look at this! [*B does not move. A strikes another match, holds it high and inspects C's face.*] Come on! Quick! [*B does not move. The match burns out, A lets it fall.*] Well I'll be . . . !

[*A takes out his handkerchief and raises it timidly towards C's face.*]

Curtain

EMBERS

A piece for radio

Sea scarcely audible.

Henry's boots on shingle. He halts.

Sea a little louder.

HENRY   On. [*Sea. Voice louder.*] On! [*He moves on. Boots on shingle. As he goes.*] Stop. [*Boots on shingle. As he goes, louder.*] Stop! [*He halts. Sea a little louder.*] Down. [*Sea. Voice louder.*] Down! [*Slither of shingle as he sits. Sea, still faint, audible throughout what follows whenever pause indicated.*] Who is beside me now? [*Pause.*] An old man, blind and foolish. [*Pause.*] My father, back from the dead, to be with me. [*Pause.*] As if he hadn't died. [*Pause.*] No, simply back from the dead, to be with me, in this strange place. [*Pause.*] Can he hear me? [*Pause.*] Yes, he must hear me. [*Pause.*] To answer me? [*Pause.*] No, he doesn't answer me. [*Pause.*] Just be with me. [*Pause.*] That sound you hear is the sea. [*Pause. Louder.*] I say that sound you hear is the sea, we are sitting on the strand. [*Pause.*] I mention it because the sound is so strange, so unlike the sound of the sea, that if you didn't see what it was you wouldn't know what it was. [*Pause.*] Hooves! [*Pause. Louder.*] Hooves! [*Sound of hooves walking on hard road.*

They die rapidly away. Pause.] Again! [*Hooves as before.
Pause. Excitedly.*] Train it to mark time! Shoe it with steel
and tie it up in the yard, have it stamp all day! [*Pause.*] A
ten-ton mammoth back from the dead, shoe it with
steel and have it tramp the world down! Listen to it!
[*Pause.*] Listen to the light now, you always loved light,
not long past noon and all the shore in shadow and the
sea out as far as the island. [*Pause.*] You would never live
this side of the bay, you wanted the sun on the water
for that evening bathe you took once too often. But
when I got your money I moved across, as perhaps you
may know. [*Pause.*] We never found your body, you
know, that held up probate an unconscionable time,
they said there was nothing to prove you hadn't run
away from us all and alive and well under a false name
in the Argentine for example, that grieved mother
greatly. [*Pause.*] I'm like you in that, can't stay away from
it, but I never go in, no, I think the last time I went in
was with you. [*Pause.*] Just be near it. [*Pause.*] Today it's
calm, but I often hear it above in the house and walking
the roads and start talking, oh just loud enough to
drown it, nobody notices. [*Pause.*] But I'd be talking now
no matter where I was, I once went to Switzerland to
get away from the cursed thing and never stopped all
the time I was there. [*Pause.*] I usen't to need anyone,
just to myself, stories, there was a great one about an
old fellow called Bolton, I never finished it, I never
finished any of them, I never finished anything,
everything always went on for ever. [*Pause.*] Bolton.
[*Pause. Louder.*] Bolton! [*Pause.*] There before the fire.
[*Pause.*] Before the fire with all the shutters . . . no,
hangings, hangings, all the hangings drawn and the
light, no light, only the light of the fire, sitting there in
the . . . no, standing, standing there on the hearthrug in

the dark before the fire with his arms on the chimney-
piece and his head on his arms, standing there waiting
in the dark before the fire in his old red dressing-gown
and no sound in the house of any kind, only the sound
of the fire. [*Pause.*] Standing there in his old red
dressing-gown might go on fire any minute like when
he was a child, no, that was his pyjamas, standing there
waiting in the dark, no light, only the light of the fire,
and no sound of any kind, only the fire, an old man in
great trouble. [*Pause.*] Ring then at the door and over he
goes to the window and looks out between the
hangings, fine old chap, very big and strong, bright
winter's night, snow everywhere, bitter cold, white
world, cedar boughs bending under load and then as
the arm goes up to ring again recognizes . . .
Holloway . . . [*long pause*] . . . yes, Holloway, recognizes
Holloway, goes down and opens. [*Pause.*] Outside all
still, not a sound, dog's chain maybe or a bough
groaning if you stood there listening long enough,
white world, Holloway with his little black bag, not a
sound, bitter cold, full moon small and white, crooked
trail of Holloway's galoshes, Vega in the Lyre very
green. [*Pause.*] Vega in the Lyre very green. [*Pause.*]
Following conversation then on the step, no, in the
room, back in the room, following conversation then
back in the room, Holloway: "My dear Bolton, it is now
past midnight, if you would be good enough—," gets
no further, Bolton: "Please! PLEASE!" Dead silence
then, not a sound, only the fire, all coal, burning down
now, Holloway on the hearthrug trying to toast his arse,
Bolton, where's Bolton, no light, only the fire, Bolton at
the window his back to the hangings, holding them a
little apart with his hand looking out, white world, even
the spire, white to the vane, most unusual, silence in

the house, not a sound, only the fire, no flames now, embers. [*Pause.*] Embers. [*Pause.*] Shifting, lapsing, furtive like, dreadful sound, Holloway on the rug, fine old chap, six foot, burly, legs apart, hands behind his back holding up the tails of his old macfarlane, Bolton at the window, grand old figure in his old red dressing-gown, back against the hangings, hand stretched out widening the chink, looking out, white world great trouble, not a sound, only the embers, sound of dying, dying glow, Holloway, Bolton, Bolton, Holloway, old men, great trouble, white world, not a sound. [*Pause.*] Listen to it! [*Pause.*] Close your eyes and listen to it, what would you think it was? [*Pause. Vehement.*] A drip! A drip! [*Sound of drip, rapidly amplified, suddenly cut off.*] Again! [*Drip again. Amplification begins.*] No! [*Drip cut off. Pause.*] Father! [*Pause. Agitated.*] Stories, stories, years and years of stories, till the need came on me, for someone, to be with me, anyone, a stranger, to talk to, imagine he hears me, years of that, and then, now, for someone who . . . knew me, in the old days, anyone, to be with me, imagine he hears me, what I am, now. [*Pause.*] No good either. [*Pause.*] Not there either. [*Pause.*] Try again. [*Pause.*] White world, not a sound. [*Pause.*] Holloway. [*Pause.*] Holloway says he'll go, damned if he'll sit up all night before a black grate, doesn't understand, call a man out, an old friend, in the cold and dark, an old friend, urgent need, bring the bag, then not a word, no explanation no heat, no light, Bolton: "Please! PLEASE!" Holloway, no refreshment, no welcome, chilled to the medulla, catch his death, can't understand, strange treatment, old friend, says he'll go, doesn't move, not a sound, fire dying, white beam from window, ghastly scene, wishes to God he hadn't come, no good, fire out, bitter cold, great trouble,

white world, not a sound, no good. [*Pause.*] No good.
[*Pause.*] Can't do it. [*Pause.*] Listen to it! [*Pause.*] Father!
[*Pause.*] You wouldn't know me now, you'd be sorry you
ever had me, but you were that already, a washout, that's
the last I heard from you, a washout. [*Pause. Imitating
father's voice.*] "Are you coming for a dip?" "No." "Come
on, come on." "No." Glare, stump to door, turn, glare. "A
washout, that's all you are, a washout!" [*Violent slam of
door. Pause.*] Again! [*Slam. Pause.*] Slam life shut like that!
[*Pause.*] Washout. [*Pause.*] Wish to Christ she had.
[*Pause.*] Never met Ada, did you, or did you, I can't
remember, no matter, no one'd know her now. [*Pause.*]
What turned her against me do you think, the child I
suppose, horrid little creature, wish to God we'd never
had her, I use to walk with her in the fields, Jesus that
was awful, she wouldn't let go my hand and I mad to
talk. "Run along now, Addie, and look at the lambs."
[*imitating Addie's voice.*] "No papa." "Go on now, go on."
[*Plaintive.*] "No papa." [*Violent.*] "Go on with you when
you're told and look at the lambs!" [*Addie's loud wail.
Pause.*] Ada too, conversation with her, that was
something, that's what hell will be like, small chat to
the babbling of Lethe about the good old days when we
wished we were dead. [*Pause.*] Price of margarine fifty
years ago. [*Pause.*] And now. [*Pause. With solemn
indignation.*] Price of blueband now! [*Pause.*] Father!
[*Pause.*] Tired of talking to you. [*Pause.*] That was always
the way, walk all over the mountains with you talking
and talking and then suddenly mum and home in
misery and not a word to a soul for weeks, sulky little
bastard, better off dead. [*Long pause.*] Ada. [*Pause.
Louder.*] Ada!

ADA   [*low remote voice throughout*] Yes.

HENRY   Have you been there long?

ADA   Some little time. [*Pause.*] Why do you stop, don't mind me. [*Pause.*] Do you want me to go away? [*Pause.*] Where is Addie?
[*Pause.*]

HENRY   With her music master. [*Pause.*] Are you going to answer me today?

ADA   You shouldn't be sitting on the cold stones, they're bad for your growths. Raise yourself up till I slip my shawl under you. [*Pause.*] Is that better?

HENRY   No comparison, no comparison. [*Pause.*] Are you going to sit down beside me?

ADA   Yes. [*No sound as she sits.*] Like that? [*Pause.*] Or do you prefer like that? [*Pause.*] You don't care. [*Pause.*] Chilly enough I imagine, I hope you put on your jaegers. [*Pause.*] Did you put on your jaegers, Henry?

HENRY   What happened was this, I put them on and then I took them off again and then I put them on again and then I took them off again and then I took them on again and then I—

ADA   Have you them on now?

HENRY   I don't know. [*Pause.*] Hooves! [*Pause. Louder.*] Hooves! [*Sound of hooves walking on hard road. They die rapidly away.*] Again!
[*Hooves as before. Pause.*]

ADA   Did you hear them?

HENRY   Not well.

ADA   Galloping?

HENRY   No. [*Pause.*] Could a horse mark time?
[*Pause.*]

ADA   I'm not sure that I know what you mean.

HENRY   [*irritably*] Could a horse be trained to stand still and mark time with its four legs?

ADA   Oh. [*Pause.*] The ones I used to fancy all did. [*She laughs. Pause.*] Laugh, Henry, it's not every day I crack a joke. [*Pause.*] Laugh, Henry do that for me.

HENRY   You wish *me* to laugh?

ADA   You laughed so charmingly once, I think that's what first attracted me to you. That and your smile. [*Pause.*] Come on, it will be like old times.
[*Pause. He tries to laugh, fails.*]

HENRY   Perhaps I should begin with the smile. [*Pause for smile.*] Did that attract you? [*Pause.*] Now I'll try again. [*Long horrible laugh.*] Any of the old charm there?

ADA   Oh Henry!
[*Pause.*]

HENRY   Listen to it! [*Pause.*] Lips and claws! [*Pause.*] Get away from it! Where it couldn't get at me! The Pampas! What?

ADA   Calm yourself.

HENRY   And I live on the brink of it! Why? Professional obligations? [*Brief laugh.*] Reasons of health? [*Brief laugh.*] Family ties? [*Brief laugh.*] A woman? [*Laugh in which she joins.*] Some old grave I cannot tear myself away from? [*Pause.*] Listen to it! What is it like?

ADA   It is like an old sound I used to hear. [*Pause.*] It is like another time, in the same place. [*Pause.*] It was rough, the spray came flying over us. [*Pause.*] Strange it should have been rough then. [*Pause.*] And calm now. [*Pause.*]

HENRY   Let us get up and go.

ADA   Go? Where? And Addie? She would be very distressed if she came and found you had gone without her. [*Pause.*] What do you suppose is keeping her?
[*Smart blow of cylindrical ruler on piano case. Unsteadily, ascending and descending, Addie plays scale of A Flat Major, hands first together, then reversed. Pause.*]

MUSIC MASTER   [*Italian accent*] Santa Cecilia!
[*Pause.*]

ADDIE   Will I play my piece now please?
[*Pause. Music Master beats two bars of waltz time with ruler on piano case. Addie plays opening bars of Chopin's 5th Waltz*

in A Flat Major, Music Master beating time lightly with ruler as she plays. In first chord of bass, bar 5, she plays E instead of F. Resounding blow of ruler on piano case. Addie stops playing.]

MUSIC MASTER [*violently*] Fa!

ADDIE [*tearfully*] What?

MUSIC MASTER [*violently*] Eff! Eff!

ADDIE [*tearfully*] Where?

MUSIC MASTER [*violently*] Qua! [*He thumps note.*] Fa!

[*Pause. Addie begins again, Music Master beating time lightly with ruler. When she comes to bar 5 she makes same mistake. Tremendous blow of ruler on piano case. Addie stops playing, begins to wail.*]

MUSIC MASTER [*frenziedly*] Eff! Eff! [*He hammers note.*] Eff! [*He hammers note.*] Eff!

[*Hammered note, "Eff!" and Addie's wail amplified to paroxysm, then suddenly cut off. Pause.*]

ADA You are silent today.

HENRY It was not enough to drag her into the world, now she must play the piano.

ADA She must learn. She shall learn. That—and riding.

[*Hooves walking.*]

RIDING MASTER Now Miss! Elbows in Miss! Hands down Miss! [*Hooves trotting.*] Now Miss! Back straight Miss! Knees in Miss! [*Hooves cantering.*] Now Miss! Tummy in Miss! Chin up Miss! [*Hooves galloping.*] Now Miss! Eyes front Miss! [*Addie begins to wail.*] Now Miss! Now Miss! [*Galloping hooves, "Now Miss!" and Addie's wail amplified to paroxysm, then suddenly cut off. Pause.*]

ADA What are you thinking of? [*Pause.*] I was never taught, until it was too late. All my life I regretted it.

HENRY What was your strong point, I forget.

ADA Oh . . . geometry I suppose, plane and solid. [*Pause.*] First plane, then solid. [*Shingle as he gets up.*] Why do you get up?

HENRY   I thought I might try and get as far as the water's edge. [*Pause. With a sigh.*] And back. [*Pause.*] Stretch my old bones.

[*Pause.*]

ADA   Well, why don't you? [*Pause.*] Don't stand there thinking about it. [*Pause.*] Don't stand there staring. [*Pause. He goes towards sea. Boots on shingle, say ten steps. He halts at water's edge. Pause. Sea a little louder. Distant.*] Don't wet your good boots.

[*Pause.*]

HENRY   Don't! don't. . . .

[*Sea suddenly rough.*]

ADA   [*twenty years earlier, imploring*] Don't! Don't!

HENRY   [*ditto, urgent*] Darling!

ADA   [*ditto, more feebly*] Don't!

HENRY   [*ditto, exultantly*] Darling!

[*Rough sea. Ada cries out. Cry and sea amplified, cut off. End of evocation. Pause. Sea calm. He goes back up deeply shelving beach. Boots laborious on shingle. He halts. Pause. He moves on. He halts. Pause. Sea calm and faint.*]

ADA   Don't stand there gaping. Sit down. [*Pause. Shingle as he sits.*] On the shawl. [*Pause.*] Are you afraid we might touch? [*Pause.*] Henry.

HENRY   Yes.

ADA   You should see a doctor about your talking, it's worse, what must it be like for Addie? [*Pause.*] Do you know what she said to me once, when she was still quite small, she said, Mummy, why does Daddy keep on talking all the time? She heard you in the lavatory. I didn't know what to answer.

HENRY   Daddy! Addie! [*Pause.*] I told you to tell her I was praying. [*Pause.*] Roaring prayers at God and his saints.

ADA   It's very bad for the child. [*Pause.*] It's silly to say it keeps you from hearing it, it doesn't keep you from hearing it and even if it does you shouldn't be hearing it, there must be something wrong with your brain. [*Pause.*]

HENRY That! I shouldn't be hearing that!

ADA I don't think you are hearing it. And if you are what's wrong with it, it's a lovely peaceful gentle soothing sound, why do you hate it? [*Pause.*] And if you hate it why don't you keep away from it? Why are you always coming down here? [*Pause.*] There's something wrong with your brain, you ought to see Holloway, he's alive still, isn't he? [*Pause.*]

HENRY [*wildly*] Thuds, I want thuds! Like this! [*He fumbles in the shingle, catches up two big stones and starts dashing them together.*] Stone! [*Clash.*] Stone! [*Clash. "Stone!" and clash amplified, cut off. Pause. He throws one stone away. Sound of its fall.*] That's life! [*He throws the other stone away. Sound of its fall.*] Not this . . . [*pause*] . . . sucking!

ADA And why life? [*Pause.*] Why life, Henry? [*Pause.*] Is there anyone about?

HENRY Not a living soul.

ADA I thought as much. [*Pause.*] When we longed to have it to ourselves there was always someone. Now that it does not matter the place is deserted.

HENRY Yes, you were always very sensitive to being seen in gallant conversation. The least feather of smoke on the horizon and you adjusted your dress and became immersed in the *Manchester Guardian*. [*Pause.*] The hole is still there, after all these years. [*Pause. Louder.*] The hole is still there.

ADA What hole? The earth is full of holes.

HENRY Where we did it at last for the first time.

ADA Ah yes, I think I remember. [*Pause.*] The place has not changed.

HENRY Oh yes it has, *I* can see it. [*Confidentially.*] There is a levelling going on! [*Pause.*] What age is she now?

ADA   I have lost count of time.

HENRY   Twelve? Thirteen? [*Pause.*] Fourteen?

ADA   I really could not tell you, Henry.

HENRY   It took us a long time to have her. [*Pause.*] Years we kept
        hammering away at it. [*Pause.*] But we did it in the end.
        [*Pause. Sigh.*] We had her in the end. [*Pause.*] Listen to it!
        [*Pause.*] It's not so bad when you get out on it. [*Pause.*]
        Perhaps I should have gone into the merchant navy.

ADA   It's only on the surface, you know. Underneath all is as
        quiet as the grave. Not a sound. All day, all night, not a
        sound. [*Pause.*]

HENRY   Now I walk about with the gramophone. But I forgot it
        today.

ADA   There is no sense in that. [*Pause.*] There is no sense in
        trying to drown it. [*Pause.*] See Holloway.
        [*Pause.*]

HENRY   Let us go for a row.

ADA   A row? And Addie? She would be very distressed if she
        came and found you had gone for a row without her.
        [*Pause.*] Who were you with just now? [*Pause.*] Before
        you spoke to me.

HENRY   I was trying to be with my father.

ADA   Oh. [*Pause.*] No difficulty about that.

HENRY   I mean I was trying to get him to be with me. [*Pause.*]
        You seem a little cruder than usual today, Ada. [*Pause.*]
        I was asking him if he had ever met you, I couldn't
        remember.

ADA   Well?

HENRY   He doesn't answer any more.

ADA   I suppose you have worn him out. [*Pause.*] You wore him
        out living and now you are wearing him out dead. [*Pause.*]
        The time comes when one cannot speak to you any more.
        [*Pause.*] The time will come when no one will speak to
        you at all, not even complete strangers. [*Pause.*] You will

be quite alone with your voice, there will be no other voice in the world but yours. [*Pause.*] Do you hear me? [*Pause.*]

HENRY   I can't remember if he met you.

ADA   You know he met me.

HENRY   No, Ada, I don't know, I'm sorry, I have forgotten almost everything connected with you.

ADA   You weren't there. Just your mother and sister. I had called to fetch you, as arranged. We were to go bathing together. [*Pause.*]

HENRY   [*irritably*] Drive on, drive on! Why do people always stop in the middle of what they are saying?

ADA   None of them knew where you were. Your bed had not been slept in. They were all shouting at one another. Your sister said she would throw herself off the cliff. Your father got up and went out, slamming the door. I left soon afterwards and passed him on the road. He did not see me. He was sitting on a rock looking out to sea. I never forgot his posture. And yet it was a common one. You used to have it sometimes. Perhaps just the stillness, as if he had been turned to stone. I could never make it out. [*Pause.*]

HENRY   Keep on, keep on! [*Imploringly.*] Keep it going, Ada, every syllable is a second gained.

ADA   That's all, I'm afraid. [*Pause.*] Go on now with your father or your stories or whatever you were doing, don't mind me any more.

HENRY   I can't! [*Pause.*] I can't do it any more!

ADA   You were doing it a moment ago, before you spoke to me.

HENRY   [*angrily*] I can't do it any more now! [*Pause.*] Christ! [*Pause.*]

ADA   Yes, you know what I mean, there are attitudes remain in one's mind for reasons that are clear, the carriage of a

head for example, bowed when one would have thought
it should be lifted, and vice versa, or a hand suspended
in mid-air, as if unowned. That kind of thing. But with
your father sitting on the rock that day nothing of the
kind, no detail you could put your finger on and say,
How very peculiar! No, I could never make it out.
Perhaps, as I said, just the great stillness of the whole
body, as if all the breath had left it. [*Pause.*] Is this
rubbish a help to you, Henry? [*Pause.*] I can try and go
on a little if you wish. [*Pause.*] No? [*Pause.*] Then I think
I'll be getting back.

HENRY   Not yet! You needn't speak. Just listen. Not even. Be with
me. [*Pause.*] Ada! [*Pause. Louder.*] Ada! [*Pause.*] Christ!
[*Pause.*] Hooves! [*Pause. Louder.*] Hooves! [*Pause.*] Christ!
[*Long pause.*] Left soon afterwards, passed you on the
road, didn't see her, looking out to.... [*Pause.*] Can't
have been looking out to *sea*. [*Pause.*] Unless you had
gone round the other side. [*Pause.*] Had you gone round
the cliff side? [*Pause.*] Father! [*Pause.*] Must have I
suppose. [*Pause.*] Stands watching you a moment, then
on down path to tram, up on open top and sits down in
front. [*Pause.*] Sits down in front. [*Pause.*] Suddenly feels
uneasy and gets down again, conductor: "Changed your
mind, Miss?," goes back up path, no sign of you. [*Pause.*]
Very unhappy and uneasy, hangs round a bit, not a soul
about, cold wind coming in off sea, goes back down
path and takes tram home. [*Pause.*] Takes tram home.
[*Pause.*] Christ! [*Pause.*] "My dear Bolton...." [*Pause.*] "If
it's an injection you want, Bolton, let down your
trousers and I'll give you one, I have a panhysterectomy
at nine," meaning of course the anaesthetic. [*Pause.*]
Fire out, bitter cold, white world, great trouble, not a
sound. [*Pause.*] Bolton starts playing with the curtain,
no, hanging, difficult to describe, draws it back no, kind

of gathers it towards him and the moon comes
flooding in, then lets it fall back, heavy velvet affair, and
pitch black in the room, then towards him again, white,
black, white, black, Holloway: "Stop that for the love of
God, Bolton, do you want to finish me?" [*Pause.*] Black,
white, black, white, maddening thing. [*Pause.*] Then he
suddenly strikes a match, Bolton does, lights a candle,
catches it up above his head, walks over and looks
Holloway full in the eye. [*Pause.*] Not a word, just the
look, the old blue eye, very glassy, lids worn thin, lashes
gone, whole thing swimming, and the candle shaking
over his head. [*Pause.*] Tears? [*Pause. Long laugh.*] Good
God no! [*Pause.*] Not a word, just the look, the old blue
eye, Holloway: "If you want a shot say so and let me get
to hell out of here." [*Pause.*] "We've had this before,
Bolton, don't ask me to go through it again." [*Pause.*]
Bolton: "Please!" [*Pause.*] "Please!" [*Pause.*] "Please,
Holloway!" [*Pause.*] Candle shaking and guttering all
over the place, lower now, old arm tired takes it in the
other hand and holds it high again, that's it, that was
always it, night, and the embers cold, and the glim
shaking in your old fist, saying, Please! Please! [*Pause.*]
Begging. [*Pause.*] Of the poor. [*Pause.*] Ada! [*Pause.*]
Father! [*Pause.*] Christ! [*Pause.*] Holds it high again,
naughty world, fixes Holloway, eyes drowned, won't ask
again, just the look, Holloway covers his face, not a
sound, white world, bitter cold, ghastly scene, old men,
great trouble, no good. [*Pause.*] No good. [*Pause.*] Christ!
[*Pause. Shingle as he gets up. He goes towards sea. Boots on
shingle. He halts. Pause. Sea a little louder.*] On. [*Pause. He
moves on. Boots on shingle. He halts at water's edge. Pause.
Sea a little louder.*] Little book. [*Pause.*] This evening. . . .
[*Pause.*] Nothing this evening. [*Pause.*] Tomorrow . . .
tomorrow . . . plumber at nine, then nothing. [*Pause.*

Puzzled.] Plumber at nine? [*Pause.*] Ah yes, the waste.
[*Pause.*] Words. [*Pause.*] Saturday . . . nothing. Sunday . . .
Sunday . . . nothing all day. [*Pause.*] Nothing, all day
nothing. [*Pause.*] All day all night nothing. [*Pause.*] Not a
sound.

ROUGH FOR RADIO I

HE   [*gloomily*] Madam.

SHE   Are you all right? [*Pause.*] You asked me to come.

HE   I ask no one to come here.

SHE   You suffered me to come.

HE   I meet my debts.
      [*Pause.*]

SHE   I have come to listen.

HE   When you please.
      [*Pause.*]

SHE   May I squat on this hassock? [*Pause.*] Thank you. [*Pause.*] May we
      have a little heat?

HE   No, madam.
      [*Pause.*]

SHE   Is it true the music goes on all the time?

HE   Yes.

SHE   Without cease?

HE   Without cease.

SHE   It's unthinkable! [*Pause.*] And the words too? All the time too?

HE   All the time.

SHE   Without cease?

HE   Yes.

SHE   It's unimaginable. [*Pause.*] So you are here all the time?

HE   Without cease.

[*Pause.*]

SHE   How troubled you look! [*Pause.*] May one see them?

HE   No, madam.

SHE   I may not go and see them?

HE   No, madam.

[*Pause.*]

SHE   May we have a little light?

HE   No, madam.

[*Pause.*]

SHE   How cold you are! [*Pause.*] Are these the two knobs?

HE   Yes.

SHE   Just push? [*Pause.*] Is it live? [*Pause.*] I ask you is it live.

HE   No, you must twist. [*Pause.*] To the right.

[*Click.*]

MUSIC   [*faint*] . . . .

[*Silence.*]

SHE   [*astonished*] But there are more than one!

HE   Yes.

SHE   How many?

[*Pause.*]

HE   To the right, madam, to the right.

[*Click.*]

VOICE   [*faint*] . . . .

SHE   [*with voice*] Louder!

VOICE   [*no louder*] . . . .

[*Silence.*]

SHE   [*astonished*] But he is alone!

HE   Yes.

SHE   All alone?

HE   When one is alone one is all alone.

[*Pause.*]

SHE   What is it like together?

[*Pause.*]

HE   To the right, madam.

        [*Click.*]

MUSIC   [*faint, brief*] ....

MUSIC ⎫
        ⎬ [*together*] ....
VOICE ⎭

        [*Silence.*]

SHE   They are not together?

HE   No.

SHE   They cannot see each other?

HE   No.

SHE   Hear each other?

HE   No.

SHE   It's inconceivable!

        [*Pause.*]

HE   To the right, madam.

        [*Click.*]

VOICE   [*faint*] ....

SHE   [*with voice*] Louder!

VOICE   [*no louder*] ....

        [*Silence.*]

SHE   And—[*faint stress*]—you like that?

HE   It is a need.

SHE   A need? *That* a need?

HE   It has become a need. [*Pause.*] To the right, madam.

        [*Click.*]

MUSIC   [*faint*] ....

SHE   [*with music*] Louder!

MUSIC   [*no louder*] ....

        [*Silence.*]

SHE   That too? [*Pause.*] That a need too?

HE   It has become a need, madam.

SHE   Are they in the same ... situation?

        [*Pause.*]

HE   I don't understand.

SHE   Are they ... subject to the same ... conditions?

HE   Yes, madam.

SHE   For instance? [*Pause.*] For instance?

HE   One cannot describe them, madam.

      [*Pause.*]

SHE   Well, I'm obliged to you.

HE   Allow me, this way.

      [*Pause.*]

SHE   [*a little off*] Is that a Turkoman?

HE   [*ditto*] Allow me.

SHE   [*a little further off*] How troubled you look! [*Pause.*] Well, I'll leave you. [*Pause.*] To your needs.

HE   [*ditto*] Goodbye, madam. [*Pause.*] To the right, madam, that's the garbage—[*faint stress*]—the *house* garbage. [*Pause.*] Goodbye, madam.

      [*Long pause. Sound of curtains violently drawn, first one, then the other, clatter of the heavy rings along the rods. Pause. Faint ping—as sometimes happens—of telephone receiver raised from cradle. Faint sound of dialling. Pause.*] Hello ... Miss ... is the doctor ... ah ... yes ... he to call me ... Macgillycuddy ... Mac-gilly-cuddy ... right ... he'll know ... and Miss ... Miss! ... urgent ... yes! ... [*shrill*] ... most urgent!

      [*Pause. Receiver put down with same faint ping. Pause. Click.*]

MUSIC [*faint*] ....

HE   [*with music*] Good God!

MUSIC [*faint*] ....

      [*Silence. Pause. Click.*]

VOICE [*faint*] ....

HE   [*with voice, shrill*] Come on! Come on!

VOICE [*faint*] ....

      [*Silence.*]

HE   [*low*] What'll I do? [*Pause. Faint ping of receiver raised again. Faint dialling. Pause.*] Hello ... Miss ... Macgillycuddy ... Mac-gilly-cuddy ... right ... I'm sorry but ... ah ... yes ... of course ...

can't reach him ... no idea ... understand ... right ...
immediately ... the moment he gets back ... what? ...
[*shrill*] ... yes! ... I told you so! ... most urgent! ... most
urgent! ... [*Pause. Low.*] Slut!
[*Sound of receiver put down violently. Pause. Click.*]

MUSIC   [*faint, brief*] ....
[*Silence. Click.*]

VOICE   [*faint, brief*]

HE   [*with voice, shrill*] It's crazy! Like one!

MUSIC }
VOICE }   [*together*] ....

[*Telephone rings. Receiver raised immediately, not more than a second's ring.*]

HE   [*with music and voice*] Yes ... wait ... [*Music and voice silent. Very
agitated.*] Yes ... yes ... no matter ... what the trouble is? ...
they're ending ... ENDING ... this morning ... what? ...
no! ... no question! ... ENDING I tell you ... nothing what? ...
to be done? ... I know there's nothing to be done ... what? ...
no! ... it's me ... ME ... what? I tell you they're ending ...
ENDING ... I can't stay like that after ... who? ... but she's left
me ... ah for God's sake ... haven't they all left me? ... did you
not know that? ... all left me ... sure? ... of course I'm sure ...
what? ... in an hour? ... not before? ... wait ... [*low*] ... there's
more ... they're together ... TOGETHER ... yes ... I don't
know ... like ... [*hesitation*] ... one ... the breathing ... I don't
know ... [*vehement*] ... no! ... never! ... meet? ... how could
they meet? ... what? ... what are all alike? ... last what? ...
gasps? ... wait ... don't go yet ... wait! ... [*Pause. Sound of
receiver put down violently. Low.*] Swine!
[*Pause. Click.*]

MUSIC   [*failing*] ....

MUSIC }
VOICE }   [*together, failing*] ....

[*Telephone rings. Receiver immediately raised.*]

HE   [*with music and voice*] Miss . . . what? . . . [*music and voice silent*] . . . a
confinement? . . . [*long pause*] . . . two confinements? . . . [*long
pause*] . . . one what? . . . what? breech? . . . what? . . . [*long
pause*] . . . tomorrow noon? . . .
[*Long pause. Faint ping as receiver put gently down. Long pause.
Click.*]

MUSIC   [*brief, failing*] . . . .

MUSIC } [*together, ending, breaking off together, resuming together more and
VOICE   more feebly*] . . . .

[*Silence. Long pause.*]

HE   [*whisper*] Tomorrow . . . noon . . .

ROUGH FOR RADIO II

Animator
Stenographer
Fox
Dick (mute)

A   Ready, miss?

S   And waiting, sir.

A   Fresh pad, spare pencils?

S   The lot, sir.

A   Good shape?

S   Tiptop, sir.

A   And you, Dick, on your toes? [*Swish of bull's pizzle. Admiringly.*] Wow! Let's hear it land. [*Swish and formidable thud.*] Good. Off with his hood. [*Pause.*] Ravishing face, ravishing! Is it not, miss?

S   Too true, sir. We know it by heart and yet the pang is ever new.

A   The gag. [*Pause.*] The blind. [*Pause.*] The plugs. [*Pause.*] Good. [*He thumps on his desk with a cylindrical ruler.*] Fox, open your eyes, readjust them to the light of day and look about you. [*Pause.*] You see, the same old team. I hope—

S   [*aflutter*] Oh!

A   What is it, miss? Vermin in the lingerie?

S   He smiled at me!

A   Good omen. [*Faint hope.*] Not the first time by any chance?

S   Heavens no, sir, what an idea!

A   [*disappointed*] I might have known. [*Pause.*] And yet it still affects you?

S   Why yes, sir, it is so sudden! So radiant! So fleeting!

A   You note it?

s   Oh no, sir, the words alone. [*Pause.*] Should one note the play of feature too?

A   I don't know, miss. Depending perhaps.

s   Me you know—

A   [*trenchant*] Leave it for the moment. [*Thump with ruler.*] Fox, I hope you have had a refreshing night and will be better inspired today than heretofore. Miss.

s   Sir.

A   Let us hear again the report on yesterday's results, it has somewhat slipped my memory.

s   [*reading*] "We the undersigned, assembled under—"

A   Skip.

s   [*reading*] ". . . note yet again with pain that these dicta—"

A   Dicta! [*Pause.*] Read on.

s   ". . . with pain that these dicta, like all those communicated to date and by reason of the same deficiencies, are totally inacceptable. The second half in particular is of such—"

A   Skip.

s   ". . . outlook quite hopeless were it not for our conviction—"

A   Skip. [*Pause.*] Well?

s   That is all, sir.

A   . . . same deficiencies . . . totally inacceptable . . . outlook quite hopeless . . . [*Disgusted.*] Well! [*Pause.*] Well!

s   That is all, sir. Unless I am to read the exhortations.

A   Read them.

s   ". . . instantly renew our standing exhortations, namely:

     1. Kindly to refrain from recording mere animal cries, they serve only to indispose us.

     2. Kindly to provide a strictly literal transcript, the meanest syllable has, or may have, its importance.

     3. Kindly to ensure full neutralization of the subject when not in session, especially with regard to the gag, its permanence and good repair. Thus rigid enforcement of the tube-feed, be it per buccam or be it on the other hand per rectum, is *absolutely*"—one word

underlined—"essential. The least word let fall in solitude and thereby in danger, as Mauthner has shown, of being no longer needed, *may be it*"—three words underlined.

"4. Kindly—"

A Enough! [*Sickened.*] Well! [*Pause.*] Well!

s It is past two, sir.

A [*roused from his prostration*] It is what?

s Past two, sir.

A [*roughly*] Then what are you waiting for? [*Pause. Gently.*] Forgive me, miss, forgive me, my cup is full. [*Pause.*] Forgive me!

s [*coldly*] Shall I open with yesterday's close?

A If you would be so good.

s [*reading*] "When I had done soaping the mole, thoroughly rinsing and drying before the embers, what next only out again in the blizzard and put him back in his chamber with his weight of grubs, at that instant his little heart was beating still I swear, ah my God my God." [*She strikes with her pencil on her desk.*] "My God."
[*Pause.*]

A Unbelievable! And there he jibbed, if I remember aright.

s Yes, sir, he would say no more.

A Dick functioned?

s Let me see . . . Yes, twice.
[*Pause.*]

A Does not the glare incommode you, miss, what if we should let down the blind?

s Thank you, sir, not on my account, it can never be too warm, never too bright, for me. But, with your permission, I shall shed my overall.

A [*with alacrity*] Please do, miss, please do. [*Pause.*] Staggering! Staggering! Ah were I but . . . forty years younger!

s [*rereading*] "Ah my God my God." [*Blow with pencil.*] "My God."

A Crabbed youth! No pity! [*Thump with ruler.*] Do you mark me? On! [*Silence.*] Dick! [*Swish and thud of pizzle on flesh. Faint cry from Fox.*] Off record, miss, remember?

s Drat it! Where's that eraser?

A Erase, miss, erase, we're in trouble enough already. [*Ruler.*] On! [*Silence.*] Dick!

F Ah yes, that for sure, live I did, no denying, all stones all sides—

A One moment.

F —walls no further—

A [*ruler*] Silence! Dick! [*Silence. Musing.*] Live I did . . . [*Pause.*] Has he used that turn before, miss?

S To what turn do you allude, sir?

A Live I did.

S Oh yes, sir, it's a notion crops up now and then. Perhaps not in those precise terms, so far, that I could not say offhand. But allusions to a life, though not common, are not rare.

A His own life?

S Yes, sir, a life all his own.

A [*disappointed*] I might have known. [*Pause.*] What a memory—mine! [*Pause.*] Have you read the Purgatory, miss, of the divine Florentine?

S Alas no, sir. I have merely flipped through the Inferno.

A [*incredulous*] Not read the Purgatory?

S Alas no, sir.

A There all sigh, I was, I was. It's like a knell. Strange, is it not?

S In what sense, sir?

A Why, one would rather have expected, I shall be. No?

S [*with tender condescension*] The creatures! [*Pause.*] It is getting on for three, sir.

A [*sigh*] Good. Where were we?

S ". . . walls no further—"

A Before, that, miss, the house is not on fire.

S ". . . live I did, no denying, all stones all sides"—inaudible—"walls—"

A [*ruler*] On! [*Silence.*] Dick!

S Sir.

A [*impatiently*] What is it, miss, can't you see that old time is aflying?

S I was going to suggest a touch of kindness, sir, perhaps just a hint of kindness.

A   So soon? And then? [*Firmly.*] No, miss, I appreciate your sentiment. But
     I have my method. Shall I remind you of it? [*Pause. Pleading.*] Don't
     say no! [*Pause.*] Oh you are an angel! You may sit, Dick. [*Pause.*] In a
     word, REDUCE the pressure instead of increasing it. [*Lyrical.*] Caress,
     fount of resipescence! [*Calmer.*] Dick, if you would. [*Swish and thud of
     pizzle on flesh. Faint cry from Fox.*] Careful, miss.

S   Have no fear, sir.

A   [*ruler*] . . . walls . . . walls what?

S   "no further," sir.

A   Right. [*Ruler.*] . . . walls no further . . . [*Ruler.*] On! [*Silence.*] Dick!

F   That for sure, no further, and there gaze, all the way up, all the way
     down, slow gaze, age upon age, up again, down again, little lichens of
     my own span, living dead in the stones, and there took to the
     tunnels. [*Silence. Ruler.*] Oceans too, that too, no denying, I drew near
     down the tunnels, blue above, blue ahead, that for sure, and there
     too, no further, ways end, all ends and farewell, farewell and fall,
     farewell seasons, till I fare again. [*Silence. Ruler.*] Farewell.
     [*Silence. Ruler. Pause.*]

A   Dick!

F   That for sure, no denying, no further, down in Spring, up in Fall, or
     inverse, such summers missed, such winters.
     [*Pause.*]

A   Nice! Nicely put! Such summers missed! So sibilant! Don't you agree,
     miss?

F ⎫
   ⎬ [*together*]   Ah that for sure—
S ⎭   Oh me you know—

A   Hsst!

F   —fatigue, what fatigue, my brother inside me, my old twin, ah to be he
     and he—but no, no no. [*Pause.*] No no. [*Silence. Ruler.*] Me get up, me
     go on, what a hope, it was he, for hunger. Have yourself opened,
     Maud would say, opened up, it's nothing, I'll give him suck if he's
     still alive, ah but no, no no. [*Pause.*] No no.
     [*Silence.*]

A   [*discouraged*] Ah dear.

s   He is weeping, sir, shall I note it?

A   I really do not know what to advise, miss.

s   Inasmuch as . . . how shall I say? . . . human trait . . . can one say in English?

A   I have never come across it, miss, but no doubt.

F   Scrabble scrabble—

A   Silence! [*Pause.*] No holding him!

s   As such . . . I feel . . . perhaps . . . at a pinch . . . [*Pause.*]

A   Are you familiar with the works of Sterne, miss?

s   Alas no, sir.

A   I may be quite wrong, but I seem to remember, there somewhere, a tear an angel comes to catch as it falls. Yes, I seem to remember . . . admittedly he was grandchild to an archbishop. [*Half rueful, half complacent.*] Ah these old spectres from the days of book reviewing, they lie in wait for one at every turn. [*Pause. Suddenly decided.*] Note it, miss, note it, and come what may. As well as for a sheep . . . [*Pause.*] Who is this woman . . . what's the name?

s   Maud. I don't know, sir, no previous mention of her has been made.

A   [*excited*] Are you sure?

s   Positive, sir. You see, my nanny was a Maud, so that the name would have struck me, had it been pronounced. [*Pause.*]

A   I may be quite wrong, but I somehow have the feeling this is the first time—oh I know it's a far call!—that he has actually . . . *named* anyone. No?

s   That may well be, sir. To make sure I would have to check through from the beginning. That would take time.

A   Kith and kin?

s   Never a word, sir. I have been struck by it. Mine play such a part, in my life!

A   And of a sudden, in the same sentence, a woman, with Christian name to boot, and a brother. I ask you!

[*Pause.*]

s   That twin, sir . . .

A   I know, not very convincing.

s   [*scandalized*] But it's quite simply impossible! Inside him! *Him!*

A   No no, such things happen, such things happen. Nature, you know . . . [*Faint laugh.*] Fortunately. A world without monsters, just imagine! [*Pause for imagining.*] No, that is not what troubles me. [*Warmly.*] Look you, miss, what counts is not so much the *thing*, in itself, that would astonish me too. No, it's the word, the notion. The notion brother is not unknown to him! [*Pause.*] But what really matters is this woman—what name did you say?

s   Maud, sir.

A   Maud!

s   And who is in milk, what is more, or about to be.

A   For mercy's sake! [*Pause.*] How does the passage go again?

s   [*rereading*] "Me get up, me go on, what a hope, it was he, for hunger. Have yourself opened, Maud would say, opened up, it's nothing, I'll give him suck if he's still alive, ah but no, no no." [*Pause.*] "No no." [*Pause.*]

A   And then the tear.

s   Exactly, sir. What I call the human trait. [*Pause.*]

A   [*low, with emotion*] Miss.

s   Sir.

A   Can it be we near our goal. [*Pause.*] Oh how bewitching you look when you show your teeth! Ah were I but . . . thirty years younger.

s   It is well after three, sir.

A   [*sigh*] Good. Where he left off. Once more.

s   "Oh but no, no—"

A   *Ah* but no. No?

s   You are quite right, sir. "Ah but no, no—"

A   [*severely*] Have a care, miss.

s   "Ah but no, no no." [*Pause.*] "No, no."

A   [*ruler*] On! [*Silence.*] Dick!

s   He has gone off, sir.

A   Just a shade lighter, Dick. [*Mild thud of pizzle.*] Ah no, you exaggerate, better than that. [*Swish and violent thud. Faint cry from Fox. Ruler.*] Ah but no, no no. On!

F   [*scream*] Let me out! Peter out in the stones!

A   Ah dear! There he goes again. Peter out in the stones!

s   It's a mercy he's tied.

A   [*gently*] Be reasonable, Fox. Stop—you may sit, Dick—stop jibbing. It's hard on you, we know. It does not lie entirely with us, we know. You might prattle away to your latest breath and still the one . . . thing remain unsaid that can give you back your darling solitudes, we know. But this much is sure: the more you say the greater your chances. Is that not so, miss?

s   It stands to reason, sir.

A   [*as to a backward pupil*] Don't ramble! Treat the subject, whatever it is! [*Snivel.*] More variety! [*Snivel.*] Those everlasting wilds may have their charm, but there is nothing there for us, that would astonish me. [*Snivel.*] Those micaceous schists, if you knew the effect [*snivel*] they can have on one, in the long run. [*Snivel.*] And your fauna! Those fodient rodents! [*Snivel.*] You wouldn't have a handkerchief, miss, you could lend me?

s   Here you are, sir.

A   Most kind. [*Blows nose abundantly.*] Much obliged.

s   Oh you may keep it, sir.

A   No no, now I'll be all right. [*To Fox.*] Of course we do not know, any more than you, what exactly it is we are after, what sign or set of words. But since you have failed so far to let it escape you, it is not by harking on the same old themes that you are likely to succeed, that would astonish me.

s   He has gone off again, sir.

A   [*warming to his point*] Someone, perhaps that is what is wanting, someone who once saw you . . . [*abating*] . . . go by. I may be quite wrong, but try, at least, what do you stand to lose? [*Beside himself.*] Even though it is not true!

s   [*shocked*] Oh sir!

A   A father, a mother, a friend, a . . . Beatrice—no, that is asking too much.
Simply someone, anyone, who once saw you . . . go by. [*Pause.*] That
woman . . . what's the name?

s   Maud, sir.

A   That Maud, for example, perhaps you once brushed against each other.
Think hard!

s   He has gone off, sir.

A   Dick!—no, wait. Kiss him, miss, perhaps that will stir some fibre.

s   Where, sir?

A   In his heart, in his entrails—or some other part.

s   No, I mean kiss him where, sir?

A   [*angry*] Why on his stinker of a mouth, What do you suppose?
[*Stenographer kisses Fox. Howl from Fox.*] Till it bleeds! Kiss it white!
[*Howl from Fox.*] Suck his gullet!
[*Silence.*]

s   He has fainted away, sir.

A   Ah . . . perhaps I went too far. [*Pause.*] Perhaps I slipped you too soon.

s   Oh no, sir, you could not have waited a moment longer, time is up.
[*Pause.*] The fault is mine, I did not go about it as I ought.

A   Come, come, miss! To the marines! [*Pause.*] Up already! [*Pained.*] I
chatter too much.

s   Come, come, sir, don't say that, it is part of your rôle, as animator.
[*Pause.*]

A   That tear, miss, do you remember?

s   Oh yes, sir, distinctly.

A   [*faint hope*] Not the first time by any chance?

s   Heavens no, sir, what an idea!

A   [*disappointed*] I might have known.

s   Last winter, now I come to think of it, he shed several, do you not
remember?

A   Last winter! But, my dear child, I don't remember yesterday, it is down
the hatch with love's young dream. Last winter! [*Pause. Low, with
emotion.*] Miss.

s   [*low*] Sir.

A   That . . . Maud.

     [*Pause.*]

s   [*encouraging*] Yes, sir.

A   Well . . . you know . . . I may be wrong . . . I wouldn't like to . . . I hardly
     dare say it . . . but it seems to me that . . . here . . . possibly . . . we
     have something at last.

s   Would to God, sir.

A   Particularly with that tear so hard behind. It is not the first, agreed. But
     in such a context!

s   And the milk, sir, don't forget the milk.

A   The breast! One can almost see it!

s   Who got her in that condition, there's another question for us.

A   What condition, miss, I fail to follow you.

s   Someone has fecundated her. [*Pause. Impatient.*] If she is in milk
     someone must have fecundated her.

A   To be sure!

s   Who?

A   [*very excited*] You mean . . .

s   I ask myself.

     [*Pause.*]

A   May we have that passage again, miss?

s   "Have yourself opened, Maud would say, opened—"

A   [*delighted*] That frequentative! [*Pause.*] Sorry, miss.

s   "Have yourself opened, Maud would say, opened—"

A   Don't skip, miss, the text in its entirety if you please.

s   I skip nothing, sir. [*Pause.*] What have I skipped, sir?

A   [*emphatically*] ". . . between two kisses . . ." [*Sarcastic.*] That mere trifle!
     [*Angry.*] How can we ever hope to get anywhere if you suppress gems
     of that magnitude?

s   But, sir, he never said anything of the kind.

A   [*angry*] ". . . Maud would say, *between two kisses,* etc." Amend.

s   But, sir, I—

A   What the devil are you deriding, miss? My hearing? My memory? My good faith? [*Thunderous.*] Amend!

S   [*feebly*] As you will, sir.

A   Let us hear how it runs now.

S   [*tremulous*] "Have yourself opened, Maud would say, between two kisses, opened up, it's nothing, I'll give him suck if he's still alive, ah but no, no no." [*Faint pencil.*] "No no."
   [*Silence.*]

A   Don't cry, miss, dry your pretty eyes and smile at me. Tomorrow, who knows, we may be free.

WORDS AND MUSIC

A piece for radio

MUSIC *Small orchestra softly tuning up.*

WORDS Please! [*Tuning. Louder.*] Please! [*Tuning dies away.*] How much
longer cooped up here in the dark? [*With loathing.*] With you!
[*Pause.*] Theme. . . . [*Pause.*] Theme . . . sloth. [*Pause. Rattled off, low.*]
Sloth is of all the passions the most powerful passion and indeed
no passion is more powerful than the passion of sloth, this is the
mode in which the mind is most affected and indeed— [*Burst of
tuning. Loud, imploring.*] Please! [*Tuning dies away. As before.*] The
mode in which the mind is most affected and indeed in no mode
is the mind more affected than in this, by passion we are to
understand a movement of the soul pursuing or fleeing real or
imagined pleasure or pain pleasure or pain real or imagined
pleasure or pain, of all these movements and who can number
them of all these movements and they are legion sloth is the
most urgent and indeed by no movement is the soul more
urged than by this by this by this to and from by no movement
the soul more urged than by this to and— [*Pause.*] From. [*Pause.*]
Listen! [*Distant sound of rapidly shuffling carpet slippers.*] At last!
[*Shuffling louder. Burst of tuning.*] Hsst!
[*Tuning dies away. Shuffling louder. Silence.*]

CROAK Joe.

WORDS [*humble*] My Lord.

CROAK   Bob.

MUSIC   *Humble muted adsum.*

CROAK   My comforts! Be friends! [*Pause.*] Bob.

MUSIC   *As before.*

CROAK   Joe.

WORDS   [*as before*] My Lord.

CROAK   Be friends! [*Pause.*] I am late, forgive. [*Pause.*] The face. [*Pause.*] On the stairs. [*Pause.*] Forgive. [*Pause.*] Joe.

WORDS   [*as before*] My Lord.

CROAK   Bob.

MUSIC   *As before.*

CROAK   Forgive. [*Pause.*] In the tower. [*Pause.*] The face. [*Long pause.*] Theme tonight. . . . [*Pause.*] Theme tonight . . . love. [*Pause.*] Love. [*Pause.*] My club. [*Pause.*] Joe.

WORDS   [*as before*] My Lord.

CROAK   Love. [*Pause. Thump of club on ground.*] Love!

WORDS   [*orotund*] Love is of all the passions the most powerful passion and indeed no passion is more powerful than the passion of love. [*Clears throat.*] This is the mode in which the mind is most strongly affected and indeed in no mode is the mind more strongly affected than in this.
[*Pause.*]

CROAK   *Rending sigh. Thump of club.*

WORDS   [*as before*] By passion we are to understand a movement of the mind pursuing or fleeing real or imagined pleasure or pain. [*Clears throat.*] Of all—

CROAK   [*anguished*] Oh!

WORDS   [*as before*] Of all these movements then and who can number them and they are legion sloth is the LOVE is the most urgent and indeed by no manner of movement is the soul more urged than by this, to and—
[*Violent thump of club.*]

CROAK   Bob.

WORDS   From.
[*Violent thump of club.*]

CROAK   Bob!

MUSIC   *As before.*

CROAK   Love!

MUSIC   *Rap of baton on stand. Soft music worthy of foregoing, great
expression, with audible groans and protestations— "No!" "Please!"
etc.—from Words. Pause.*

CROAK   [*anguished*] Oh! [*Thump of club.*] Louder!

MUSIC   *Loud rap of baton and as before fortissimo, all expression gone,
drowning Words' protestations. Pause.*

CROAK   My comforts! [*Pause.*] Joe sweet.

WORDS   [*as before*] Arise then and go now the manifest unanswerable—

CROAK   *Groans.*

WORDS   —to wit this love what is this love that more than all the cursed
deadly or any other of its great movers so moves the soul and
soul what is this soul that more than by any of its great movers
is by love so moved? [*Clears throat. Prosaic.*] Love of woman, I
mean, if that is what my Lord means.

CROAK   Alas!

WORDS   What? [*Pause. Very rhetorical.*] Is love the word? [*Pause. Do.*] Is soul
the word? [*Pause. Do.*] Do we mean love, when we say love?
[*Pause. Pause. Do.*] Soul, when we say soul?

CROAK   [*anguished*] Oh! [*Pause.*] Bob dear.

WORDS   Do we? [*With sudden gravity.*] Or don't we?

CROAK   [*imploring*] Bob!

MUSIC   *Rap of baton. Love and soul music, with just audible protestations—
"No!" "Please!" "Peace!" etc.—from Words. Pause.*

CROAK   [*anguished*] Oh! [*Pause.*] My balms! [*Pause.*] Joe.

WORDS   [*humble*] My Lord.

CROAK   Bob.

MUSIC   *Adsum as before.*

CROAK   My balms! [*Pause.*] Age. [*Pause.*] Joe. [*Pause. Thump of club.*] Joe.

WORDS   [*as before*] My Lord.

CROAK   Age!
         [*Pause.*]

WORDS   [*faltering*] Age is . . . age is when . . . old age I mean . . . if that is

what my Lord means ... is when ... if you're a man ... were a
man ... huddled ... nodding ... the ingle ... waiting—
[*Violent thump of club.*]

CROAK   Bob. [*Pause.*] Age. [*Pause. Violent thump of club.*] Age!

MUSIC   *Rap of baton. Age music, soon interrupted by violent thump.*

CROAK   Together. [*Pause. Thump.*] Together! [*Pause. Violent thump.*]
         Together, dogs!

MUSIC   *Long la.*

WORDS   [*imploring*] No!
         [*Violent thump.*]

CROAK   Dogs!

MUSIC   *La.*

WORDS   [*trying to sing*] Age is when ... to a man ...

MUSIC   *Improvement of above.*

WORDS   [*trying to sing this*] Age is when to a man ...

MUSIC   *Suggestion for following.*

WORDS   [*trying to sing this*] Huddled o'er ... the ingle. ... [*Pause. Violent
         thump. Trying to sing.*] Waiting for the hag to put the ... pan in
         the bed ...

MUSIC   *Improvement of above.*

WORDS   [*trying to sing this*] Waiting for the hag to put the pan in the bed.

MUSIC   *Suggestion for following.*

WORDS   [*trying to sing this*] And bring the ... arrowroot. ... [*Pause. Violent
         thump. As before.*] And bring the toddy. ...
         [*Pause. Tremendous thump.*]

CROAK   Dogs!

MUSIC   *Suggestion for following.*

WORDS   [*trying to sing this*] She comes in the ashes. ... [*Imploring.*] No!

MUSIC   *Repeats suggestion.*

WORDS   [*trying to sing this*] She comes in the ashes who loved could not
         be ... won or ...
         [*Pause.*]

MUSIC   *Repeats end of previous suggestion.*

WORDS   [*trying to sing this*] Or won not loved ... [*wearily*] ... or some other trouble. . . . [*Pause. Trying to sing.*] Comes in the ashes like in that old—

MUSIC   *Interrupts with improvement of this and brief suggestion.*

WORDS   [*trying to sing this*] Comes in the ashes like in that old light . . . her face . . . in the ashes. . . .

[*Pause.*]

CROAK   *Groans.*

MUSIC   *Suggestion for following.*

WORDS   [*trying to sing this*] That old moonlight . . . on the earth . . . again.

[*Pause.*]

MUSIC   *Further brief suggestion.*

[*Silence.*]

CROAK   *Groans.*

MUSIC   *Plays air through alone, then invites Words with opening, pause, invites again and finally accompanies very softly.*

WORDS   [*trying to sing, softly*]

Age is when to a man
Huddled o'er the ingle
Shivering for the hag
To put the pan in the bed
And bring the toddy
She comes in the ashes
Who loved could not be won
Or won not loved
Or some other trouble
Comes in the ashes
Like in that old light
The face in the ashes
That old starlight
On the earth again.

[*Long pause.*]

CROAK   [*murmur*] The face. [*Pause.*] The face. [*Pause.*] The face. [*Pause.*] The face.

MUSIC   *Rap of baton and warmly sentimental, about one minute.*

[*Pause.*]

CROAK   The face.

WORDS   [*cold*] Seen from above in that radiance so cold and faint. . . .

[*Pause.*]

MUSIC   *Warm suggestion from above for above.*

WORDS   [*disregarding, cold*] Seen from above at such close quarters in that radiance so cold and faint with eyes so dimmed by . . . what had passed, its quite . . . piercing beauty is a little. . . .

[*Pause.*]

MUSIC   *Renews timidly previous suggestion.*

WORDS   [*interrupting, violently*] Peace!

CROAK   My comforts! Be friends!

[*Pause.*]

WORDS   . . . blunted. Some moments later however, such are the powers of recuperation at this age, the head is drawn back to a distance of two or three feet, the eyes widen to a stare and begin to feast again. [*Pause.*] What then is seen would have been better seen in the light of day, that is incontestable. But how often it has, in recent months, how often, at all hours, under all angles, in cloud and shine, been seen I mean. And there is, is there not, in that clarity of silver . . . that clarity of silver . . . is there not . . . my Lord. . . . [*Pause.*] Now and then the rye, swayed by a light wind, casts and withdraws its shadow.

[*Pause.*]

CROAK   *Groans.*

WORDS   Leaving aside the features or lineaments proper, matchless severally and in their ordonnance—

CROAK   *Groans.*

WORDS   —flare of the black disordered hair as though spread wide on water, the brows knitted in a groove suggesting pain but simply concentration more likely all things considered on some consummate inner process, the eyes of course closed in keeping with this, the lashes . . . [*pause*] . . . the nose . . . [*pause*] . . . nothing, a little pinched perhaps, the lips. . . .

CROAK   [*anguished*] Lily!

WORDS   ... tight, a gleam of tooth biting on the under, no coral, no swell, whereas normally. . . .

CROAK   *Groans.*

WORDS   ... the whole so blanched and still that were it not for the great white rise and fall of the breasts, spreading as they mount and then subsiding to their natural ... aperture—

MUSIC   *Irrepressible burst of spreading and subsiding music with vain protestations— "Peace!" "No!" "Please!" etc. —from Words. Triumph and conclusion.*

WORDS   [*gently expostulatory*] My Lord! [*Pause. Faint thump of club.*] I resume, so wan and still and so ravished away that it seems no more of the earth than Mira in the Whale, at her tenth and greatest magnitude on this particular night shining coldly down—as we say, looking up. [*Pause.*] Some moments later however, such are the powers—

CROAK   [*anguished*] No!

WORDS   —the brows uncloud, the lips part and the eyes ... [*pause*] ... the brows uncloud, the nostrils dilate, the lips part and the eyes ... [*pause*] ... a little colour comes back into the cheeks and the eyes ... [*reverently*] ... open. [*Pause.*] Then down a little way ... [*Pause. Change to poetic tone. Low.*]

> Then down a little way
> Through the trash
> To where ... towards where. . . .

[*Pause.*]

MUSIC   *Discreet suggestion for above.*

WORDS   [*trying to sing this*]

> Then down a little way
> Through the trash
> Towards where ...

[*Pause.*]

MUSIC   *Discreet suggestion for following.*

WORDS   [*trying to sing this*]

> All dark no begging
> No giving no words
> No sense no need. . . .

[*Pause.*]

MUSIC   *More confident suggestion for following.*

WORDS   [*trying to sing this*]

> Through the scum
> Down a little way
> To where one glimpse
> Of that wellhead.

[*Pause.*]

MUSIC   *Invites with opening, pause, invites again and finally accompanies very softly.*

WORDS   [*trying to sing, softly*]

> Then down a little way
> Through the trash
> Towards where
> All dark no begging
> No giving no words
> No sense no need
> Through the scum
> Down a little way
> To whence one glimpse
> Of that wellhead.

[*Pause. Shocked.*] My Lord! [*Sound of club let fall. As before.*] My Lord! [*Shuffling slippers, with halts. They die away. Long pause.*] Bob. [*Pause.*] Bob!

MUSIC   *Brief rude retort.*

WORDS   Music. [*Imploring.*] Music!

[*Pause.*]

MUSIC   *Rap of baton and statement with elements already used or wellhead alone.*

[*Pause.*]

WORDS   Again. [*Pause. Imploring.*] Again!

MUSIC   *As before or only very slightly varied.*

[*Pause.*]

WORDS   *Deep sigh.*

Curtain

CASCANDO

A radio piece for music and voice

OPENER   [*cold*] It is the month of May . . . for me.

[*Pause.*]

Correct.

[*Pause.*]

I open.

VOICE   [*low, panting*] —story . . . if you could finish it . . . you could rest . . . sleep . . . not before . . . oh I know . . . the ones I've finished . . . thousands and one . . . all I ever did . . . in my life . . . with my life . . . saying to myself . . . finish this one . . . it's the right one . . . then rest . . . sleep . . . no more stories . . . no more words . . . and finished it . . . and not the right one . . . couldn't rest . . . straight away another . . . to begin . . . to finish . . . saying to myself . . . finish this one . . . then rest . . . this time . . . it's the right one . . . this time . . . you have it . . . and finished it . . . and not the right one . . . couldn't rest . . . straight away another . . . but this one . . . it's different . . . I'll finish it . . . I've got it . . . Woburn . . . I resume . . . a long life . . . already . . . say what you like . . . a few misfortunes . . . that's enough . . . five years later . . . ten . . . I don't know . . . Woburn . . . he's changed . . . not enough . . . recognizable . . . in the shed . . . yet another . . . waiting for night . . . night to fall . . . to go out . . . go on . . . elsewhere . . . sleep elsewhere . . .

it's slow . . . he lifts his head . . . now and then . . . his eyes . . .
to the window . . . it's darkening . . . earth darkening . . . it's
night . . . he gets up . . . knees first . . . then up . . . on his
feet . . . slips out . . . Woburn . . . same old coat . . . right the
sea . . . left the hills . . . he has the choice . . . he has only—

OPENER   [*with Voice*] And I close.

    [*Silence.*]

    I open the other.

MUSIC   . . . .

OPENER   [*with Music*] And I close.

    [*Silence.*]

    I open both.

VOICE ⎫   —on . . . getting on . . . finish . . . don't
     ⎬ [*together*]
MUSIC ⎭ . . . .

give up . . . then rest . . . sleep . . . not before . . . finish
. . . .

this time . . . it's the right one . . . you have it . . . you've got
. . . .

it . . . it's there . . . somewhere . . . you've got him . . . follow . . .
. . . .

him . . . don't lose him . . . Woburn story . . . getting on . . .
. . . .

finish . . . then sleep . . . no more stories . . . no more words
. . . .

. . . come on . . . next thing . . . he—
. . . .

OPENER   [*with Voice and Music*] And I close.

    [*Silence.*]

    I start again.

VOICE   —down . . . gentle slopes . . . boreen . . . giant aspens . . . wind in
the boughs . . . faint sea . . . Woburn . . . same old coat . . . he
goes on . . . stops . . . not a soul . . . not yet . . . night too
bright . . . say what you like . . . he goes on . . . hugging the
bank . . . same old stick . . . he goes down . . . falls . . . on

purpose or not . . . can't see . . . he's down . . . that's what
counts . . . face in the mud . . . arms spread . . . that's the
idea . . . already . . . there already . . . no not yet . . . he gets
up . . . knees first . . . hands flat . . . in the mud . . . head
sunk . . . then up . . . on his feet . . . huge bulk . . . come on . . .
he goes on . . . he goes down . . . come on . . . in his head . . .
what's in his head . . . a hole . . . a shelter . . . a hollow . . . in the
dunes . . . a cave . . . vague memory . . . in his head . . . of a
cave . . . he goes down . . . no more trees . . . no more bank . . .
he's changed . . . not enough . . . night too bright . . . soon the
dunes . . . no more cover . . . not a soul . . . not—
[*Silence.*]

MUSIC   . . . .

[*Silence.*]

VOICE }
MUSIC } [*together*] —rest . . . sleep . . . no more stories . . .
. . . .

no more words . . . don't give up . . . this time . . . it's the
. . . .

right one . . . we're there . . . I'm there . . . somewhere . . .
. . . .

Woburn . . . I've got him . . . don't lose him . . . follow him
. . . .

. . . to the end . . . come on . . . this time . . . it's the right one
. . . .

. . . finish . . . sleep . . . Woburn . . . come on—
. . . .

[*Silence.*]

OPENER   So, at will.
They say, It's in his head.
No. I open.

VOICE   —falls . . . again . . . on purpose or not . . . can't see . . . he's
down . . . that's what matters . . . face in the sand . . . arms
spread . . . bare dunes . . . not a scrub . . . same old coat . . .
night too bright . . . say what you like . . . sea louder . . .

thunder ... manes of foam ... Woburn ... his head ... what's in his head ... peace ... peace again ... in his head ... no further ... no more searching ... sleep ... no not yet ... he gets up ... knees first ... hands flat ... in the sand ... head sunk ... then up ... on his feet ... huge bulk ... same old broadbrim ... jammed down ... come on ... he goes on ... ton weight ... in the sand ... knee-deep ... he goes down ... sea—

OPENER   [*with Voice*] And I close.

[*Silence.*]

I open the other.

MUSIC   . . . .

OPENER   [*with Music*] And I close.

[*Silence.*]

So, at will.

It's my life, I live on that.

[*Pause.*]

Correct.

[*Pause.*]

What do I open?

They say, He opens nothing, he has nothing to open, it's in his head.

They don't see me, they don't see what I do, they don't see what I have, and they say, He opens nothing, he has nothing to open, it's in his head.

I don't protest any more, I don't say any more,

There is nothing in my head.

I don't answer any more.

I open and close.

VOICE   —lights ... of the land ... the island ... the sky ... he need only ... lift his head ... his eyes ... he'd see them ... shine on him ... but no ... he—

[*Silence.*]

MUSIC   [*brief*] . . . .

[*Silence.*]

OPENER   They say, That is not his life, he does not live on that. They don't
          see me, they don't see what my life is, they don't see what I live
          on, and they say, That is not his life, he does not live on that.
          [*Pause.*]
          I have lived on it . . . till I'm old.
          Old enough.
          Listen.

VOICE   [*weakening*] —this time . . . I'm there . . . Woburn . . . it's him . . .
          I've seen him . . . I've got him . . . come on . . . same old coat . . .
          he goes down . . . falls . . . falls again . . . on purpose or not . . .
          can't see . . . he's down . . . that's what counts . . . come on—

OPENER   [*with Voice*] Full strength.

VOICE   —face . . . in the stones . . . no more sand . . . all stones . . . that's
          the idea . . . we're there . . . this time . . . no not yet . . . he gets
          up . . . knees first . . . hands flat . . . in the stones . . . head
          sunk . . . then up . . . on his feet . . . huge bulk . . . Woburn . . .
          faster . . . he goes on . . . he goes down . . . he—
          [*Silence.*]

MUSIC   [*weakening*] . . . .

OPENER   [*with Music*] Full strength.

MUSIC   . . . .
          [*Silence.*]

OPENER   That's not all.
          I open both.
          Listen.

VOICE ⎫   —sleep . . . no further . . . no more
      ⎬ [*together*]
MUSIC ⎭   . . . .

          searching . . . to find him . . . in the dark . . . to see him . . .
          . . . .

          to say to him . . . for whom . . . that's it . . . no matter . . .
          . . . .

          never him . . . never right . . . start again . . . in the dark . . .
          . . . .

          done with that . . . this time . . . it's the right one . . . we're

. . . .

there . . . nearly . . . finish—

. . . .

[*Silence.*]

OPENER   From one world to another, it's as though they drew together.
We have not much further to go. Good.

VOICE ⎫
        ⎬ [*together*]   —nearly . . . I've got him . . . I've seen
MUSIC ⎭   . . . .

him . . . I've said him . . . we're there . . . nearly . . . no more

. . . .

stories . . . all false . . . this time . . . it's the right one . . . I

. . . .

have it . . . finish . . . sleep . . . Woburn . . . it's him . . . I've

. . . .

got him . . . follow him . . . to—

. . . .

[*Silence.*]

OPENER   Good.

[*Pause.*]

Yes, correct, the month of May.

You know, the reawakening.

[*Pause.*]

I open.

VOICE   —no tiller . . . no thwarts . . . no oars . . . afloat . . . sucked out . . .
then back . . . aground . . . drags free . . . out . . . Woburn . . . he
fills it . . . flat out . . . face in the bilge . . . arms spread . . . same
old coat . . . hands clutching . . . the gunnels . . . no . . . I don't
know . . . I see him . . . he clings on . . . out to sea . . . heading
nowhere . . . for the island . . . then no more . . . else—

[*Silence.*]

MUSIC   . . . .

[*Silence.*]

OPENER   They said, It's his own, it's his voice, it's in his head.

[*Pause.*]

VOICE —faster ... out ... driving out ... rearing ... plunging ...
heading nowhere ... for the island ... then no more ...
elsewhere ... anywhere ... heading anywhere ... lights—
[*Pause.*]

OPENER No resemblance.
I answered, And that ...

MUSIC [*brief*] ....
[*Silence.*]

OPENER ... is that mine too?
But I don't answer any more.
And they don't say anything any more.
They have quit.
Good.
[*Pause.*]
Yes, correct, the month of May, the close of May.
The long days.
[*Pause.*]
I open.
[*Pause.*]
I'm afraid to open.
But I must open.
So I open.

VOICE —come on ... Woburn ... arms spread ... same old coat ... face
in the bilge ... he clings on ... island gone ... far astern ...
heading out ... open sea ... land gone ... his head ... what's
in his head ... Woburn—

OPENER [*with Voice*] Come on! Come on!

VOICE —at last ... we're there ... no further ... no more searching
... in the dark ... elsewhere ... always elsewhere ... we're
there ... nearly ... Woburn ... hang on ... don't let go ... lights
gone ... of the land ... all gone ... nearly all ... too far ... too
late ... of the sky ... those ... if you like ... he need only ...
turn over ... he'd see them ... shine on him ... but no ... he
clings on ... Woburn ... he's changed ... nearly enough—

[*Silence.*]

MUSIC   . . . .

OPENER   [*with Music*] God.

MUSIC   . . . .

[*Silence.*]

OPENER   God God.

[*Pause.*]

There was a time I asked myself, What is it.

There were times I answered, It's the outing.

Two outings.

Then the return.

Where?

To the village.

To the inn.

Two outings, then at last the return, to the village, to the inn, by the only road that leads there.

An image, like any other.

But I don't answer any more.

I open.

VOICE ⎫   —don't let go . . . finish . . . it's the
MUSIC ⎭ [*together*]   . . . .

right one . . . this time . . . I have it . . . we're there . . .

. . . .

Woburn . . . nearly—

. . . .

OPENER   [*with Voice and Music*] As though they had linked their arms.

VOICE ⎫   —sleep . . . no more stories . . . come on
MUSIC ⎭ [*together*]   . . . .

. . . Woburn . . . it's him . . . see him . . . say him . . . to the

. . . .

end . . . don't let go—

OPENER   [*with Voice and Music*] Good.

VOICE ⎫   —nearly . . . just a few more . . . a few
MUSIC ⎭ [*together*]   . . . .

more . . . I'm there . . . nearly . . . Woburn . . . it's him . . . it

. . . .

was him . . . I've got him . . . nearly—

OPENER   [*with Voice and Music, fervently*] Good!

VOICE ⎫
         ⎬ [*together*]   —this time . . . it's the right one . . .
MUSIC ⎭

. . . .

finish . . . no more stories . . . sleep . . . we're there . . . nearly

. . . .

. . . just a few more . . . don't let go . . . Woburn . . . he clings . . .

. . . .

on . . . come on . . . come on—

. . . .

[*Silence.*]

Curtain

PLAY

A play in one act

Front centre, touching one another, three identical grey urns (see page 367) about one yard high. From each a head protrudes, the neck held fast in the urn's mouth. The heads are those, from left to right as seen from auditorium, of W 2, M and W 1. They face undeviatingly front throughout the play. Faces so lost to age and aspect as to seem almost part of urns. But no masks.

Their speech is provoked by a spotlight projected on faces alone (see page 366).

The transfer of light from one face to another is immediate. No blackout, i.e. return to almost complete darkness of opening, except where indicated.

The response to light is immediate.

Faces impassive throughout. Voices toneless except where an expression is indicated.

Rapid tempo throughout.

The curtain rises on a stage in almost complete darkness. Urns just discernible. Five seconds.

Faint spots simultaneously on three faces. Three seconds. Voices faint, largely unintelligible.

W1 — Yes, strange, darkness best, and the darker the worse, till all dark, then all well, for the time, but it will come, the time will come, the thing is there, you'll see it, get off me, keep off me, all dark, all still, all over, wiped out—

W2 — Yes, perhaps, a shade gone, I suppose, some might say, poor thing, a shade gone, just a shade, in the head—[*faint wild laugh*]—just a shade, but I doubt it, I doubt it, not really, I'm all right, still all right, do my best, all I can—

[*together, see page 367*]

M — Yes, peace, one assumed, all out, all the pain, all as if... never been, it will come—[*hiccup*]—pardon, no sense in this, oh I know... none the less, one assumed, peace... I mean... not merely all over, but as if... never been—

[*Spots off. Blackout. Five seconds. Strong spots simultaneously on three faces. Three seconds. Voices normal strength.*]

W1 — I said to him, Give her up—

W2 — [*together*]   One morning as I was sitting—

M — We were not long together—

[*Spots off. Blackout. Five seconds. Spot on W1.*]

W1 I said to him, Give her up. I swore by all I held most sacred—
[*Spot from W1 to W2.*]

W2 One morning as I was sitting stitching by the open window she burst in and flew at me. Give him up, she screamed, he's mine. Her photographs were kind to her. Seeing her now for the first time full length in the flesh I understood why he preferred me.
[*Spot from W2 to M.*]

M We were not long together when she smelled the rat. Give up that whore, she said, or I'll cut my throat—[*hiccup*] pardon—so help me God. I knew she could have no proof. So I told her I did not know what she was talking about.
[*Spot from M to W2.*]

W2 What are you talking about? I said, stitching away. Someone yours? Give up whom? I smell you off him, she screamed, he stinks of bitch.
[*Spot from W2 to W1.*]

W1   Though I had him dogged for months by a first-rate man, no
      shadow of proof was forthcoming. And there was no denying that
      he continued as . . . assiduous as ever. This, and his horror of the
      merely Platonic thing, made me sometimes wonder if I were not
      accusing him unjustly. Yes.
      [Spot from W1 to M.]

M   What have you to complain of? I said. Have I been neglecting you?
      How could we be together in the way we are if there were someone
      else? Loving her as I did, with all my heart, I could not but feel
      sorry for her.
      [Spot from M to W2.]

W2   Fearing she was about to offer me violence I rang for Erskine and
      had her shown out. Her parting words, as he could testify, if he is
      still living, and has not forgotten, coming and going on the earth,
      letting people in, showing people out, were to the effect that she
      would settle my hash. I confess this did alarm me a little, at the
      time.
      [Spot from W2 to M.]

M   She was not convinced. I might have known. I smell her off you,
      she kept saying. There was no answer to this. So I took her in my
      arms and swore I could not live without her. I meant it, what is
      more. Yes, I am sure I did. She did not repulse me.
      [Spot from M to W1.]

W1   Judge then of my astonishment when one fine morning, as I was
      sitting stricken in the morning room, he slunk in, fell on his knees
      before me, buried his face in my lap and . . . confessed.
      [Spot from W1 to M.]

M   She put a bloodhound on me, but I had a little chat with him. He
      was glad of the extra money.
      [Spot from M to W2.]

W2   Why don't you get out, I said, when he started moaning about his
      home life, there is obviously nothing between you any more. Or is
      there?
      [Spot from W2 to W1.]

W1   I confess my first feeling was one of wonderment. What a male!
      [*Spot from W1 to M. He opens his mouth to speak. Spot from M to W2.*]

W2   Anything between us, he said, what do you take me for, a
      something machine? And of course with him no danger of the . . .
      spiritual thing. Then why don't you get out? I said. I sometimes
      wondered if he was not living with her for her money.
      [*Spot from W2 to M.*]

M   The next thing was the scene between them. I can't have her
      crashing in here, she said, threatening to take my life. I must have
      looked incredulous. Ask Erskine, she said, if you don't believe me.
      But she threatens to take her own, I said. Not yours? she said. No, I
      said, hers. We had fun trying to work this out.
      [*Spot from M to W1.*]

W1   Then I forgave him. To what will love not stoop! I suggested a little
      jaunt to celebrate, to the Riviera or our darling Grand Canary. He
      was looking pale. Peaked. But this was not possible just then.
      Professional commitments.
      [*Spot from W1 toW2.*]

W2   She came again. Just strolled in. All honey. Licking her lips. Poor
      thing. I was doing my nails, by the open window. He has told me
      all about it, she said. Who he, I said filing away, and what it? I know
      what torture you must be going through, she said, and I have
      dropped in to say I bear you no ill-feeling. I rang for Erskine.
      [*Spot from W2 to M.*]

M   Then I got frightened and made a clean breast of it. She was
      looking more and more desperate. She had a razor in her vanity-
      bag. Adulterers, take warning, never admit.
      [*Spot from M to W1.*]

W1   When I was satisfied it was all over I went to have a gloat. Just a
      common tart. What he could have found in her when he had me—
      [*Spot from W1 to W2.*]

W2   When he came again we had it out. I felt like death. He went on
      about why he had to tell her. Too risky and so on. That meant he
      had gone back to her. Back to that!
      [*Spot from W2 to W1.*]

W1   Pudding face, puffy, spots, blubber mouth, jowls, no neck, dugs you could—

[*Spot from W1 to W2.*]

W2   He went on and on. I could hear a mower. An old hand mower. I stopped him and said that whatever I might feel I had no silly threats to offer—but not much stomach for her leavings either. He thought that over for a bit.

[*spot from W2 to W1.*]

W1   Calves like a flunkey—

[*Spot from W1 to M.*]

M   When I saw her again she knew. She was looking—[*hiccup*]— wretched. Pardon. Some fool was cutting grass. A little rush, then another. The problem was how to convince her that no . . . revival of intimacy was involved. I couldn't. I might have known. So I took her in my arms and said I could not go on living without her. I don't believe I could have.

[*Spot from M to W2.*]

W2   The only solution was to go away together. He swore we should as soon as he had put his affairs in order. In the meantime we were to carry on as before. By that he meant as best we could.

[*Spot from W2 to W1.*]

W1   So he was mine again. All mine. I was happy again. I went about singing. The world—

[*Spot from W1 to M.*]

M   At home all heart to heart, new leaf and bygones bygones. I ran into your ex-doxy, she said one night, on the pillow, you're well out of that. Rather uncalled for, I thought. I am indeed, sweetheart, I said, I am indeed. God what vermin women. Thanks to you, angel, I said.

[*Spot from M to W1.*]

W1   Then I began to smell her off him again. Yes.

[*Spot from W1 to W2.*]

W2   When he stopped coming I was prepared. More or less.

[*Spot from W2 to M.*]

M   Finally it was all too much. I simply could no longer—

[*Spot from M to W1.*]

W1   Before I could do anything he disappeared. That meant she had
      won. That slut! I couldn't credit it. I lay stricken for weeks. Then I
      drove over to her place. It was all bolted and barred. All grey with
      frozen dew. On the way back by Ash and Snodland—
      [*Spot from W1 to M.*]

M   I simply could no longer—
      [*Spot from M to W2.*]

W2   I made a bundle of his things and burnt them. It was November
      and the bonfire was going. All night I smelt them smouldering.
      [*Spot off W2. Blackout. Five seconds. Spots half previous strength
      simultaneously on three faces. Three seconds. Voices proportionately lower.*]

W1   ⎫   Mercy, mercy—
W2   ⎬ [*together*]   To say I am—
M   ⎭   When first this change—
      [*Spots off. Blackout. Five seconds. Spot on M.*]

M   When first this change I actually thanked God. I thought, It is
      done, it is said, now all is going out—
      [*Spot from M to W1.*]

W1   Mercy, mercy, tongue still hanging out for mercy. It will come. You
      haven't seen me. But you will. Then it will come.
      [*Spot from W1 to W2.*]

W2   To say I am not disappointed, no, I am. I had anticipated
      something better. More restful.
      [*Spot from W2 to W1.*]

W1   Or you will weary of me.
      [*Spot from W1 to M.*]

M   Down, all going down, into the dark, peace is coming, I thought,
      after all, at last, I was right, after all, thank God, when first this
      change.
      [*Spot from M to W2.*]

W2   Less confused. Less confusing. At the same time I prefer this to . . .
      the other thing. Definitely. There are endurable moments.
      [*Spot from W2 to M.*]

M   I thought.

[*Spot from M to W2.*]

W2 When you go out—and I go out. Some day you will tire of me and go out . . . for good.

[*Spot from W2 to W1.*]

W1 Hellish half-light.

[*Spot from W1 to M.*]

M Peace, yes, I suppose, a kind of peace, and all that pain as if . . . never been.

[*Spot from M to W2.*]

W2 Give me up, as a bad job. Go away and start poking and pecking at someone else. On the other hand—

[*Spot from W2 to W1.*]

W1 Get off me! Get off me!

[*Spot from W1 to M.*]

M It will come. Must come. There is no future in this.

[*Spot from M to W2.*]

W2 On the other hand things may disimprove, there is that danger.

[*Spot from W2 to M.*]

M Oh of course I know now—

[*Spot from M to W1.*]

W1 Is it that I do not tell the truth, is that it, that some day somehow I may tell the truth at last and then no more light at last, for the truth?

[*Spot from W1 to W2.*]

W2 You might get angry and blaze me clean out of my wits. Mightn't you?

[*Spot from W2 to M.*]

M I know now, all that was just . . . play. And all this? When will all this—

[*Spot from M to W1.*]

W1 Is that it?

[*Spot from W1 to W2.*]

W2 Mightn't you?

[*Spot from W2 to M.*]

M All this, when will all this have been . . . just play?

[*Spot from M to W1.*]

W1   I can do nothing . . . for anybody . . . any more . . . thank God. So it must be something I have to say. How the mind works still!
[*Spot from W1 to W2.*]

W2   But I doubt it. It would not be like you somehow. And you must know I am doing my best. Or don't you?
[*Spot from W2 to M.*]

M   Perhaps they have become friends. Perhaps sorrow—
[*Spot from M to W1.*]

W1   But I have said all I can. All you let me. All I—
[*Spot from W1 to M*]

M   Perhaps sorrow has brought them together.
[*Spot from M to W2.*]

W2   No doubt I make the same mistake as when it was the sun that shone, of looking for sense where possibly there is none.
[*Spot from W2 to M.*]

M   Perhaps they meet, and sit, over a cup of that green tea they both so loved, without milk or sugar, not even a squeeze of lemon—
[*Spot from M to W2.*]

W2   Are you listening to me? Is anyone listening to me? Is anyone looking at me? Is anyone bothering about me at all?
[*Spot from W2 to M.*]

M   Not even a squeeze of—
[*Spot from M to W1.*]

W1   Is it something I should do with my face, other than utter? Weep?
[*Spot from W1 to W2.*]

W2   Am I taboo, I wonder. Not necessarily, now that all danger is averted. That poor creature—I can hear her—that poor creature—
[*Spot from W2 to W1.*]

W1   Bite off my tongue and swallow it? Spit it out? Would that placate you? How the mind works still to be sure!
[*Spot from W1 to M.*]

M   Meet, and sit, now in the one dear place, now in the other, and sorrow together, and *compare*—[*hiccup*]—pardon—happy memories.

[*Spot from M to W1.*]

W1   If only I could think, There is no sense in this . . . either, none whatsoever. I can't.

[*Spot from W1 to W2.*]

W2   That poor creature who tried to seduce you, what ever became of her, do you suppose?—I can hear her. Poor thing.

[*Spot from W2 to M.*]

M   Personally I always preferred Lipton's.

[*Spot from M to W1.*]

W1   And that all is falling, all fallen, from the beginning, on empty air. Nothing being asked at all. No one asking me for anything at all.

[*Spot from W1 to W2.*]

W2   They might even feel sorry for me, if they could see me. But never so sorry as I for them.

[*Spot from W2 to W1.*]

W1   I can't.

[*Spot from W1 to W2.*]

W2   Kissing their sour kisses.

[*Spot from W2 to M.*]

M   I pity them in any case, yes, compare my lot with theirs, however blessed, and—

[*Spot from M to W1.*]

W1   I can't. The mind won't have it. It would have to go. Yes.

[*Spot from W1 to M.*]

M   Pity them.

[*Spot from M to W2.*]

W2   What do you do when you go out? Sift?

[*Spot from W2 to M.*]

M   Am I hiding something? Have I lost—

[*Spot from M to W1.*]

W1   She had means, I fancy, though she lived like a pig.

[*Spot from W1 to W2.*]

W2   Like dragging a great roller, on a scorching day. The strain . . . to get it moving, momentum coming—

[*Spot off* W2. *Blackout. Three seconds. Spot on* W2.]

W2 Kill it and strain again.

[*Spot from* W2 *to* M.]

M Have I lost . . . the thing you want? Why go out? Why go—

[*Spot from* M *to* W2.]

W2 And you perhaps pitying me, thinking, Poor thing, she needs a rest.

[*Spot from* W2 *to* W1.]

W1 Perhaps she has taken him away to live . . . somewhere in the sun.

[*Spot from* W1 *to* M.]

M Why go down? Why not—

[*Spot from* M *to* W2.]

W2 I don't know.

[*Spot from* W2 *to* W1.]

W1 Perhaps she is sitting somewhere, by the open window, her hands folded in her lap, gazing down out over the olives—

[*Spot from* W1 *to* M.]

M Why not keep on glaring at me without ceasing? I might start to rave and—[*hiccup*]—bring it up for you. Par—

[*Spot from* M *to* W2.]

W2 No.

[*Spot from* W2 *to* M.]

M —don.

[*Spot from* M *to* W1.]

W1 Gazing down out over the olives, then the sea, wondering what can be keeping him, growing cold. Shadow stealing over everything. Creeping. Yes.

[*Spot from* W1 *to* M.]

M To think we were never together.

[*Spot from* M *to* W2.]

W2 Am I not perhaps a little unhinged already?

[*Spot from* W2 *to* W1.]

W1 Poor creature. Poor creatures.

[*Spot from* W1 *to* M.]

M Never woke together, on a May morning, the first to wake to wake the other two. Then in a little dinghy—

[*Spot from M to W1.*]

W1   Penitence, yes, at a pinch, atonement, one was resigned, but no, that does not seem to be the point either.
[*Spot from W1 to W2.*]

W2   I say, Am I not perhaps a little unhinged already? [*Hopefully.*] Just a little? [*Pause.*] I doubt it.
[*Spot from W2 to M.*]

M   A little dinghy—
[*Spot from M to W1.*]

W1   Silence and darkness were all I craved. Well, I get a certain amount of both. They being one. Perhaps it is more wickedness to pray for more.
[*Spot from W1 to M.*]

M   A little dinghy, on the river, I resting on my oars, they lolling on air-pillows in the stern . . . sheets. Drifting. Such fantasies.
[*Spot from M to W1.*]

W1   Hellish half-light.
[*Spot from W1 to W2.*]

W2   A shade gone. In the head. Just a shade. I doubt it.
[*Spot from W2 to M.*]

M   We were not civilized.
[*Spot from M to W1.*]

W1   Dying for dark—and the darker the worse. Strange.
[*Spot from W1 to M.*]

M   Such fantasies. Then. And now—
[*Spot from M to W2.*]

W2   I doubt it.
[*Pause. Peal of wild low laughter from W2 cut short as spot from her to W1.*]

W1   Yes, and the whole thing there, all there, staring you in the face. You'll see it. Get off me. Or weary.
[*Spot from W1 to M.*]

M   And now, that you are . . . mere eye. Just looking. At my face. On and off.
[*Spot from M to W1.*]

W1   Weary of playing with me. Get off me. Yes.

[*Spot from W1 to M.*]

M Looking for something. In my face. Some truth. In my eyes. Not even.

[*Spot from M to W2. Laugh as before from W2 cut short as spot from her to M.*]

M Mere eye. No mind. Opening and shutting on me. Am I as much—

[*Spot off M. Blackout. Three seconds. Spot on M.*]

Am I as much as . . . being seen?

[*Spot off M. Blackout. Five seconds. Faint spots simultaneously on three faces. Three seconds. Voices faint, largely unintelligible.*]

W1 ⎫
W2 ⎬ [*together*]   Yes, strange, etc.
M ⎭   Yes, perhaps, etc.
                     Yes, peace, etc.

[*Repeat play.*]

M [*Closing repeat.*] Am I as much as . . . being seen?

[*Spot off M. Blackout. Five seconds. Strong spots simultaneously on three faces. Three seconds. Voices normal strength.*]

W1 ⎫
W2 ⎬ [*together*]   I said to him, Give her up—
M ⎭   One morning as I was sitting—
                     We were not long together—

[*Spots off. Blackout. Five seconds. Spot on M.*]

M We were not long together—

[*Spot off M. Blackout. Five seconds.*]

Curtain

The source of light is single and must not be situated outside the ideal space (stage) occupied by its victims.

The optimum position for the spot is at the centre of the footlights, the faces being thus lit at close quarters and from below.

When exceptionally three spots are required to light the three faces simultaneously, they should be as a single spot branching into three.

Apart from these moments a single mobile spot should be used, swivelling at maximum speed from one face to another as required.

The method consisting in assigning to each face a separate fixed spot is unsatisfactory in that it is less expressive of a unique inquisitor than the single mobile spot.

CHORUS

w1	Yes strange	darkness best	and the darker	the worse
w2	Yes perhaps	a shade gone	I suppose	some might say
M	Yes peace	one assumed	all out	all the pain

w1	till all dark	then all well	for the time	but it will come
w2	poor thing	a shade gone	just a shade	in the head
M	all as if	never been	it will come	[*Hiccup.*] pardon

w1	the time will come	the thing is there		you'll see it
w2	[*Laugh* - - - - - -]	just a shade		but I doubt it
M	no sense in this	oh I know		none the less

w1	get off me	keep off me	all dark	all still
w2	I doubt it	not really	I'm all right	still all right
M	one assumed	peace I mean	not merely	all over

w1	all over	wiped out—
w2	do my best	all I can—
M	but as if	never been—

URNS

In order for the urns to be only one yard high, it is necessary either that traps be used, enabling the actors to stand below stage level, or that they kneel throughout play, the urns being open at the back.

Should traps be not available, and the kneeling posture found impracticable, the actors should stand, the urns be enlarged to full length and moved back from front to mid-stage, the tallest actor setting the height, the broadest the breadth, to which the three urns should conform.

The sitting posture results in urns of unacceptable bulk and is not to be considered.

REPEAT

The repeat may be an exact replica of first statement or it may present an element of variation.

In other words, the light may operate the second time exactly as it did the first (exact replica) or it may try a different method (variation).

The London production (and in a lesser degree the Paris production) opted for the variation with following deviations from first statement:

1. Introduction of an abridged chorus, cut short on laugh of W2, to open fragment of second repeat.

2. Light less strong in repeat and voices correspondingly lower, giving the following schema, where A is the highest level of light and voice and E the lowest:

C First chorus.
A First part of 1.   } 1
B Second part of 1.

D Second chorus.
B First part of Repeat 1.   } Repeat 1
C Second part of Repeat 1.

E Abridged chorus.
C Fragment of Repeat 2   } Fragment of Repeat 2

3. Breathless quality in voices from beginning of Repeat 1 and increasing to end of play.

4. Changed order of speeches in repeat as far as this is compatible with unchanged continuity for actors. E.g. the order of interrogation W1, W2, M, W2, W1, M at opening of 1 becomes W2, W1, M, W2, M, W1 at opening of repeat, and so on if and as desired.

FILM

Throughout first two parts all perception is E's. E is the camera. But in third part there is O's perception of room and contents and at the same time E's continued perception of O. This poses a problem of images which I cannot solve without technical help. See below, note 8.

The film is divided into three parts. 1. The street (about eight minutes). 2. The stairs (about five minutes). 3. The room (about seventeen minutes).

The film is entirely silent except for the "sssh!" in part one.

Climate of film comic and unreal. O should invite laughter throughout by his way of moving. Unreality of street scene (see notes to this section).

GENERAL

Esse est percipi.

All extraneous perception suppressed, animal, human, divine, self-perception maintains in being.

Search of non-being in flight from extraneous perception breaking down in inescapability of self-perception.

No truth value attaches to above, regarded as of merely structural and dramatic convenience.

In order to be figured in this situation the protagonist is sundered into object (O) and eye (E), the former in flight, the latter in pursuit.

It will not be clear until end of film that pursuing perceiver is not extraneous, but self.

Until end of film O is perceived by E from behind and at an angle not exceeding 45°. Convention: O enters *percipi* = experiences anguish of perceivedness, only when this angle is exceeded.

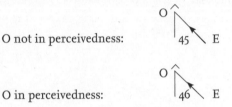

O not in perceivedness:

O in perceivedness:

E is therefore at pains, throughout pursuit, to keep within this "angle of immunity" and only exceeds it (1) inadvertently at beginning of part one when he first sights O (2) inadvertently at beginning of part two when he follows O into vestibule and (3) deliberately at end of part three when O is cornered. In first two cases he hastily reduces angle.

OUTLINE

1. The street

Dead straight. No sidestreets or intersections. Period: about 1929. Early summer morning. Small factory district. Moderate animation of workers going unhurriedly to work. All going in same direction and all in couples. No automobiles. Two bicycles ridden by men with girl passengers (on crossbar). One cab, cantering nag, driver standing brandishing whip. All persons in opening scene to be shown in some way perceiving—one another, an object, a shop window, a poster, etc., i.e. all contentedly in *percipere* and *percipi*. First view of above is by E motionless and searching with his eyes for O. He may be supposed at street edge of wide (4 yards) sidewalk. O finally comes into view hastening blindly along sidewalk, hugging the wall on his left, in opposite direction to all the others. Long dark overcoat (whereas all others in light summer dress) with collar up, hat pulled down over eyes, briefcase in left hand, right hand shielding exposed side of face. He storms along in comic foundered precipitancy. E's searching eye, turning left from street to sidewalk, picks him up at an angle exceeding that of immunity (O's unperceivedness according to convention) (1). O, entering perceivedness, reacts (after just sufficient onward movement for his gait to be established) by halting and cringing aside towards wall. E immediately draws back to close the angle (2) and O, released from perceivedness, hurries on. E lets him get about 10 yards ahead and then starts after him (3). Street elements from now on incidental (except for episode of couple) in the sense that only registered in so far as they happen to enter field of pursuing eye fixed on O.

Episode of couple (4). In his blind haste O jostles an elderly couple of shabby genteel aspect, standing on sidewalk, peering together at a newspaper. They should be discovered by E a few yards before collision. The woman is holding a pet monkey under her left arm. E follows O an instant as he hastens blindly on, then registers couple recovering from shock, comes up with them, passes them slightly and halts to observe them (5). Having recovered they turn and look after O, the woman raising a lorgnon to her eyes, the man taking off his pince-nez fastened to his coat by a ribbon. They then look at each other, she lowering her lorgnon, he resuming his pince-nez. He opens his mouth to vituperate. She checks him with a gesture and soft "sssh!" He turns again, taking off his pince-nez, to look after O. She feels the gaze of E upon them and turns, raising her lorgnon, to look at him. She nudges her companion who turns back towards her, resuming his pince-nez, follows direction of her gaze and, taking off his pince-nez, looks at E. As they both stare at E the expression gradually comes over their faces which will be that of the flower-woman in the stairs scene and that of O at the end of film, an expression only to be described as corresponding to an agony of perceivedness. Indifference of monkey, looking up into face of its mistress. They close their eyes, she lowering her lorgnon, and hasten away in direction of all the others, i.e. that opposed to O and E (6).

E turns back towards O by now far ahead and out of sight. Immediate acceleration of E in pursuit (blurred transit of encountered elements). O comes into view, grows rapidly larger until E settles down behind him at same angle and remove as before. O disappears suddenly through open housedoor on his left. Immediate acceleration of E who comes up with O in vestibule at foot of stairs.

2. Stairs

Vestibule about 4 yards square with stairs at inner righthand angle. Relation of streetdoor to stairs such that E's first perception of O (E near door, O motionless at foot of stairs, right hand on banister, body shaken by panting) is from an angle a little exceeding that of immunity. O, entering perceivedness (according to convention), transfers right hand from banister to exposed side of face and cringes aside towards wall on his left. E immediately draws back to close the angle and O, released, resumes his pose at foot of stairs, hand on banister. O mounts a few steps (E remaining near door), raises head, listens, redescends hastily backwards and crouches down in angle of stairs and wall on his right, invisible to one descending (7). E registers him there, then transfers to stairs. A frail old woman appears on bottom landing. She carries a tray of flowers slung from her neck by a strap. She descends slowly, with fumbling feet, one hand steadying the tray, the other holding the banister. Absorbed by difficulty of descent she does not become aware of E until she is quite down and making for the door. She halts and looks full at E. Gradually same expression as that of couple in street. She closes her eyes, then sinks to the ground and lies with face in scattered flowers. E lingers on this a moment, then transfers to where O last registered. He is no longer there, but hastening up the stairs. E transfers to stairs and picks up O as he reaches first landing. Bound forward and up of E who overtakes O on second flight and is literally at his heels when he reaches second landing and opens with key door of room. They enter room together, E turning with O as he turns to lock the door behind him.

3. The room

Here we assume problem of dual perception solved and enter O's perception (8). E must so manoeuvre throughout what follows, until investment proper, that O is always seen from behind, at most convenient remove, and from an angle never exceeding that of immunity, i.e. preserved from perceivedness.

Small barely furnished room (9). Side by side on floor a large cat and small dog. Unreal quality. Motionless till ejected. Cat bigger than dog. On a table against wall a parrot in a cage and a goldfish in a bowl. This room sequence falls into three parts.

1. Preparation of room (occlusion of window and mirror, ejection of dog and cat, destruction of God's image, occlusion of parrot and goldfish).

2. Period in rocking-chair. Inspection and destruction of photographs.

3. Final investment of O by E and dénouement.

1. O stands near door with case in hand and takes in room. Succession of images: dog and cat, side by side, staring at him; mirror; window; couch with rug; dog and cat staring at him; parrot and goldfish, parrot staring at him; rocking-chair; dog and cat staring at him. He sets down case, approaches window from side and draws curtain. He turns towards dog and cat, still staring at him, then goes to couch and takes up rug. He turns towards dog and cat, still staring at him. Holding rug before him he approaches mirror from side and covers it with rug. He turns towards parrot and goldfish, parrot still staring at him. He goes to rocking-chair, inspects it from front. Insistent image of curiously carved headrest (10). He turns towards dog and cat still staring at him. He puts them out of room (11). He takes up case and is moving towards chair when rug falls from mirror. He drops briefcase, hastens to wall between couch and mirror, follows walls past window, approaches mirror from side, picks up rug and, holding it before him, covers mirror with it again. He returns to briefcase, picks it up, goes to chair, sits down and is opening case when disturbed by print, pinned to wall before him, of the face of God the Father, the eyes staring at him severely. He sets down case on floor to his left, gets up and inspects print. Insistent image of wall, paper hanging off in strips (10). He tears print from wall, tears it in four, throws down the pieces and grinds them underfoot. He turns back to chair, image again of its curious headrest, sits down, image again of tattered wall-paper, takes case on his knees, takes out a folder, sets down case on floor to his left and is opening folder when disturbed by parrot's eye. He lays folder on case, gets up, takes off overcoat, goes to parrot, close-up of parrot's eye, covers cage with coat, goes back to chair, image again of headrest, sits down, image again of tattered wall-paper, takes up folder and is opening it when

disturbed by fish's eye. He lays folder on case, gets up, goes to fish, close-up of fish's eye, extends coat to cover bowl as well as cage, goes back to chair, image again of headrest, sits down, image again of wall, takes up folder, takes off hat and lays it on case to his left. Scant hair or bald to facilitate identification of narrow black elastic encircling head.

When O sits up and back his head is framed in headrest which is a narrower extension of backrest. Throughout scene of inspection and destruction of photographs E may be supposed immediately behind chair looking down over O's left shoulder (12).

2. O opens folder, takes from it a packet of photographs (13), lays folder on case and begins to inspect photographs. He inspects them in order 1 to 7. When he has finished with 1 he lays it on his knees, inspects 2, lays it on top of 1, and so on, so that when he has finished inspecting them all 1 will be at the bottom of the pile and 7—or rather 6, for he does not lay down 7—at the top. He gives about six seconds each to 1–4, about twice as long to 5 and 6 (trembling hands). Looking at 6 he touches with fore-finger little girl's face. After six seconds of 7 he tears it in four and drops pieces on floor on his left. He takes up 6 from top of pile on his knees, looks at it again for about three seconds, tears it in four and drops pieces on floor to his left. So on for the others, looking at each again for about three seconds before tearing it up. 1 must be on tougher mount for he has difficulty in tearing it across. Straining hands. He finally succeeds, drops pieces on floor and sits, rocking slightly, hands holding armrests (14).

3. Investment proper. Perception from now on, if dual perception fea-sible, E's alone, except perception of E by O at end. E moves a little back (image of headrest from back), then starts circling to his left, approaches maximum angle and halts. From this open angle, beyond which he will enter *percipi*, O can be seen beginning to doze off. His visible hand relaxes on armrest, his head nods and falls forward, the rock approaches stillness. E advances, opening angle beyond limit of immunity, his gaze pierces the light sleep and O starts awake. The start revives the rock, immediately arrested by foot to floor. Tension of hand on armrest. Turning his head to right, O cringes away from perceivedness. E draws back to reduce the angle and after a moment, reassured, O turns back front and resumes his

pose. The rock resumes, dies down slowly as O dozes off again. E now begins a much wider encirclement. Images of curtained window, walls and shrouded mirror to indicate his path and that he is not yet looking at O. Then brief image of O seen by E from well beyond the angle of immunity, i.e. from near the table with shrouded bowl and cage. O is now seen to be fast asleep, his head sunk on his chest and his hands, fallen from the armrests, limply dangling. E resumes his cautious approach. Images of shrouded bowl and cage and tattered wall adjoining, with same indication as before. Halt and brief image, not far short of full-face, of O still fast asleep. E advances last few yards along tattered wall and halts directly in front of O. Long image of O, full-face, against ground of headrest, sleeping. E's gaze pierces the sleep, O starts awake, stares up at E. Patch over O's left eye now seen for the first time. Rock revived by start, stilled at once by foot to ground. Hand clutches armrests. O half starts from chair, then stiffens, staring up at E. Gradually that look. Cut to E, of whom this very first image (face only, against ground of tattered wall). It is O's face (with patch) but with very different expression, impossible to describe, neither severity nor benignity, but rather acute *intentness*. A big nail is visible near left temple (patch side). Long image of the unblinking gaze. Cut back to O, still half risen, staring up, with that look. O closes his eyes and falls back in chair, starting off rock. He covers his face with his hands. Image of O rocking, his head in his hands but not yet bowed. Cut back to E. As before. Cut back to O. He sits, bowed forward, his head in his hands, gently rocking. Hold it as the rocking dies down.

End

NOTES

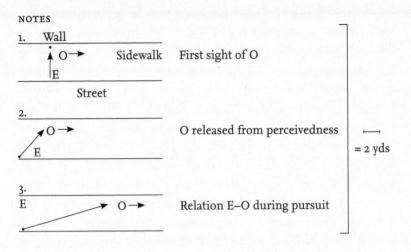

1.

Wall

O→   Sidewalk   First sight of O

E

Street

2.

O→   O released from perceivedness

E   ⊢⊣ = 2 yds

3.

E   O→   Relation E–O during pursuit

4. The purpose of this episode, undefendable except as a dramatic convenience, is to suggest as soon as possible unbearable quality of E's scrutiny. Reinforced by episode of flower-woman in stairs sequence.

5.

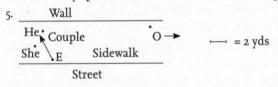

Wall

He⋅ Couple   ⋅O →   ⊢⊣ = 2 yds
She ⋅E   Sidewalk

Street

6. Expression of this episode, like that of animals' ejection in part three, should be as precisely stylized as possible. The purpose of the monkey, either unaware of E or indifferent to him, is to anticipate behaviour of animals in part three, attentive to O exclusively.

7. Suggestion for vestibule with (1) O in *percipi* (2) released (3) hiding from flower-woman. Note that even when E exceeds angle of immunity O's face never really seen because of immediate turn aside and (here) hand to shield face.

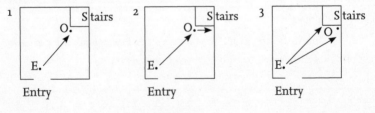

1   S|tairs   2   S|tairs   3   S|tairs
O⋅   O⋅→   O⋅
E⋅   E⋅   E⋅
Entry   Entry   Entry

8. Up till now the perceptions of O, hastening *blindly* to illusory sanc-
tuary, have been neglected and must in fact have been negligible. But in
the room, until he falls asleep and the investment begins, they must be
recorded. And at the same time E's perceiving of O must continue to be
given. E is concerned only with O, not with the room, or only incidentally
with the room in so far as its elements happen to enter the field of his
gaze fastened on O. We see O in the room thanks to E's perceiving and the
room itself thanks to O's perceiving. In other words this room sequence,
up to the moment of O's falling asleep, is composed of two independent sets of images. I feel that any attempt to express them in simultane-
ity (composite images, double frame, superimposition, etc.) must prove
unsatisfactory. The presentation in a single image of O's perception of
the print, for example, and E's perception of O perceiving it—no doubt
feasible technically—would perhaps

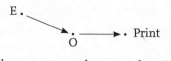

make impossible for the spectator a clear apprehension of either. The
solution might be in a succession of images of different *quality*, corresponding on the one hand to E's perception of O and on the other to
O's perception of the room. This difference of quality might perhaps be
sought in different degrees of development, the passage from the one to
the other being from greater to lesser and lesser to greater definition or
luminosity. The dissimilarity, however obtained, would have to be fla-
grant. Having been up till now exclusively in the E quality, we would suddenly pass, with O's first survey of the room, into this quite different O
quality. Then back to the E quality when O is shown moving to the window. And so on throughout the sequence, switching from the one to the
other as required. Were this the solution adopted it might be desirable
to establish, by means of brief sequences, the O quality in parts one and
two.

This seems to be the chief problem of the film, though I perhaps
exaggerate its difficulty through technical ignorance.

9.

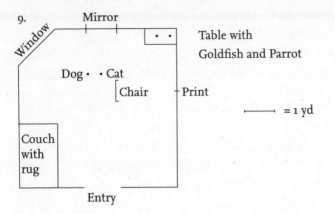

Suggestion for room.

This obviously cannot be O's room. It may be supposed it is his mother's room, which he has not visited for many years and is now to occupy momentarily, to look after the pets, until she comes out of hospital. This has no bearing on the film and need not be elucidated.

10. At close of film face E and face O can only be distinguished (1) by different expressions (2) by fact of O looking up and E down and (3) by difference of ground (for O headrest of chair, for E wall). Hence insistence on headrest and tattered wall.

11. Foolish suggestion for eviction of cat and dog. Also see Note 6.

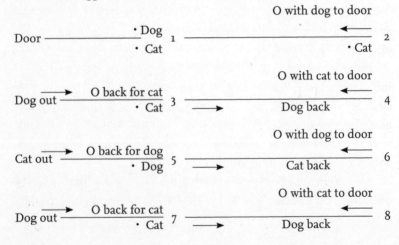

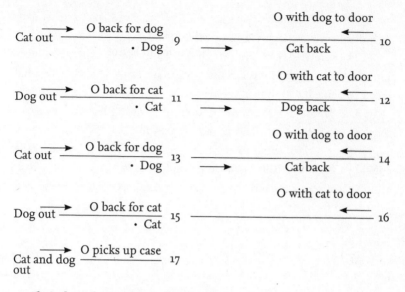

12. Chair from front during photo sequence.

13. Description of photographs.

1. Male infant. 6 months. His mother holds him in her arms. Infant smiles front. Mother's big hands. Her severe eyes devouring him. Her big old-fashioned beflowered hat.

2. The same. 4 years. On a veranda, dressed in loose nightshirt, kneeling on a cushion, attitude of prayer, hands clasped, head bowed, eyes closed. Half profile. Mother on chair beside him, big hands on knees, head bowed towards him, severe eyes, similar hat to 1.

3. The same. 15 years. Bareheaded. School blazer. Smiling. Teaching a dog to beg. Dog on its hind legs looking up at him.

4. The same. 20 years. Graduation day. Academic gown. Mortar-board under arm. On a platform, receiving scroll from Rector. Smiling. Section of public watching.

5. The same. 21 years. Bareheaded. Smiling. Small moustache. Arm round fiancée. A young man takes a snap of them.

6. The same. 25 years. Newly enlisted. Bareheaded. Uniform. Bigger moustache. Smiling. Holding a little girl in his arms. She looks into his face, exploring it with finger.

7. The same. 30 years. Looking over 40. Wearing hat and overcoat. Patch over left eye. Cleanshaven. Grim expression.

14. Profit by rocking-chair to emotionalize inspection, e.g. gentle steady rock for 1 to 4, rock stilled (foot to ground) after two seconds of 5, rock resumed between 5 and 6, rock stilled after two seconds of 6, rock resumed after 6 and for 7 as for 1–4.

THE OLD TUNE

An adaptation

Background of street noises, in the foreground a barrel-organ playing an old tune. 20 seconds. The mechanism jams. Thumps on the box to set it off again. No result.

GORMAN [*old man's cracked voice, frequent pauses for breath even in the middle of a word, speech indistinct for want of front teeth, whistling sibilants*] There we go, bust again. [*Sound of lid raised. Scraping inside box.*] Cursed bloody music! [*Scraping. Creaking of handle. Thumps on box. The mechanism starts off again.*] Ah about time! [*Tune resumes. 10 seconds. Sound of faltering steps approaching.*]

CREAM [*old man's cracked voice, stumbling speech, pauses in the middle of sentences, whistling sibilants due to ill-fitting denture*] Well, if it isn't—[*the tune stops*]—Gorman my old friend Gorman, do you recognize me Cream father of the judge, Cream you remember Cream.

GORMAN Mr. Cream! Well, I'll be! Mr. Cream! [*Pause.*] Sit you down, sit you down, here, there. [*Pause.*] Great weather for the time of day Mr. Cream, eh.

CREAM My old friend Gorman, it's a sight to see you again after all these years, all these years.

GORMAN Yes indeed, Mr. Cream, yes indeed, that's the way it is. [*Pause.*] And you, tell me.

CREAM I was living with my daughter and she died, then I came here to live with the other.

GORMAN Miss Miss what?

CREAM Bertha. You know she got married, yes, Moody the nurseryman, two children.

GORMAN Grand match, Mr. Cream, grand match, more power to you. But tell me then the poor soul she was taken then was she.

CREAM Malignant, tried everything, lingered three years, that's how it goes, the young pop off and the old hang on.

GORMAN Ah dear oh dear Mr. Cream, dear oh dear.

[Pause.]

CREAM And you your wife?

GORMAN Still in it, still in it, but for how long.

CREAM Poor Daisy yes.

GORMAN Had she children?

CREAM Three, three children, Johnny, the eldest, then Ronnie, then a baby girl, Queenie, my favourite, Queenie, a baby girl.

GORMAN Darling name.

CREAM She's so quick for her years you wouldn't believe it, do you know what she came out with to me the other day ah only the other day poor Daisy.

GORMAN And your son-in-law?

CREAM Eh?

GORMAN Ah dear oh dear, Mr. Cream, dear oh dear. [Pause.] Ah yes children that's the way it is. [Roar of motor engine.] They'd tear you to flitters with their flaming machines.

CREAM Shocking crossing, sudden death.

GORMAN As soon as look at you, tear you to flitters.

CREAM Ah in our time Gorman this was the outskirts, you remember, peace and quiet.

GORMAN Do I remember, fields it was, fields, bluebells, over there, on the bank, bluebells. When you think. . . . [Suddenly complete silence. 10 seconds. The tune resumes, falters, stops. Silence. The street noises resume.] Ah the horses, the carriages, and the

barouches, ah the barouches, all that's the dim distant past,
Mr. Cream.

CREAM And the broughams, remember the broughams, there was style
for you, the broughams.

[*Pause.*]

GORMAN The first car I remember I saw it here, here, on the corner, a
Pic-Pic she was.

CREAM Not a Pic-Pic, Gorman, not a Pic-Pic, a Dee Dyan Button.

GORMAN A Pic-Pic, a Pic-Pic, don't I remember it well, just as I was
coming out of Swan's the bookseller's beyond there on the
corner, Swan's the bookseller's that was, just as I was coming
out with a rise of fourpence ah there wasn't much money in
it in those days.

CREAM A Dee Dyan, a Dee Dyan.

GORMAN You had to work for your living in those days, it wasn't at six
you knocked off, nor at seven neither, eight it was, eight
o'clock, yes by God. [*Pause.*] Where was I? [*Pause.*] Ah yes eight
o'clock as I was coming out of Swan's there was the crowd
gathered and the car wheeling round the bend.

CREAM A Dee Dyan Gorman, a Dee Dyan, I can remember the man
himself from Wougham he was the vintner what's this his
name was.

GORMAN Bush, Seymour Bush.

CREAM Bush that's the man.

GORMAN One way or t'other, Mr. Cream, one way or t'other no matter it
wasn't the likes of nowadays, their flaming machines they'd
tear you to shreds.

CREAM My dear Gorman do you know what it is I'm going to tell you,
all this speed do you know what it is has the whole place
ruinated, no living with it any more, the whole place
ruinated, even the weather. [*Roar of engine.*] Ah when you
think of the springs in our time remember the springs we
had, the heat there was in them, and the summers remember
the summers would destroy you with the heat.

GORMAN Do I remember, there was one year back there seems like
        yesterday must have been round 95 when we were still out at
        Cruddy, didn't we water the roof of the house every evening
        with the rubber jet to have a bit of cool in the night, yes
        summer 95.

CREAM   That would surprise me Gorman, remember in those days the
        rubber hose was a great luxury a great luxury, wasn't till after
        the war the rubber hose.

GORMAN You may be right.

CREAM   No may be about it. I tell you the first we ever had round here
        was in Drummond's place, old Da Drummond, that was after
        the war 1920 maybe, still very exorbitant it was at the time,
        don't you remember watering out of the can you must with
        that bit of garden you had didn't you, wasn't it your father
        owned that patch out on the Marston Road.

GORMAN The Sheen Road Mr. Cream but true for you the watering
        you're right there, me and me hose how are you when we had
        no running water at the time or had we.

CREAM   The Sheen Road, that's the one out beyond Shackleton's sawpit.

GORMAN We didn't get it in till 1925 now it comes back to me the wash-
        hand basin and jug.
        [*Roar of engine.*]

CREAM   The Sheen Road you saw what they've done to that I was out on
        it yesterday with the son-in-law, you saw what they've done
        our little gardens and the grand sloe hedges.

GORMAN Yes all those gazebos springing up like thistles there's trash for
        you if you like, collapse if you look at them am I right.

CREAM   Collapse is the word, when you think of the good stone made
        the cathedrals nothing to come up to it.

GORMAN And on top of all no foundations, no cellars, no nothing, how
        are you going to live without cellars I ask you, on piles if you
        don't mind, piles, like in the lake age, there's progress for you.

CREAM   Ah Gorman you haven't changed a hair, just the same old wag
        he always was. Getting on for seventy-five is it?

GORMAN   Seventy-three, seventy-three, soon due for the knock.

CREAM   Now Gorman none of that, none of that, and me turning seventy-six, you're a young man Gorman.

GORMAN   Ah Mr. Cream, always a great one for a crack.

CREAM   Here Gorman while we're at it have a fag, here. [*Pause.*] The daughter must have whipped them again, doesn't want me to be smoking, mind her own damn business. [*Pause.*] Ah I have them, here, have one.

GORMAN   I wouldn't leave you short.

CREAM   Short for God's sake, here, have one.
[*Pause.*]

GORMAN   They're packed so tight they won't come out.

CREAM   Take hold of the packet. [*Pause.*] Ah what ails me all bloody thumbs. Can you pick it up.
[*Pause.*]

GORMAN   Here we are. [*Pause.*] Ah yes a nice puff now and again but it's not what it was their gaspers now not worth a fiddler's, remember in the forces the shag remember the black shag that was tobacco for you.

CREAM   Ah the black shag my dear Gorman the black shag, fit for royalty the black shag fit for royalty. [*Pause.*] Have you a light on you.

GORMAN   Well then I haven't, the wife doesn't like me to be smoking.
[*Pause.*]

CREAM   Must have whipped my lighter too the bitch, my old tinder jizzer.

GORMAN   Well no matter I'll keep it and have a draw later on.

CREAM   The bitch sure as a gun she must have whipped it too that's going beyond the beyonds, beyond the beyonds, nothing you can call your own. [*Pause.*] Perhaps we might ask this gentleman. [*Footsteps approach.*] Beg your pardon Sir trouble you for a light.
[*Footsteps recede.*]

GORMAN   Ah the young nowadays Mr. Cream very wrapped up they are the young nowadays, no thought for the old. When you think, when you think. . . . [*Suddenly complete silence. 10 seconds. The tune resumes, falters, stops. Silence. The street noises resume.*] Where were we? [*Pause.*] Ah yes the forces, you went in in 1900, 1900, 1902, am I right?

CREAM   1903, 1903, and you 1906 was it?

GORMAN   1906 yes at Chatham.

CREAM   The Gunners?

GORMAN   The Foot, the Foot.

CREAM   But the Foot wasn't Chatham don't you remember, there it was the Gunners, you must have been at Caterham, Caterham, the Foot.

GORMAN   Chatham I tell you, isn't it like yesterday, Morrison's pub on the corner.

CREAM   Harrison's. Harrison's Oak Lounge, do you think I don't know Chatham. I used to go there on holiday with Mrs. Cream, I know Chatham backwards Gorman, inside and out, Harrison's Oak Lounge on the corner of what was the name of the street, on a rise it was, it'll come back to me, do you think I don't know Harrison's Oak Lounge there on the corner of dammit I'll forget my own name next and the square it'll come back to me.

GORMAN   Morrison or Harrison we were at Chatham.

CREAM   That would surprise me greatly, the Gunners were Chatham do you not remember that?

GORMAN   I was in the Foot, at Chatham, in the Foot.

CREAM   The Foot, that's right the Foot at Chatham.

GORMAN   That's what I'm telling you, Chatham the Foot.

CREAM   That would surprise me greatly, you must have it mucked up with the war, the mobilization.

GORMAN   The mobilization have a heart it's as clear in my mind as yesterday the mobilization, we were shifted straight away to Chesham, was it, no, Chester, that's the place, Chester, there was Morrison's pub on the corner and a chamber-maid what was her name, Joan, Jean, Jane, the very start of the war when we still didn't believe it, Chester, ah those are happy memories.

CREAM Happy memories, happy memories, I wouldn't go so far as that.

GORMAN I mean the start up, the start up at Chatham, we still didn't believe it, and that chamber-maid what was her name it'll come back to me. [*Pause.*] And your son by the same token. [*Roar of engine.*]

CREAM Eh?

GORMAN Your son the judge.

CREAM He has rheumatism.

GORMAN Ah rheumatism, rheumatism runs in the blood Mr. Cream.

CREAM What are you talking about, I never had rheumatism.

GORMAN When I think of my poor old mother, only sixty and couldn't move a muscle. [*Roar of engine.*] Rheumatism they never found the remedy for it yet, atom rockets is all they care about, I can thank my lucky stars touch wood. [*Pause.*] Your son yes he's in the papers the Carton affair, the way he managed that case he can be a proud man, the wife read it again in this morning's *Lark*.

CREAM What do you mean the Barton affair.

GORMAN The Carton affair Mr. Cream, the sex fiend, on the Assizes.

CREAM That's not him, he's not the Assizes my boy isn't, he's the County Courts, you mean Judge . . . Judge . . . what's this his name was in the Barton affair.

GORMAN Ah I thought it was him.

CREAM Certainly not I tell you, the County Courts my boy, not the Assizes, the County Courts.

GORMAN Oh you know the Courts and the Assizes it was always all six of one to me.

CREAM Ah but there's a big difference Mr. Gorman, a power of difference, a civil case and a criminal one, quite another how d'you do, what would a civil case be doing in the *Lark* now I ask you.

GORMAN All that machinery you know I never got the swing of it and now it's all six of one to me.

CREAM   Were you never in the Courts?

GORMAN   I was once all right when my niece got her divorce that was
         when was it now thirty years ago yes thirty years, I was greatly
         put about I can tell you the poor little thing divorced after two
         years of married life, my sister was never the same after it.

CREAM   Divorce is the curse of society you can take it from me, the
         curse of society, ask my boy if you don't believe me.

GORMAN   Ah there I'm with you the curse of society look at what it leads
         up to, when you think my niece had a little girl as good as
         never knew her father.

CREAM   Did she get alimony.

GORMAN   She was put out to board and wasted away to a shadow, that's a
         nice thing for you.

CREAM   Did the mother get alimony.

GORMAN   Divil the money. [*Pause.*] So that's your son ladling out the
         divorces.

CREAM   As a judge he must, as a father it goes to his heart.

GORMAN   Has he children.

CREAM   Well in a way he had one, little Herbert, lived to be four months
         then passed away, how long is it now, how long is it now.

GORMAN   Ah dear oh dear, Mr. Cream, dear oh dear and did they never
         have another?
         [*Roar of engine.*]

CREAM   Eh?

GORMAN   Other children.

CREAM   Didn't I tell you, I have my daughters' children, my two
         daughters. [*Pause.*] Talking of that your man there Barton the
         sex boyo isn't that nice carryings on for you showing himself
         off like that without a stitch on him to little children might just
         as well have been ours Gorman, our own little grandchildren.
         [*Roar of engine.*]

GORMAN   Mrs. Cream must be a proud woman too to be a grandmother.

CREAM   Mrs. Cream is in her coffin these twenty years Mr. Gorman.

GORMAN   Oh God forgive me what am I talking about, I'm getting you wouldn't know what I'd be talking about, that's right you were saying you were with Miss Daisy.

CREAM With my daughter Bertha, Mr. Gorman, my daughter Bertha, Mrs. Rupert Moody.

GORMAN Your daughter Bertha that's right so she married Moody, gallous garage they have there near the slaughter-house.

CREAM Not him, his brother the nurseryman.

GORMAN Grand match, more power to you, have they children? [*Roar of engine.*]

CREAM Eh?

GORMAN Children.

CREAM Two dotey little boys, little Johnny I mean Hubert and the other, the other.

GORMAN But tell me your daughter poor soul she was taken then was she. [*Pause.*] That cigarette while we're at it might try this gentleman. [*Footsteps approach.*] Beg your pardon Sir trouble you for a light. [*Footsteps recede.*] Ah the young are very wrapped up Mr. Cream.

CREAM Little Hubert and the other, the other, what's this his name is. [*Pause.*] And Mrs. Gorman.

GORMAN Still in it.

CREAM Ah you're the lucky jim Gorman, you're the lucky jim, Mrs. Gorman by gad, fine figure of a woman Mrs. Gorman, fine handsome woman.

GORMAN Handsome, all right, but you know, age. We have our health thanks be to God touch wood. [*Pause.*] You know what it is Mr. Cream, that'd be the way to pop off chatting away like this of a sunny morning.

CREAM None of that now Gorman, who's talking of popping off with the health you have as strong as an ox and a comfortable wife, ah I'd give ten years of mine to have her back do you hear me, living with strangers isn't the same.

GORMAN Miss Bertha's so sweet and good you're on the pig's back for God's sake, on the pig's back.

CREAM   It's not the same you can take it from me, can't call your soul your own, look at the cigarettes, the lighter.

GORMAN   Miss Bertha so sweet and good.

CREAM   Sweet and good, all right, but dammit if she doesn't take me for a doddering old drivelling dotard. [*Pause.*] What did I do with those cigarettes?

GORMAN   And tell me your poor dear daughter-in-law what am I saying your daughter-in-law.

CREAM   My daughter-in-law, my daughter-in-law, what about my daughter-in-law.

GORMAN   She had private means, it was said she had private means.

CREAM   Private means ah they were the queer private means, all swallied up in the war every ha'penny do you hear me, all in the bank the private means not as much land as you'd tether a goat. [*Pause.*] Land Gorman there's no security like land but that woman you might as well have been talking to the bedpost, a mule she was that woman was.

GORMAN   Ah well it's only human nature, you can't always pierce into the future.

CREAM   Now now Gorman don't be telling me, land wouldn't you live all your life off a bit of land damn it now wouldn't you any fool knows that unless they take the fantasy to go and build on the moon the way they say, ah that's all fantasy Gorman you can take it from me all fantasy and delusion, they'll smart for it one of these days by God they will.

GORMAN   You don't believe in the moon what they're experimenting at.

CREAM   My dear Gorman the moon is the moon and cheese is cheese what do they take us for, didn't it always exist the moon wasn't it always there as large as life and what did it ever mean only fantasy and delusion Gorman, fantasy and delusion. [*Pause.*] Or is it our forefathers were a lot of old bags maybe now is that on the cards I ask you, Bacon, Wellington, Washington, for them the moon was always in their opinion damn it I ask you you'd think to hear them talk

no one ever bothered his arse with the moon before, make a
cat swallow his whiskers they think they've discovered the
moon as if as if. [*Pause.*] What was I driving at?
[*Roar of engine.*]

GORMAN   So you're against progress are you.

CREAM   Progress, progress, progress is all very fine and grand, there's
such a thing I grant you, but it's scientific, progress,
scientific, the moon's not progress, lunacy, lunacy.

GORMAN   Ah there I'm with you progress is scientific and the moon, the
moon, that's the way it is.

CREAM   The wisdom of the ancients that's the trouble they don't give a
rap or a snap for it any more, and the world going to rack
and ruin, wouldn't it be better now to go back to the old
maxims and not be gallivanting off killing one another in
China over the moon, ah when I think of my poor father.

GORMAN   Your father that reminds me I knew your father well. [*Roar of
engine.*] There was a man for you old Mr. Cream, what he had
to say he lashed out with it straight from the shoulder and no
humming and hawing, now it comes back to me one year
there on the town council my father told me must have been
wait now till I see 95, 95 or 6, a short while before he resigned,
95 that's it the year of the great frost.

CREAM   Ah I beg your pardon, the great frost was 93 I'd just turned ten,
93 Gorman the great frost.
[*Roar of engine.*]

GORMAN   My father used to tell the story how Mr. Cream went hell for
leather for the mayor who was he in those days, must have
been Overend, yes Overend.

CREAM   Ah there you're mistaken my dear Gorman, my father went on
the council with Overend in 97, January 97.

GORMAN   That may be, that may be, but it must have been 95 or 6 just the
same seeing as how my father went off in 96, April 96, there
was a set against him and he had to give in his resignation.

CREAM   Well then your father was off when it happened, all I know is mine went on with Overend in 97 the year Marrable was burnt out.

GORMAN   Ah Marrable it wasn't five hundred yards from the door five hundred yards Mr. Cream, I can still hear my poor mother saying to us ah poor dear Maria she was saying to me again only last night, January 96 that's right.

CREAM   97 I tell you, 97, the year my father was voted on.

GORMAN   That may be but just the same the clout he gave Overend that's right now I have it.

CREAM   The clout was Oscar Bliss the butcher in Pollox Street.

GORMAN   The butcher in Pollox Street, there's a memory from the dim distant past for you, didn't he have a daughter do you remember.

CREAM   Helen, Helen Bliss, pretty girl, she'd be my age, 83 saw the light of day.

GORMAN   And Rosie Plumpton bonny Rosie staring up at the lid these thirty years she must be now and Molly Berry and Eva what was her name Eva Hart that's right Eva Hart didn't she marry a Crumplin.

CREAM   Her brother, her brother Alfred married Gertie Crumplin great one for the lads she was you remember, Gertie great one for the lads.

GORMAN   Do I remember, Gertie Crumplin great bit of skirt by God, hee hee hee great bit of skirt.

CREAM   You old dog you!

[*Roar of engine.*]

GORMAN   And Nelly Crowther there's one came to a nasty end.

CREAM   Simon's daughter that's right, the parents were greatly to blame you can take it from me.

GORMAN   They reared her well then just the same bled themselves white for her so they did, poor Mary used to tell us all we were very close in those days lived on the same landing you know, poor Mary yes she used to say what a drain it was having the child boarding out at Saint Theresa's can you imagine, very classy, daughters of the gentry Mr. Cream, even taught French they were the young ladies.

CREAM   Isn't that what I'm telling you, reared her like a princess of the blood they did, French now I ask you, French.

GORMAN   Would you blame them Mr. Cream, the best of parents, you can't deny it, education.

CREAM   French, French, isn't that what I'm saying.

[*Roar of engine.*]

GORMAN   They denied themselves everything, take the bits out of their mouths they would for their Nelly.

CREAM   Don't be telling me they had her on a string all the same the said young lady, remember that Holy Week 1912 was it or 13.

[*Roar of engine.*]

GORMAN   Eh?

CREAM   When you think of Simon the man he was don't be telling me that. [*Pause.*] Holy Week 1913 now it all comes back to me is that like as if they had her on a string what she did then.

GORMAN   Peace to her ashes Mr. Cream.

CREAM   Principles, Gorman, principles without principles I ask you. [*Roar of engine.*] Wasn't there an army man in it?

GORMAN   Eh?

CREAM   Wasn't there an army man in it?

GORMAN   In the car?

CREAM   Eh?

GORMAN   An army man in the car?

CREAM   In the Crowther blow-up.

[*Roar of engine.*]

GORMAN   You mean the Lootnant St. John Fitzball.

CREAM   St. John Fitzball that's the man, wasn't he mixed up in it?

GORMAN   They were keeping company all right. [*Pause.*] He died in 14. Wounds.

CREAM   And his aunt Miss Hester.

GORMAN   Dead then these how many years is it now how many.

CREAM   She was a great old one, a little on the high and mighty side perhaps you might say.

GORMAN   Take fire like gunpowder but a heart of gold if you only knew. [*Roar of engine.*] Her niece has a chip of the old block wouldn't you say.

CREAM   Her niece? No recollection.

GORMAN   No recollection, Miss Victoria, come on now, she was to have married an American and she's in the Turrets yet.

CREAM   I thought they'd sold.

GORMAN   Sell the Turrets is it they'll never sell, the family seat three centuries and maybe more, three centuries Mr. Cream.

CREAM   You might be their historiographer Gorman to hear you talk, what you don't know about those people.

GORMAN   Histryographer no Mr. Cream I wouldn't go so far as that but Miss Victoria right enough I know her through and through we stop and have a gas like when her aunt was still in it, ah yes nothing hoity-toity about Miss Victoria you can take my word she has a great chip of the old block.

CREAM   Hadn't she a brother.

GORMAN   The Lootnant yes, died in 14. Wounds.
         [*Deafening roar of engine.*]

CREAM   The bloody cars such a thing as a quiet chat I ask you. [*Pause.*] Well I'll be slipping along I'm holding you back from your work.

GORMAN   Slipping along what would you want slipping along and we only after meeting for once in a blue moon.

CREAM   Well then just a minute and smoke a quick one. [*Pause.*] What did I do with those cigarettes? [*Pause.*] You fire ahead don't mind me.

GORMAN   When you think, when you think. . . .
         [*Suddenly complete silence. 10 seconds. The tune resumes. The street noises resume and submerge tune a moment. Street noises and tune together crescendo. Tune finally rises above them triumphant.*]

COME AND GO

A dramaticule

For John Calder

Flo
Vi
Ru
(Ages undeterminable)

Sitting centre side by side stage right to left Flo, Vi and Ru.
    Very erect, facing front, hands clasped in laps.
    Silence.

VI   Ru.

RU   Yes.

VI   Flo.

FLO   Yes.

VI   When did we three last meet?

RU   Let us not speak.
    [*Silence.*
    Exit Vi right.
    Silence.]

FLO   Ru.

RU   Yes.

FLO   What do you think of Vi?

RU   I see little change. [*Flo moves to centre seat, whispers in Ru's ear.*
    Appalled.] Oh! [*They look at each other. Flo puts her finger to her lips.*]
    Does she not realize?

FLO   God grant not.
    [*Enter Vi. Flo and Ru turn back front, resume pose. Vi sits right. Silence.*]
    Just sit together as we used to, in the playground at Miss Wade's.

RU   On the log.

[*Silence.*

Exit Flo left.

Silence.]

Vi.

VI   Yes.

RU   How do you find Flo?

VI   She seems much the same. [*Ru moves to centre seat, whispers in Vi's ear.
Appalled.*] Oh! [*They look at each other. Ru puts her finger to her lips.*]
Has she not been told?

RU   God forbid.

[*Enter Flo. Ru and Vi turn back front, resume pose. Flo sits left.*]
Holding hands . . . that way.

FLO   Dreaming of . . . love.

[*Silence.*

Exit Ru right.

Silence.]

VI   Flo.

FLO   Yes.

VI   How do you think Ru is looking?

FLO   One sees little in this light. [*Vi moves to centre seat, whispers in Flo's
ear. Appalled.*] Oh! [*They look at each other. Vi puts her finger to her lips.*]
Does she not know?

VI   Please God not.

[*Enter Ru. Vi and Flo turn back front, resume pose. Ru sits right.*

Silence.]

May we not speak of the old days? [*Silence.*] Of what came after?
[*Silence.*] Shall we hold hands in the old way?

[*After a moment they join hands as follows: Vi's right hand with Ru's right
hand, Vi's left hand with Flo's left hand, Flo's right hand with Ru's left
hand, Vi's arms being above Ru's left arm and Flo's right arm. The three
pairs of clasped hands rest on the three laps. Silence.*]

FLO   I can feel the rings.

[*Silence.*]

Curtain

NOTES

Successive positions

1	Flo	Vi	Ru
2 ⌈	Flo		Ru
⌊		Flo	Ru
3	Vi	Flo	Ru
4 ⌈	Vi		Ru
⌊	Vi	Ru	
5	Vi	Ru	Flo
6 ⌈	Vi		Flo
⌊		Vi	Flo
7	Ru	Vi	Flo

Hands

Ru   Vi   Flo

Lighting

Soft, from above only and concentrated on playing area. Rest of stage as dark as possible.

Costume

Full-length coats, buttoned high, dull violet (Ru), dull red (Vi), dull yellow (Flo). Drab nondescript hats with enough brim to shade faces. Apart from colour differentiation three figures as alike as possible. Light shoes with rubber soles. Hands made up to be as visible as possible. No rings apparent.

Seat

Narrow benchlike seat, without back, just long enough to accommodate three figures almost touching. As little visible as possible. It should not be clear what they are sitting on.

Exits

The figures are not seen to go off stage. They should disappear a few steps from lit area. If dark not sufficient to allow this, recourse should be had to screens or drapes as little visible as possible. Exits and entrances slow, without sound of feet.

Ohs

Three very different sounds.

Voices

As low as compatible with audibility. Colourless except for three "ohs" and two lines following.

EH JOE

A piece for television

Joe, late fifties, grey hair, old dressing-gown, carpet slippers, in his room.

    1. Joe seen from behind sitting on edge of bed, intent pose, getting up, going to window, opening window, looking out, closing window, drawing curtain, standing intent.

    2. Joe do. (= from behind) going from window to door, opening door, looking out, closing door, locking door, drawing hanging before door, standing intent.

    3. Joe do. going from door to cupboard, opening cupboard, looking in, closing cupboard, locking cupboard, drawing hanging before cupboard, standing intent.

    4. Joe do. going from cupboard to bed, kneeling down, looking under bed, getting up, sitting down on edge of bed as when discovered, beginning to relax.

    5. Joe seen from front sitting on edge of bed, relaxed, eyes closed. Hold, then dolly slowly in to close-up of face. First word of text stops this movement.

Camera

Joe's opening movements followed by camera at constant remove, Joe full length in frame throughout. No need to record room as whole. After this opening pursuit, between first and final close-up of face, camera has nine slight moves in towards face, say four inches each time. Each move is stopped by voice resuming, never camera move and voice together. This would give position of camera when dolly stopped by first word of text as one yard from maximum close-up of face. Camera does not move between paragraphs till clear that pause (say three seconds) longer than between phrases. Then four inches in say four seconds when movement stopped by voice resuming.

Voice
Low, distinct, remote, little colour, absolutely steady rhythm, slightly slower than normal. Between phrases a beat of one second at least. Between paragraphs about seven, i.e. three before camera starts to advance and four for advance before it is stopped by voice resuming.

Face
Practically motionless throughout, eyes unblinking during paragraphs, impassive except in so far as it reflects mounting tension of listening. Brief zones of relaxation between paragraphs when perhaps voice has relented for the evening and intentness may relax variously till restored by voice resuming.

WOMAN'S VOICE
Joe . . .
[*Eyes open, resumption of intentness.*]
Joe . . .
[*Full intentness.*]
Thought of everything? . . . Forgotten nothing? . . . You're all right now, eh? . . . No one can see you now. . . . No one can get at you now. . . . Why don't you put out that light? . . . There might be a louse watching you. . . . Why don't you go to bed? . . . What's wrong with that bed, Joe? . . . You changed it, didn't you? . . . Made no difference? . . . Or is the heart already? . . . Crumbles when you lie down in the dark. . . . Dry rotten at last. . . . Eh Joe?

Camera move 1

The best's to come, you said, that last time. . . . Hurrying me into my coat. . . . Last I was favoured with from you. . . . Say it you now, Joe, no one'll hear you. . . . Come on, Joe, no one can say it like you, say it again now and listen to yourself. . . . The best's to come. . . . You were right for once. . . . In the end.

Camera move 2

You know that penny farthing hell you call your mind. . . . That's where you think this is coming from, don't you? . . . That's where you heard your father. . . . Isn't that what you told me? . . . Started in on you one June night and went on for years. . . . On and off. . . . Behind the eyes. . . . That's how you were able to throttle him in the end. . . . Mental thuggee you called it. . . . One of your happiest fancies. . . . Mental thuggee. . . . Otherwise he'd be plaguing you yet. . . . Then your mother when her hour came. . . . "Look up, Joe, look up, we're watching you." . . . Weaker and weaker till you laid her too. . . . Others. . . . All the others. . . . Such love he got. . . . God knows why. . . . Pitying love. . . . None to touch it. . . . And look at him now. . . . Throttling the dead in his head.

Camera move 3

Anyone living love you now, Joe? . . . Anyone living sorry for you now? . . . That slut that comes on Saturday, you pay her, don't you? . . . Penny a hoist tuppence as long as you like. . . . Watch yourself you don't run short, Joe. . . . Ever think of that? . . . Eh Joe? . . . What it'd be if you ran out of us. . . . Not another soul to still. . . . Sit there in his stinking old wrapper hearing himself. . . . That lifelong adorer. . . . Weaker and weaker till not a gasp left there either. . . . Is it that you want? . . . Well preserved for his age and the silence of the grave. . . . That old paradise you were always harping on. . . . No Joe. . . . Not for the likes of us.

Camera move 4

I was strong myself when I started. . . . In on you. . . . Wasn't I, Joe? . . . Normal strength. . . . Like those summer evenings in the Green. . . . In the early days. . . . Of our idyll. . . . When we sat watching the

ducks. . . . Holding hands exchanging vows. . . . How you admired my
elocution! . . . Among other charms. . . . Voice like flint glass. . . . To
borrow your expression. . . . Powerful grasp of language you had. . . .
Flint glass. . . . You could have listened to it for ever. . . . And now
this. . . . Squeezed down to this. . . . How much longer would you
say? . . . Till the whisper. . . . You know. . . . When you can't hear the
words. . . . Just the odd one here and there. . . . That's the worst. . . .
Isn't it, Joe? . . . Isn't that what you told me. . . . Before we expire. . . .
The odd word. . . . Straining to hear. . . . Why must you do that? . . .
When you're nearly home. . . . What matter then. . . . What we
mean. . . . It should be the best. . . . Nearly home again. . . . Another
stilled. . . . And it's the worst. . . . Isn't that what you said? . . . The
whisper. . . . The odd word. . . . Straining to hear. . . . Brain tired
squeezing. . . . It stops in the end. . . . You stop it in the end. . . .
Imagine if you couldn't. . . . Ever think of that? . . . If it went on. . . .
The whisper in your head. . . . Me whispering at you in your head. . . .
Things you can't catch. . . . On and off. . . . Till you join us. . . . Eh Joe?

Camera move 5

How's your Lord these days? . . . Still worth having? . . . Still lapping
it up? . . . The passion of our Joe. . . . Wait till He starts talking to
you. . . . When you're done with yourself. . . . All your dead dead. . . .
Sitting there in your foul old wrapper. . . . Very fair health for a man
of your years. . . . Just that lump in your bubo. . . . Silence of the
grave without the maggots. . . . To crown your labours. . . . Till one
night. . . . "Thou fool thy soul." . . . Put your thugs on that. . . . Eh
Joe? . . . Ever think of that? . . . When He starts in on you. . . . When
you're done with yourself. . . . If you ever are.

Camera move 6

Yes, great love God knows why. . . . Even me. . . . But I found a
better. . . . As I hope you heard. . . . Preferable in all respects. . . .

Kinder. . . . Stronger. . . . More intelligent. . . . Better looking. . . .
Cleaner. . . . Truthful. . . . Faithful. . . . Sane. . . . Yes. . . . I did all right.

Camera move 7

But there was one didn't. . . . You know the one I mean, Joe. . . . The
green one. . . . The narrow one. . . . Always pale. . . . The pale eyes. . . .
Spirit made light. . . . To borrow your expression. . . . The way they
opened after. . . . Unique. . . . Are you with me now? . . . Eh Joe? . . .
There was love for you. . . . The best's to come, you said. . . . Bundling
her into her Avoca sack. . . . Her fingers fumbling with the big horn
buttons. . . . Ticket in your pocket for the first morning flight. . . .
You've had her, haven't you? . . . You've laid her? . . . Of course he
has. . . . She went young. . . . No more old lip from her.

Camera move 8

Ever know what happened? . . . She didn't say? . . . Just the
announcement in the *Independent*. . . . "On Mary's beads we plead her
needs and in the Holy Mass." . . . Will I tell you? . . . Not
interested? . . . Well I will just the same. . . . I think you should
know. . . . That's right, Joe, squeeze away. . . . Don't lose heart now. . . .
When you're nearly home. . . . I'll soon be gone. . . . The last of
them. . . . Unless that poor old slut loves you. . . . Then yourself. . . .
That old bonfire. . . . Years of that stink. . . . Then the silence. . . . A
dollop of that. . . . To crown all. . . . Till His Nibs. . . . One dirty winter
night. . . . "Mud thou art."

Camera move 9

All right. . . . Warm summer night. . . . All sleeping. . . . Sitting on the
edge of her bed in her lavender slip. . . . You know the one. . . . Ah she
knew you, heavenly powers! . . . Faint lap of sea through open
window. . . . Gets up in the end and slips out as she is. . . . Moon. . . .

Stock. . . . Down the garden and under the viaduct. . . . Sees from the
seaweed the tide is flowing. . . . Goes on down to the edge and lies
down with her face in the wash. . . . Cut a long story short doesn't
work. . . . Gets up in the end sopping wet and back up to the
house. . . . Gets out the Gillette. . . . The make you recommended for
her body hair. . . . Back down the garden and under the viaduct. . . .
Takes the blade from the holder and lies down at the edge on her
side. . . . Cut another long story short doesn't work either. . . . You
know how she always dreaded pain. . . . Tears a strip from the slip
and ties it round the scratch. . . . Gets up in the end and back up to
the house. . . . Slip clinging the way wet silk will. . . . This all new to
you, Joe? . . . Eh Joe? . . . Gets the tablets and back down the garden
and under the viaduct. . . . Takes a few on the way. . . . Unconscionable
hour by now. . . . Moon going off the shore behind the hill. . . .
Stands a bit looking at the beaten silver. . . . Then starts along the
edge to a place further down near the Rock. . . . Imagine what in her
mind to make her do that. . . . Imagine. . . . Trailing her feet in the
water like a child. . . . Takes a few more on the way. . . . Will I go on,
Joe? . . . Eh Joe? . . . Lies down in the end with her face a few feet
from the tide. . . . Clawing at the shingle now. . . . Has it all worked
out this time. . . . Finishes the tube. . . . There's love for you. . . . Eh
Joe? . . . Scoops a little cup for her face in the stones. . . . The green
one. . . . The narrow one. . . . Always pale. . . . The pale eyes. . . . The
look they shed before. . . . The way they opened after. . . . Spirit made
light. . . . Wasn't that your description, Joe? . . .
[*Voice drops to whisper, almost inaudible except words in italics.*]
All right. . . . You've had the best. . . . Now *imagine.* . . . Before she
goes. . . . Face in the cup. . . . Lips on a *stone.* . . . Taking Joe with
her. . . . Light gone. . . . *"Joe Joe."* . . . No sound. . . . To the *stones.* . . .
Say it you now, no one'll hear you. . . . Say "Joe" it parts the *lips.* . . .
Imagine the hands. . . . The *solitaire.* . . . Against a *stone.* . . . Imagine
the *eyes.* . . . Spiritlight. . . . Month of June. . . . What year of your
Lord? . . . *Breasts* in the stones. . . . And the *hands.* . . . Before they

go. . . . *Imagine* the hands. . . . What are they at? . . . In the *stones.* . . .
[*Image fades, voice as before.*]
What are they fondling? . . . Till they go. . . . *There's love for you.* . . .
Isn't it, Joe? . . . Wasn't it, Joe? . . . *Eh Joe?* . . . Wouldn't you say? . . .
Compared to us. . . . Compared to Him. . . . *Eh Joe?* . . .
[*Voice and image out. End.*]

BREATH

Curtain

1. Faint light on stage littered with miscellaneous rubbish. Hold about five seconds.
2. Faint brief cry and immediately inspiration and slow increase of light together reaching maximum together in about ten seconds. Silence and hold about five seconds.
3. Expiration and slow decrease of light together reaching minimum together (light as in 1) in about ten seconds and immediately cry as before. Silence and hold about five seconds.

Curtain

RUBBISH

No verticals, all scattered and lying.

CRY

Instant of recorded vagitus. Important that two cries be identical, switching on and off strictly synchronized light and breath.

BREATH

Amplified recording.

MAXIMUM LIGHT

Not bright. If 0 = dark and 10 = bright, light should move from about 3 to 6 and back.

NOT I

NOTE
Movement: this consists in simple sideways raising of arms from sides and their falling back, in a gesture of helpless compassion. It lessens with each recurrence till scarcely perceptible at third. There is just enough pause to contain it as Mouth recovers from vehement refusal to relinquish third person.

Stage in darkness but for Mouth, upstage audience right, about 8 feet above stage level, faintly lit from close-up and below, rest of face in shadow. Invisible microphone.

   Auditor, downstage audience left, tall standing figure, sex undeterminable, enveloped from head to foot in loose black djellaba, with hood, fully faintly lit, standing on invisible podium about 4 feet high shown by attitude alone to be facing diagonally across stage intent on Mouth, dead still throughout but for four brief movements where indicated. See Note. As house lights down Mouth's voice unintelligible behind curtain. House lights out. Voice continues unintelligible behind curtain, 10 seconds. With rise of curtain ad-libbing from text as required leading when curtain fully up and attention sufficient into:

MOUTH   ... out ... into this world ... this world ... tiny little thing ...
       before its time ... in a godfor— ... what? ... girl? ... yes ...
       tiny little girl ... into this ... out into this ... before her

time . . . godforsaken hole called . . . called . . . no matter . . .
parents unknown . . . unheard of . . . he having vanished . . .
thin air . . . no sooner buttoned up his breeches . . . she
similarly . . . eight months later . . . almost to the tick . . . so no
love . . . spared that . . . no love such as normally vented on
the . . . speechless infant . . . in the home . . . no . . . nor indeed
for that matter any of any kind . . . no love of any kind . . . at
any subsequent stage . . . so typical affair . . . nothing of any
note till coming up to sixty when—. . . what? . . seventy? . . .
good God! . . . coming up to seventy . . . wandering in a field . . .
looking aimlessly for cowslips . . . to make a ball . . . a few steps
then stop . . . stare into space . . . then on . . . a few more . . .
stop and stare again . . . so on . . . drifting around . . . when
suddenly . . . gradually . . . all went out . . . all that early April
morning light . . . and she found herself in the—. . . what? . . .
who? . . . no! . . . she! . . . [*pause and movement 1*] . . . found
herself in the dark . . . and if not exactly . . . insentient . . .
insentient . . . for she could still hear the buzzing . . . so-
called . . . in the ears . . . and a ray of light came and went . . .
came and went . . . such as the moon might cast . . . drifting . . .
in and out of cloud . . . but so dulled . . . feeling . . . feeling so
dulled . . . she did not know . . . what position she was in . . .
imagine! . . . what position she was in! . . . whether standing . . .
or sitting . . . but the brain—. . . what? . . . kneeling? . . . yes . . .
whether standing . . . or sitting . . . or kneeling . . . but the
brain—. . . what? . . . lying? . . . yes . . . whether standing . . . or
sitting . . . or kneeling . . . or lying . . . but the brain still . . .
still . . . in a way . . . for her first thought was . . . oh long
after . . . sudden flash . . . brought up as she had been to
believe . . . with the other waifs . . . in a merciful . . . [*Brief
laugh.*] . . . God . . . [*Good laugh.*] . . . first thought was . . . oh
long after . . . sudden flash . . . she was being punished . . . for
her sins . . . a number of which then . . . further proof if proof
were needed . . . flashed through her mind . . . one after

another ... then dismissed as foolish ... oh long after ... this
thought dismissed ... as she suddenly realized ... gradually
realized ... she was not suffering ... imagine! ... not
suffering! ... indeed could not remember ... off-hand ...
when she had suffered less ... unless of course she was ...
meant to be suffering ... ha! ... *thought* to be suffering ... just
as the odd time ... in her life ... when clearly intended to be
having pleasure ... she was in fact ... having none ... not the
slightest ... in which case of course ... that notion of
punishment ... for some sin or other ... or for the lot ... or
no particular reason ... for its own sake ... thing she
understood perfectly ... that notion of punishment ... which
had first occurred to her ... brought up as she had been to
believe ... with the other waifs ... in a merciful ... [*Brief
laugh.*] ... God ... [*Good laugh.*] ... first occurred to her ...
then dismissed ... as foolish ... was perhaps not so foolish ...
after all ... so on ... all that ... vain reasonings ... till another
thought ... oh long after ... sudden flash ... very foolish
really but— ... what? ... the buzzing? ... yes ... all the time
the buzzing ... so-called ... in the ears ... though of course
actually ... not in the ears at all ... in the skull ... dull roar in
the skull ... and all the time this ray or beam ... like
moonbeam ... but probably not ... certainly not ... always the
same spot ... now bright ... now shrouded ... but always the
same spot ... as no moon could ... no ... no moon ... just all
part of the same wish to ... torment ... though actually in
point of fact ... not in the least ... not a twinge ... so far ...
ha! ... so far ... this other thought then ... oh long after ...
sudden flash ... very foolish really but so like her ... in a
way ... that she might do well to ... groan ... on and off ...
writhe she could not ... as if in actual agony ... but could
not ... could not bring herself ... some flaw in her make-up ...
incapable of deceit ... or the machine ... more likely the
machine ... so disconnected ... never got the message ... or

powerless to respond . . . like numbed . . . couldn't make the
sound . . . not any sound . . . no sound of any kind . . . no
screaming for help for example . . . should she feel so
inclined . . . scream . . . [*screams*] . . . then listen . . . [*silence*] . . .
scream again . . . [*screams again*] . . . then listen again . . .
[*silence*] . . . no . . . spared that . . . all silent as the grave . . . no
part— . . . what? . . . the buzzing? . . . yes . . . all silent but for
the buzzing . . . so-called . . . no part of her moving . . . that she
could feel . . . just the eyelids . . . presumably . . . on and off . . .
shut out the light . . . reflex they call it . . . no feeling of any
kind . . . but the lids . . . even best of times . . . who feels
them? . . . opening . . . shutting . . . all that moisture . . . but the
brain still . . . still sufficiently . . . oh very much so! . . . at this
stage . . . in control . . . under control . . . to question even
this . . . for on that April morning . . . so it reasoned . . . that
April morning . . . she fixing with her eye . . . a distant bell . . .
as she hastened towards it . . . fixing it with her eye . . . lest it
elude her . . . had not all gone out . . . all that light . . . of
itself . . . without any . . . any . . . on her part . . . so on . . . so on
it reasoned . . . vain questionings . . . and all dead still . . . sweet
silent as the grave . . . when suddenly . . . gradually . . . she
realiz— . . . what? . . . the buzzing? . . . yes . . . all dead still but
for the buzzing . . . when suddenly she realized . . . words
were— . . . what? . . . who? . . . no! . . . she! . . . [*pause and
movement 2*] . . . realized . . . words were coming . . . imagine!
. . . words were coming . . . a voice she did not recognize . . . at
first . . . so long since it had sounded . . . then finally had to
admit . . . could be none other . . . than her own . . . certain
vowel sounds . . . she had never heard . . . elsewhere . . . so that
people would stare . . . the rare occasions . . . once or twice a
year . . . always winter some strange reason . . . stare at her
uncomprehending . . . and now this stream . . . steady
stream . . . she who had never . . . on the contrary . . .
practically speechless . . . all her days . . . how she survived! . . .

even shopping . . . out shopping . . . busy shopping centre . . .
supermart . . . just hand in the list . . . with the bag . . . old
black shopping bag . . . then stand there waiting . . . any length
of time . . . middle of the throng . . . motionless . . . staring
into space . . . mouth half open as usual . . . till it was back in
her hand . . . the bag back in her hand . . . then pay and go . . .
not as much as goodbye . . . how she survived! . . . and now this
stream . . . not catching the half of it . . . not the quarter . . . no
idea . . . what she was saying . . . imagine! . . . no idea what she
was saying! . . . till she began trying to . . . delude herself . . . it
was not hers at all . . . not her voice at all . . . and no doubt
would have . . . vital she should . . . was on the point . . . after
long efforts . . . when suddenly she felt . . . gradually she
felt . . . her lips moving . . . imagine! . . . her lips moving! . . .
as of course till then she had not . . . and not alone the
lips . . . the cheeks . . . the jaws . . . the whole face . . . all
those— . . . what? . . . the tongue? . . . yes . . . the tongue in the
mouth . . . all those contortions without which . . . no speech
possible . . . and yet in the ordinary way . . . not felt at all . . . so
intent one is . . . on what one is saying . . . the whole being . . .
hanging on its words . . . so that not only she had . . . had
she . . . not only had she . . . to give up . . . admit hers alone . . .
her voice alone . . . but this other awful thought . . . oh long
after . . . sudden flash . . . even more awful if possible . . . that
feeling was coming back . . . imagine! . . . feeling coming
back! . . . starting at the top . . . then working down . . . the
whole machine . . . but no . . . spared that . . . the mouth
alone . . . so far . . . ha! . . . so far . . . then thinking . . . oh long
after . . . sudden flash . . . it can't go on . . . all this . . . all
that . . . steady stream . . . straining to hear . . . make something of it . . . and her own thoughts . . . make something of
them . . . all— . . . what? . . . the buzzing? . . . yes . . . all the time
the buzzing . . . so-called . . . all that together . . . imagine! . . .
whole body like gone . . . just the mouth . . . lips . . . cheeks . . .

jaws ... never— ... what? ... tongue? ... yes ... lips ...
cheeks ... jaws ... tongue ... never still a second ... mouth
on fire ... stream of words ... in her ear ... practically in her
ear ... not catching the half ... not the quarter ... no idea
what she's saying ... imagine! ... no idea what she's saying! ...
and can't stop ... no stopping it ... she who but a moment
before ... but a moment! ... could not make a sound ... no
sound of any kind ... now can't stop ... imagine! ... can't stop
the stream ... and the whole brain begging ... something
begging in the brain ... begging the mouth to stop ... pause a
moment ... if only for a moment ... and no response ... as if
it hadn't heard ... or couldn't ... couldn't pause a second ...
like maddened ... all that together ... straining to hear ...
piece it together ... and the brain ... raving away on its
own ... trying to make sense of it ... or make it stop ... or in
the past ... dragging up the past ... flashes from all over ...
walks mostly ... walking all her days ... day after day ... a few
steps then stop ... stare into space ... then on ... a few
more ... stop and stare again ... so on ... drifting around ...
day after day ... or that time she cried ... the one time she
could remember ... since she was a baby ... must have cried
as a baby ... perhaps not ... not essential to life ... just the
birth cry to get her going ... breathing ... then no more till
this ... old hag already ... sitting staring at her hand ...
where was it? ... Croker's Acres ... one evening on the way
home ... home! ... a little mound in Croker's Acres ...
dusk ... sitting staring at her hand ... there in her lap ...
palm upward ... suddenly saw it wet ... the palm ... tears
presumably ... hers presumably ... no one else for miles ...
no sound ... just the tears ... sat and watched them dry ... all
over in a second ... or grabbing at straw ... the brain ...
flickering away on its own ... quick grab and on ... nothing
there ... on to the next ... bad as the voice ... worse ... as
little sense ... all that together ... can't— ... what? ... the

buzzing? ... yes ... all the time the buzzing ... dull roar like
falls ... and the beam ... flickering on and off ... starting to
move around ... like moonbeam but not ... all part of the
same ... keep an eye on that too ... corner of the eye ... all
that together ... can't go on ... God is love ... she'll be
purged ... back in the field ... morning sun ... April ... sink
face down in the grass ... nothing but the larks ... so on ...
grabbing at the straw ... straining to hear ... the odd word ...
make some sense of it ... whole body like gone ... just the
mouth ... like maddened ... and can't stop ... no stopping
it ... something she— ... something she had to— ...
what? ... who? ... no! ... she! ... [*pause and movement 3*] ...
something she had to— ... what? ... the buzzing? ... yes ...
all the time the buzzing ... dull roar ... in the skull ... and
the beam ... ferreting around ... painless ... so far ... ha! ...
so far ... then thinking ... oh long after ... sudden flash ...
perhaps something she had to ... had to ... tell ... could that
be it? ... something she had to ... tell ... tiny little thing ...
before its time ... godforsaken hole ... no love ... spared
that ... speechless all her days ... practically speechless ...
how she survived! ... that time in court ... what had she to say
for herself ... guilty or not guilty ... stand up woman ...
speak up woman ... stood there staring into space ... mouth
half open as usual ... waiting to be led away ... glad of the
hand on her arm ... now this ... something she had to tell ...
could that be it? ... something that would tell ... how it
was ... how she— ... what? ... had been? ... yes ...
something that would tell how it had been ... how she had
lived ... lived on and on ... guilty or not ... on and on ... to
be sixty ... something she— ... what? ... seventy? ... good
God! ... on and on to be seventy ... something she didn't
know herself ... wouldn't know if she heard ... then
forgiven ... God is love ... tender mercies ... new every
morning ... back in the field ... April morning ... face in the

grass . . . nothing but the larks . . . pick it up there . . . get on
with it from there . . . another few— . . . what? . . . not that? . . .
nothing to do with that? . . . nothing she could tell? . . . all
right . . . nothing she could tell . . . try something else . . . think
of something else . . . oh long after . . . sudden flash . . . not
that either . . . all right . . . something else again . . . so on . . .
hit on it in the end . . . think everything keep on long
enough . . . then forgiven . . . back in the— . . . what? . . . not
that either? . . . nothing to do with that either? . . . nothing she
could think? . . . all right . . . nothing she could tell . . . nothing
she could think . . . nothing she— . . . what? . . . who? . . .
no! . . . she! . . . [*pause and movement 4*] . . . tiny little thing . . .
out before its time . . . godforsaken hole . . . no love . . . spared
that . . . speechless all her days . . . practically speechless . . .
even to herself . . . never out loud . . . but not completely . . .
sometimes sudden urge . . . once or twice a year . . . always
winter some strange reason . . . the long evenings . . . hours of
darkness . . . sudden urge to . . . tell . . . then rush out stop the
first she saw . . . nearest lavatory . . . start pouring it out . . .
steady stream . . . mad stuff . . . half the vowels wrong . . . no
one could follow . . . till she saw the stare she was getting . . .
then die of shame . . . crawl back in . . . once or twice a year . . .
always winter some strange reason . . . long hours of
darkness . . . now this . . . this . . . quicker and quicker . . . the
words . . . the brain . . . flickering away like mad . . . quick grab
and on . . . nothing there . . . on somewhere else . . . try
somewhere else . . . all the time something begging . . .
something in her begging . . . begging it all to stop . . .
unanswered . . . prayer unanswered . . . or unheard . . . too
faint . . . so on . . . keep on . . . trying . . . not knowing what . . .
what she was trying . . . what to try . . . whole body like gone . . .
just the mouth . . . like maddened . . . so on . . . keep— . . .
what? . . . the buzzing? . . . yes . . . all the time the buzzing . . .
dull roar like falls . . . in the skull . . . and the beam . . . poking

around ... painless ... so far ... ha! ... so far ... all that ...
keep on ... not knowing what ... what she was— ... what? ...
who? ... no! ... she! ... SHE! ... [*pause*] ... what she was
trying ... what to try ... no matter ... keep on ... [*curtain starts
down*] ... hit on it in the end ... then back ... God is love ...
tender mercies ... new every morning ... back in the field ...
April morning ... face in the grass ... nothing but the
larks ... pick it up—

[*Curtain fully down. House dark. Voice continues behind curtain,
unintelligible, 10 seconds, ceases as house lights up.*]

THAT TIME

NOTE
Moments of one and the same voice A B C relay one another without solution of continuity—apart from the two 10-second breaks. Yet the switch from one to another must be clearly faintly perceptible. If three-fold source and context prove insufficient to produce this effect it should be assisted mechanically (e.g. threefold pitch).

Curtain. Stage in darkness. Fade up to Listener's Face about 10 feet above stage level midstage off centre.

   Old white face, long flaring white hair as if seen from above outspread.

   Voices A B C are his own coming to him from both sides and above. They modulate back and forth without any break in general flow except where silence indicated. See note. Silence 7 seconds. Listener's Eyes are open. His breath audible, slow and regular.

A that time you went back that last time to look was the ruin still there where you hid as a child when was that [*eyes close*] grey day took the eleven to the end of the line and on from there no no trams then all gone long ago that time you went back to look was the ruin still there where you hid as a child that last time not a tram left in the place only the old rails when was that

C when you went in out of the rain always winter then always raining that time in the Portrait Gallery in off the street out of the cold and rain slipped in when no one was looking and through the rooms shivering and dripping till you found a seat marble slab and sat down to rest and dry off and on to hell out of there when was that

B   on the stone together in the sun on the stone at the edge of the little wood and as far as eye could see the wheat turning yellow vowing every now and then you loved each other just a murmur not touching or anything of that nature you one end of the stone she the other long low stone like millstone no looks just there on the stone in the sun with the little wood behind gazing at the wheat or eyes closed all still no sign of life not a soul abroad no sound

A   straight off the ferry and up with the nightbag to the high street neither right nor left not a curse for the old scenes the old names straight up the rise from the wharf to the high street and there not a wire to be seen only the old rails all rust when was that was your mother ah for God's sake all gone long ago that time you went back that last time to look was the ruin still there where you hid as a child someone's folly

C   was your mother ah for God's sake all gone long ago all dust the lot you the last huddled up on the slab in the old green greatcoat with your arms round you whose else hugging you for a bit of warmth to dry off and on to hell out of there and on to the next not a living soul in the place only yourself and the odd attendant drowsing around in his felt shufflers not a sound to be heard only every now and then a shuffle of felt drawing near then dying away

B   all still just the leaves and ears and you too still on the stone in a daze no sound not a word only every now and then to vow you loved each other just a murmur one thing could ever bring tears till they dried up altogether that thought when it came up among the others floated up that scene

A   Foley was it Foley's Folly bit of a tower still standing all the rest rubble and nettles where did you sleep no friend all the homes gone was it that kip on the front where you no she was with you then still with you then just the one night in any case off the ferry one morning and back on her the next to look was the ruin still there where none

ever came where you hid as a child slip off when no one was looking
and hide there all day long on a stone among the nettles with your
picture-book

c   till you hoisted your head and there before your eyes when they
opened a vast oil black with age and dirt someone famous in his
time some famous man or woman or even child such as a young
prince or princess some young prince or princess of the blood black
with age behind the glass where gradually as you peered trying to
make it out gradually of all things a face appeared had you swivel on
the slab to see who it was there at your elbow

b   on the stone in the sun gazing at the wheat or the sky or the eyes
closed nothing to be seen but the wheat turning yellow and the blue
sky vowing every now and then you loved each other just a murmur
tears without fail till they dried up altogether suddenly there in
whatever thoughts you might be having whatever scenes perhaps
way back in childhood or the womb worst of all or that old
Chinaman long before Christ born with long white hair

c   never the same after that never quite the same but that was nothing
new if it wasn't this it was that common occurrence something you
could never be the same after crawling about year after year sunk in
your lifelong mess muttering to yourself who else you'll never be the
same after this you were never the same after that

a   or talking to yourself who else out loud imaginary conversations there
was childhood for you ten or eleven on a stone among the giant
nettles making it up now one voice now another till you were hoarse
and they all sounded the same well on into the night some moods in
the black dark or moonlight and they all out on the roads looking
for you

b   or by the window in the dark harking to the owl not a thought in your
head till hard to believe harder and harder to believe you ever told
anyone you loved them or anyone you till just one of those things
you kept making up to keep the void out just another of those old
tales to keep the void from pouring in on top of you the shroud
[*Silence 10 seconds. Breath audible. After 3 seconds eyes open.*]

c   never the same but the same as what for God's sake did you ever say I
to yourself in your life come on now [*eyes close*] could you ever say I
to yourself in your life turning-point that was a great word with you
before they dried up altogether always having turning-points and
never but the one the first and last that time curled up worm in
slime when they lugged you out and wiped you off and straightened
you up never another after that never looked back after that was that
the time or was that another time

B   muttering that time altogether on the stone in the sun or that time
together on the towpath or that time together in the sand that time
that time making it up from there as best you could always together
somewhere in the sun on the towpath facing downstream into the
sun sinking and the bits of flotsam coming from behind and
drifting on or caught in the reeds the dead rat it looked like came
on you from behind and went drifting on till you could see it no
more

A   that time you went back to look was the ruin still there where you hid
as a child that last time straight off the ferry and up the rise to the
high street to catch the eleven neither right nor left only one
thought in your head not a curse for the old scenes the old names
just head down press on up the rise to the top and there stood
waiting with the nightbag till the truth began to dawn

c   when you started not knowing who you were from Adam trying how
that would work for a change not knowing who you were from Adam
no notion who it was saying what you were saying whose skull you
were clapped up in whose moan had you the way you were was that
the time or was that another time there alone with the portraits of
the dead black with dirt and antiquity and the dates on the frames in
case you might get the century wrong not believing it could be you
till they put you out in the rain at closing-time

B   no sight of the face or any other part never turned to her nor she to
you always parallel like on an axle-tree never turned to each other
just blurs on the fringes of the field no touching or anything of that
nature always space between if only an inch no pawing in the

manner of flesh and blood no better than shades no worse if it wasn't for the vows

A   no getting out to it that way so what next no question of asking not another word to the living as long as you lived so foot it up in the end to the station bowed half double get out to it that way all closed down and boarded up Doric terminus of the Great Southern and Eastern all closed down and the colonnade crumbling away so what next

C   the rain and the old rounds trying making it up that way as you went along how it would work that way for a change never having been how never having been would work the old rounds trying to wangle you into it tottering and muttering all over the parish till the words dried up and the head dried up and the legs dried up whosever they were or it gave up whoever it was

B   stock still always stock still like that time on the stone or that time in the sand stretched out parallel in the sand in the sun gazing up at the blue or eyes closed blue dark blue dark stock still side by side scene float up and there you were wherever it was

A   gave it up gave up and sat down on the steps in the pale morning sun no those steps got no sun somewhere else then gave up and off somewhere else and down on a step in the pale sun a doorstep say someone's doorstep for it to be time to get on the night ferry and out to hell out of there no need sleep anywhere not a curse for the old scenes the old names the passers pausing to gape at you quick gape then pass pass on pass by on the other side

B   stock still side by side in the sun then sink and vanish without your having stirred any more than the two knobs on a dumbbell except the lids and every now and then the lips to vow and all around all still all sides wherever it might be no stir or sound only faintly the leaves in the little wood behind or the ears or the bent or the reeds as the case might be of man no sight of man or beast no sight or sound

C   always winter then always raining always slipping in somewhere when no one would be looking in off the street out of the cold and rain in

the old green holeproof coat your father left you places you hadn't to
pay to get in like the Public Library that was another great thing free
culture far from home or the Post Office that was another another
place another time

A   huddled on the doorstep in the old green greatcoat in the pale sun
with the nightbag needless on your knees not knowing where you
were little by little not knowing where you were or when you were or
what for place might have been uninhabited for all you knew like
that time on the stone the child on the stone where none ever came
[*Silence 10 seconds. Breath audible. After 3 seconds eyes open.*]

B   or alone in the same the same scenes making it up that way to keep it
going keep it out on the stone [*eyes close*] alone on the end of the
stone with the wheat and blue or the towpath alone on the towpath
with the ghosts of the mules the drowned rat or bird or whatever it
was floating off into the sunset till you could see it no more nothing
stirring only the water and the sun going down till it went down and
you vanished all vanished

A   none ever came but the child on the stone among the giant nettles
with the light coming in where the wall had crumbled away poring
on his book well on into the night some moods the moonlight and
they all out on the roads looking for him or making up talk breaking
up two or more talking to himself being together that way where
none ever came

C   always winter then endless winter year after year as if it couldn't end
the old year never end like time could go no further that time in the
Post Office all bustle Christmas bustle in off the street when no one
was looking out of the cold and rain pushed open the door like
anyone else and straight for the table neither right nor left with all
the forms and the pens on their chains sat down first vacant seat and
were taking a look round for a change before drowsing away

B   or that time alone on your back in the sand and no vows to break the
peace when was that an earlier time a later time before she came
after she went or both before she came after she was gone and you
back in the old scene wherever it might be might have been the

same old scene before as then then as after with the rat or the wheat
the yellowing ears or that time in the sand the glider passing over
that time you went back soon after long after

A   eleven or twelve in the ruin on the flat stone among the nettles in the
dark or moonlight muttering away now one voice now another there
was childhood for you till there on the step in the pale sun you
heard yourself at it again not a curse for the passers pausing to gape
at the scandal huddled there in the sun where it had no warrant
clutching the nightbag drooling away out loud eyes closed and the
white hair pouring out down from under the hat and so sat on in
that pale sun forgetting it all

C   perhaps fear of ejection having clearly no warrant in the place to say
nothing of the loathsome appearance so this look round for once at
your fellow bastards thanking God for once bad and all as you were
you were not as they till it dawned that for all the loathing you were
getting you might as well not have been there at all the eyes passing
over you and through you like so much thin air was that the time or
was that another time another place another time

B   the glider passing over never any change same blue skies nothing ever
changed but she with you there or not on your right hand always the
right hand on the fringe of the field and every now and then in the
great peace like a whisper so faint she loved you hard to believe you
even you made up that bit till the time came in the end

A   making it all up on the doorstep as you went along making yourself all
up again for the millionth time forgetting it all where you were and
what for Foley's Folly and the lot the child's ruin you came to look
was it still there to hide in again till it was night and time to go till
that time came

C   the Library that was another place another time that time you slipped
in off the street out of the cold and rain when no one was looking
what was it then you were never the same after never again after
something to do with dust something the dust said sitting at the big
round table with a bevy of old ones poring on the page and not a
sound

B   that time in the end when you tried and couldn't by the window in the dark and the owl flown to hoot at someone else or back with a shrew to its hollow tree and not another sound hour after hour hour after hour not a sound when you tried and tried and couldn't any more no words left to keep it out so gave it up gave up there by the window in the dark or moonlight gave up for good and let it in and nothing the worse a great shroud billowing in all over you on top of you and little or nothing the worse little or nothing

A   back down to the wharf with the nightbag and the old green greatcoat your father left you trailing the ground and the white hair pouring out down from under the hat till that time came on down neither right nor left not a curse for the old scenes the old names not a thought in your head only get back on board and away to hell out of it and never come back or was that another time all that another time was there ever any other time but that time away to hell out of it all and never come back

C   not a sound only the old breath and the leaves turning and then suddenly this dust whole place suddenly full of dust when you opened your eyes from floor to ceiling nothing only dust and not a sound only what was it it said come and gone was that it something like that come and gone come and gone no one come and gone in no time gone in no time

[*Silence 10 seconds. Breath audible. After 3 seconds eyes open. After 5 seconds smile, toothless for preference. Hold 5 seconds till fade out and curtain.*]

FOOTFALLS

May (M), *dishevelled grey hair, worn grey wrap hiding feet, trailing.*
Woman's Voice (V) *from dark upstage.*

Strip: downstage, parallel with front, length nine steps, width one metre, a little off centre audience right.

$$L \; \frac{\overset{\text{r l r l r l r l r} \leftarrow}{}}{\underset{\rightarrow \text{l r l r l r l r l}}{}} R$$

Pacing: starting with right foot (r), from right (R) to left (L), with left foot (l) from L to R.

Turn: rightabout at L, leftabout at R.

Steps: clearly audible rhythmic tread.

Lighting: dim, strongest at floor level, less on body, least on head.

Voices: both low and slow throughout.

Curtain. Stage in darkness.

Faint single chime. Pause as echoes die.

Fade up to dim on strip. Rest in darkness.

M discovered pacing towards L. Turns at L. paces three more lengths, halts, facing front at R.

Pause.

M   Mother. [*Pause. No louder.*] Mother.
     [*Pause.*]

V   Yes, May.

M   Were you asleep?

V   Deep asleep. [*Pause.*] I heard you in my deep sleep. [*Pause.*] There is no
     sleep so deep I would not hear you there. [*Pause. M resumes pacing.*

Four lengths. After first length, synchronous with steps.] One two three four five six seven wheel one two three four five six seven wheel. [*Free.*] Will you not try to snatch a little sleep?
[M *halts facing front at R. Pause.*]

M   Would you like me to inject you again?

V   Yes, but it is too soon.
    [*Pause.*]

M   Would you like me to change your position again?

V   Yes, but it is too soon.
    [*Pause.*]

M   Straighten your pillows? [*Pause.*] Change your drawsheet?
    [*Pause.*] Pass you the bedpan? [*Pause.*] The warming-pan?
    [*Pause.*] Dress your sores? [*Pause.*] Sponge you down?
    [*Pause.*] Moisten your poor lips? [*Pause.*] Pray with you?
    [*Pause.*] For you? [*Pause.*] Again.
    [*Pause.*]

V   Yes, but it is too soon.
    [*Pause.*]

M   What age am I now?

V   And I? [*Pause. No louder.*] And I?

M   Ninety.

V   So much?

M   Eighty-nine, ninety.

V   I had you late. [*Pause.*] In life. [*Pause.*] Forgive me again. [*Pause. No louder.*] Forgive me again.
    [M *resumes pacing. After one length halts facing front at L. Pause.*]

M   What age am I now?

V   In your forties.

M   So little?

V   I'm afraid so. [*Pause. M resumes pacing. After first turn at L.*] May. [*Pause. No louder.*] May.

M   [*pacing*] Yes, Mother.

V   Will you never have done? [*Pause.*] Will you never have done . . . revolving it all?

M [halting] It?

V It all. [Pause.] In your poor mind. [Pause.] It all. [Pause.] It all.
[M resumes pacing. Five seconds. Fade out on strip.
All in darkness. Steps cease.
Pause.
Chime a little fainter. Pause for echoes.
Fade up to a little less on strip. Rest in darkness.
M discovered facing front at R.
Pause.]

V I walk here now. [Pause.] Rather I come and stand. [Pause.] At nightfall.
[Pause.] She fancies she is alone. [Pause.] See how still she stands, how
stark, with her face to the wall. [Pause.] How outwardly unmoved.
[Pause.] She has not been out since girlhood. [Pause.] Not out since
girlhood. [Pause.] Where is she, it may be asked. [Pause.] Why, in the
old home, the same where she— [Pause.] The same where she began.
[Pause.] Where it began. [Pause.] It all began. [Pause.] But this, this,
when did this begin? [Pause.] When other girls of her age were out
at . . . lacrosse she was already here. [Pause.] At this. [Pause.] The floor
here, now bare, once was— [M begins pacing. Steps a little slower.] But
let us watch her move, in silence. [M paces. Towards end of second
length.] Watch how feat she wheels. [M turns, paces. Synchronous with
steps third length.] Seven, eight, nine, wheel. [M turns at L, paces one
more length, halts facing front at B.] I say the floor here, now bare, this
strip of floor, once was carpeted, a deep pile. Till one night, while
still little more than a child, she called her mother and said, Mother,
this is not enough. The mother: Not enough? May—the child's given
name—May: Not enough. The mother: What do you mean, May, not
enough, what can you possibly mean, May, not enough? May: I mean,
Mother, that I must hear the feet, however faint they fall. The
mother: The motion alone is not enough? May: No, Mother, the
motion alone is not enough, I must hear the feet, however faint they
fall. [Pause. M resumes pacing. With pacing.] Does she still sleep, it may
be asked? Yes, some nights she does, in snatches, bows her poor head
against the wall and snatches a little sleep. [Pause.] Still speak? Yes,

some nights she does, when she fancies none can hear. [*Pause.*] Tells
how it was. [*Pause.*] Tries to tell how it was. [*Pause.*] It all. [*Pause.*] It all.
[*M continues pacing. Five seconds. Fade out on strip.*
All in darkness, steps cease.
Pause.
Chime a little fainter still. Pause for echoes.
Fade up to a little less still on strip. Rest in darkness.
M discovered facing front at R.
Pause.]

M   Sequel. [*Pause. Begins pacing. Steps a little slower still. After two lengths*
halts facing front at R. Pause.] Sequel. A little later, when she was quite
forgotten, she began to— [*Pause.*] A little later, when as though she
had never been, it never been, she began to walk. [*Pause.*] At
nightfall. [*Pause.*] Slip out at nightfall and into the little church by
the north door, always locked at that hour, and walk, up and down,
up and down, his poor arm. [*Pause.*] Some nights she would halt, as
one frozen by some shudder of the mind, and stand stark still till
she could move again. But many also were the nights when she
paced without pause, up and down, up and down, before vanishing
the way she came. [*Pause.*] No sound. [*Pause.*] None at least to be
heard. [*Pause.*] The semblance. [*Pause. Resumes pacing. After two*
lengths halts facing front at R. Pause.] The semblance. Faint, though by
no means invisible, in a certain light. [*Pause.*] Given the right light.
[*Pause.*] Grey rather than white, a pale shade of grey. [*Pause.*]
Tattered. [*Pause.*] A tangle of tatters. [*Pause.*] Watch it pass—[*pause*]—
watch her pass before the candelabrum, how its flames, their
light . . . like moon through passing rack. [*Pause.*] Soon then after
she was gone, as though never there, began to walk, up and down,
up and down, that poor arm. [*Pause.*] At nightfall. [*Pause.*] That is to
say, at certain seasons of the year, during Vespers. [*Pause.*]
Necessarily. [*Pause. Resumes pacing. After one length halts facing front at*
L. Pause.] Old Mrs. Winter, whom the reader will remember, old
Mrs. Winter, one late autumn Sunday evening, on sitting down to

supper with her daughter after worship, after a few half-hearted mouthfuls laid down her knife and fork and bowed her head. What is it, Mother, said the daughter, a most strange girl, though scarcely a girl any more . . . [*brokenly*] . . . dreadfully un— . . . [*Pause. Normal voice.*] What is it, Mother, are you not feeling yourself? [*Pause.*] Mrs. W. did not at once reply. But finally, raising her head and fixing Amy—the daughter's given name, as the reader will remember—raising her head and fixing Amy full in the eye she said—[*pause*]—she murmured, fixing Amy full in the eye she murmured, Amy did you observe anything . . . strange at Evensong? Amy: No, Mother, I did not. Mrs. W: Perhaps it was just my fancy. Amy: Just what exactly, Mother, did you perhaps fancy it was? [*Pause.*] Just what exactly, Mother, did you perhaps fancy this . . . strange thing was you observed? [*Pause.*] Mrs. W: You yourself observed nothing . . . strange? Amy: No, Mother, I myself did not, to put it mildly. Mrs. W: What do you mean, Amy, to put it mildly, what can you possibly mean, Amy, to put it mildly? Amy: I mean, Mother, that to say I observed nothing . . . strange is indeed to put it mildly. For I observed nothing of any kind, strange or otherwise. I saw nothing, heard nothing, of any kind. I was not there. Mrs. W: Not there? Amy: Not there. Mrs. W: But I heard you respond. [*Pause.*] I heard you say Amen. [*Pause.*] How could you have responded if you were not there? [*Pause.*] How could you possibly have said Amen if, as you claim, you were not there? [*Pause.*] The love of God, and the fellowship of the Holy Ghost, be with us all, now, and for evermore. Amen. [*Pause.*] I heard you distinctly. [*Pause. Resumes pacing. After three steps halts without facing front. Long pause. Resumes pacing, halts facing front at R. Long pause.*] Amy. [*Pause. No louder.*] Amy. [*Pause.*] Yes, Mother. [*Pause.*] Will you never have done? [*Pause.*] Will you never have done . . . revolving it all? [*Pause.*] It? [*Pause.*] It all. [*Pause.*] In your poor mind. [*Pause.*] It all. [*Pause.*] It all.
[*Pause. Fade out on strip. All in darkness.
Pause.*]

Chime even a little fainter still. Pause for echoes.
Fade up to even a little less still on strip.
No trace of May.
Hold ten seconds.
Fade out.]

                                                            Curtain

GHOST TRIO

A play for television

Female Voice (V)
Male Figure (F)

I   Pre-action
II Action
III Re-action

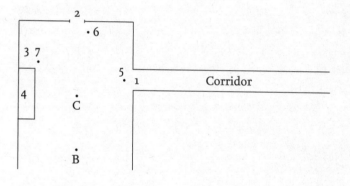

Room: 6 m × 5 m

1 Door.
2 Window.
3 Mirror.
4 Pallet.
5 F seated by door.
6 F at window.
7 F at head of pallet.
A Position general view.
B Position medium shot.
C Position near shot of 5 and 1, 6 and 2, 7 and 3.

I

1. *Fade up to general view from A. 10 seconds.*

2. v Good evening. Mine is a faint voice. Kindly tune accordingly. [*Pause.*] Good evening. Mine is a faint voice. Kindly tune accordingly. [*Pause.*] It will not be raised, nor lowered, whatever happens. [*Pause.*] Look. [*Long pause.*] The familiar chamber. [*Pause.*] At the far end a window. [*Pause.*] On the right the indispensable door. [*Pause.*] On the left, against the wall, some kind of pallet. [*Pause.*] The light: faint, omnipresent. No visible source. As if all luminous. Faintly luminous. No shadow. [*Pause.*] No shadow. Colour: none. All grey. Shades of grey. [*Pause.*] The colour grey if you wish, shades of the colour grey. [*Pause.*] Forgive my stating the obvious. [*Pause.*] Keep that sound down. [*Pause.*] Now look closer. [*Pause.*] Floor.

3. *Cut to close-up of floor. Smooth grey rectangle 0.70 m × 1.50 m. 5 seconds.*

4. v Dust. [*Pause.*] Having seen that specimen of floor you have seen it all. Wall.

5. *Cut to close-up of wall. Smooth grey rectangle 0.70 m × 1.50 m. 5 seconds.*

6. v Dust. [*Pause.*] Knowing this, the kind of wall—

7. *Close-up of wall continued. 5 seconds.*

8. v The kind of floor—

9. *Cut to close-up of floor. 5 seconds.*

10. v Look again.

11. *Cut to general view from A. 5 seconds.*

12. v Door.

13. *Cut to close-up of whole door. Smooth grey rectangle 0.70 m × 2 m. Imperceptibly ajar. No knob. Faint music. 5 seconds.*

14. v Window.

15. *Cut to close-up of whole window. Opaque sheet of glass 0.70 m × 1.50 m. Imperceptibly ajar. No knob. 5 seconds.*

16. v Pallet.

17. *Cut to close-up from above of whole pallet. 0.70 m × 2 m. Grey sheet. Grey rectangular pillow at window end. 5 seconds.*

18. v Knowing all this, the kind of pallet—

19.   *Close-up of whole pallet continued. 5 seconds.*

20. v The kind of window—

21.   *Cut to close-up of whole window. 5 seconds.*

22. v The kind of door—

23.   *Cut to close-up of whole door. Faint music. 5 seconds.*

24. v The kind of wall—

25.   *Cut to close-up of wall as before. 5 seconds.*

26. v The kind of floor.

27.   *Cut to close-up of floor as before. 5 seconds.*

28. v Look again.

29.   *Cut to general view. 5 seconds.*

30. v Sole sign of life a seated figure.

31.   *Move in slowly from A to B whence medium shot of F and door. F is
       seated on a stool, bowed forward, face hidden, clutching with both hands
       a small cassette not identifiable as such at this range. Faint music.
       5 seconds.*

32.   *Move in from B to C whence near shot of F and door. Cassette now
       identifiable. Music slightly louder, 5 seconds.*

33.   *Move in from C to close-up of head, hands, cassette. Clutching hands,
       head bowed, face hidden. Music slightly louder. 5 seconds.*

34.   *Move slowly back to A via C and B (no stops). Music progressively
       fainter till at level of B it ceases to be heard.*

35.   *General view from A. 5 seconds.*

II

All from A except 26–29

1. v   He will now think he hears her.
2.   *F raises head sharply, turns still crouched to door, fleeting face, tense pose. 5 seconds.*
3. v   No one.
4.   *F relapses into opening pose, bowed over cassette. 5 seconds.*
5. v   Again.
6.   *Same as 2.*
7. v   Now to door.
8.   *F gets up, lays cassette on stool, goes to door, listens with right ear against door, back to camera. 5 seconds.*
9. v   No one. [*Pause 5 seconds.*] Open.
10.   *With right hand F pushes door open halfway clockwise, looks out, back to camera. 2 seconds.*
11. v No one.
12.   *F removes hand from door which closes slowly of itself, stands irresolute, back to camera. 2 seconds.*
13. v Now to window.
14.   *F goes to window, stands irresolute, back to camera. 5 seconds.*
15. v Open.
16.   *With right hand F pushes window open halfway clockwise, looks out, back to camera. 5 seconds.*
17. v No one.
18.   *F removes hand from window which closes slowly of itself, stands irresolute, back to camera. 2 seconds.*
19. v Now to pallet.
20.   *F goes to head of pallet (window end), stands looking down at it. 5 seconds.*
21.   *F turns to wall at head of pallet, goes to wall, looks at his face in mirror hanging on wall, invisible from A.*
22. v [*surprised*] Ah!
23.   *After 5 seconds F bows his head, stands before mirror with bowed head. 2 seconds.*

24. v Now to door.

25.   *F goes to stool, takes up cassette, sits, settles into opening pose, bowed over cassette. 2 seconds.*

26.   *Same as I.31.*

27.   *Same as I.32.*

28.   *Same as I.33.*

29.   *Same as I.34.*

30.   *Same as I.35.*

31. v He will now again think he hears her.

32.   *Same as II.2.*

33.   *F gets up, lays cassette on stool, goes to door, opens it as before, looks out, stoops forward. 10 seconds.*

34.   *F straightens up, releases door which closes slowly of itself, stands irreso-lute, goes to stool, takes up cassette, sits irresolute, settles finally into opening pose, bowed over cassette. 5 seconds.*

35.   *Faint music audible for first time at A. It grows louder. 5 seconds.*

36. v Stop.

37.   *Music stops. General view from A. 5 seconds.*

38. v Repeat.

III

1. *Immediately after "Repeat" cut to near shot from C of F and door. Music audible. 5 seconds.*

2. *Move in to close-up of head, hands, cassette. Music slightly louder. 5 seconds.*

3. *Music stops. Action II.2. 5 seconds.*

4. *Action II.4. Music resumes. 5 seconds.*

5. *Move back to near shot from C of F and door. Music audible. 5 seconds.*

6. *Music stops. Action II.2. Near shot from C of F and door. 5 seconds.*

7. *Action II.8. Near shot from C of stool, cassette, F with right ear to door. 5 seconds.*

8. *Action II.10. Crescendo creak of door opening. Near shot from C of stool, cassette, F with right hand holding door open. 5 seconds.*

9. *Cut to view of corridor seen from door. Long narrow (0.70 m) grey rectangle between grey walls, empty, far end in darkness. 5 seconds.*

10. *Cut back to near shot from C of stool, cassette, F holding door open. 5 seconds.*

11. *Action II.12. Decrescendo creak of door slowly closing. Near shot from C of stool, cassette, F standing irresolute, door. 5 seconds.*

12. *Cut to close-up from above of cassette on stool, small grey rectangle on larger rectangle of seat. 5 seconds.*

13. *Cut back to near shot of stool, cassette, F standing irresolute, door. 5 seconds.*

14. *Action II.14 seen from C. Near shot from C of F and window. 5 seconds.*

15. *Action II.16 seen from C. Crescendo creak of window opening. Faint sound of rain. Near shot from C of F with right hand holding window open. 5 seconds.*

16. *Cut to view from window. Night. Rain falling in dim light. Sound of rain slightly louder. 5 seconds.*

17. *Cut back to near shot from C of F with right hand holding window open. Faint sound of rain. 5 seconds.*

18. *Action II.18 seen from C. Decrescendo creak of window slowly closing. Near shot from C of F and window. 5 seconds.*

19. *Action II.20 seen from C. Near shot from C of F, mirror, head of pallet.*

20. Cut to close-up from above of whole pallet.

21. Move down to tighter close-up of pallet moving slowly from pillow to foot and back to pillow. 5 seconds on pillow.

22. Move back to close-up from above of whole pallet. 5 seconds.

23. Cut back to near shot from C of F, mirror, head of pallet. 5 seconds.

24. Cut to close-up of mirror reflecting nothing. Small grey rectangle (same dimensions as cassette) against larger rectangle of wall. 5 seconds.

25. Cut back to near shot from C of F, mirror, head of pallet. 5 seconds.

26. Action II.21 seen from C. Near shot from C of F and mirror. 5 seconds.

27. Cut to close-up of F's face in mirror. 5 seconds. Eyes close. 5 seconds. Eyes open. 5 seconds. Head bows. Top of head in mirror. 5 seconds.

28. Cut back to near shot from C of F with bowed head, mirror, head of pallet. 5 seconds.

29. Action II.25 seen from C. Near shot from C of F settling into opening pose. Music audible once settled. 10 seconds.

30. Music stops. Action II.2 seen from C. Faint sound of steps approaching. They stop. Faint sound of knock on door. 5 seconds. Second knock, no louder. 5 seconds.

31. Action II.33 seen from C. Crescendo creak of door slowly opening. Near shot from C of stool, cassette, F holding door open, stooping forward. 10 seconds.

32. Cut to near shot of small boy full length in corridor before open door. Dressed in black oilskin with hood glistening with rain. White face raised to invisible F. 5 seconds. Boy shakes head faintly. Face still, raised. 5 seconds. Boy shakes head again. Face still, raised. 5 seconds. Boy turns and goes. Sound of receding steps. Register from the same position his slow recession till he vanishes in dark at end of corridor. 5 seconds on empty corridor.

33. Cut back to near shot from C of stool, cassette, F holding door open. 5 seconds.

34. Action II.34 seen from C. Decrescendo creak of door slowly closing. 5 seconds.

35. Cut to general view from A. 5 seconds.

36. Music audible at A. It grows. 10 seconds.

37.   *With growing music move in slowly to close-up of head bowed right down over cassette now held in arms and invisible. Hold till end of Largo.*

38.   *Silence. F raises head. Face seen clearly for second time. 10 seconds.*

39.   *Move slowly back to A.*

40.   *General view from A. 5 seconds.*

41.   *Fade out.*

MUSIC

From Largo of Beethoven's Fifth Piano Trio (*The Ghost*):

I.13	*beginning bar 47*
I.23	*beginning bar 49*
I.31–34	*beginning bar 19*
II.26–29	*beginning bar 64*
II.35–36	*beginning bar 71*
III.1–2, 4–5	*beginning bar 26*
III.29	*beginning bar 64*
III.36 to end	*beginning bar 82*

...but the clouds...

A play for television

M   Near shot from behind of man sitting on invisible stool bowed over invisible table. Light grey robe and skullcap. Dark ground. Same shot throughout.

M1   M in set. Hat and greatcoat dark, robe and skullcap light.

W   Close-up of woman's face reduced as far as possible to eyes and mouth. Same shot throughout.

S   Long shot of set empty or with M1. Same shot throughout.

V   M's voice.

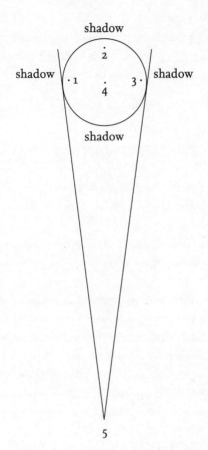

Set: circular, about 5 m diameter, surrounded by deep shadow.

Lighting: a gradual lightening from dark periphery to maximum light at centre.

    1. West, roads.

    2. North, sanctum.

    3. East, closet.

    4. Standing position.

    5. Camera.

1. *Dark. 5 seconds.*
2. *Fade up to M. 5 seconds.*
3. v When I thought of her it was always night. I came in—
4. *Dissolve to S empty. 5 seconds. M1 in hat and greatcoat emerges from west shadow, advances five steps and stands facing east shadow. 2 seconds.*
5. v No—
6. *Dissolve to M. 2 seconds.*
7. v No, that is not right. When she appeared it was always night. I came in—
8. *Dissolve to S empty. 5 seconds. M1 in hat and greatcoat emerges from west shadow, advances five steps and stands facing east shadow. 5 seconds.*
9. v Right. Came in, having walked the roads since break of day, brought night home, stood listening [5 seconds], finally went to closet—
10. *M1 advances five steps to disappear in east shadow. 2 seconds.*
11. v Shed my hat and greatcoat, assumed robe and skull, reappeared—
12. *M1 in robe and skullcap emerges from east shadow, advances five steps and stands facing west shadow. 5 seconds.*
13. v Reappeared and stood as before, only facing the other way, exhibiting the other outline [5 seconds], finally turned and vanished—
14. *M1 turns right and advances five steps to disappear in north shadow. 5 seconds.*
15. v Vanished within my little sanctum and crouched, where none could see me, in the dark.
16. *Dissolve to M. 5 seconds.*
17. v Let us now make sure we have got it right.
18. *Dissolve to S empty. 2 seconds. M1 in hat and greatcoat emerges from west shadow, advances five steps and stands facing east shadow. 2 seconds. He advances five steps to disappear in east shadow. 2 seconds. He emerges in robe and skullcap from east shadow, advances five steps and stands facing west shadow. 2 seconds. He turns right and advances five steps to disappear in north shadow. 2 seconds.*

19. v Right.

20.   *Dissolve to M. 2 seconds.*

21. v Then crouching there, in my little sanctum, in the dark, where none could see me, I began to beg, of her, to appear, to me. Such had long been my use and wont. No sound, a begging of the mind, to her, to appear, to me. Deep down into the dead of night, until I wearied, and ceased. Or of course until—

22.   *Dissolve to W. 2 seconds.*

23.   *Dissolve to M. 2 seconds.*

24. v For had she never once appeared, all that time, would I have, could I have, gone on begging, all that time? Not just vanished within my little sanctum and busied myself with something else, or with nothing, busied myself with nothing? Until the time came, with break of day, to issue forth again, shed robe and skull, resume my hat and greatcoat, and issue forth again, to walk the roads.

25.   *Dissolve to S empty. 2 seconds. M1 in robe and skullcap emerges from north shadow, advances five steps and stands facing camera. 2 seconds. He turns left and advances five steps to disappear in east shadow. 2 seconds. He emerges in hat and greatcoat from east shadow, advances five steps and stands facing west shadow. 2 seconds. He advances five steps to disappear in west shadow. 2 seconds.*

26. v Right.

27.   *Dissolve to M. 5 seconds.*

28. v Let us now distinguish three cases. One: she appeared and—

29.   *Dissolve to W. 2 seconds.*

30.   *Dissolve to M. 2 seconds.*

31. v In the same breath was gone. *2 seconds.* Two: she appeared and—

32.   *Dissolve to W. 5 seconds.*

33. v Lingered. *5 seconds.* With those unseeing eyes I so begged when alive to look at me. *5 seconds.*

34.   *Dissolve to M. 2 seconds.*

35. v Three: she appeared and—

36.   *Dissolve to W. 5 seconds.*

37. v After a moment—

38.   *W's lips move, uttering inaudibly:* "... clouds ... but the clouds ...
       of the sky ...," *V murmuring, synchronous with lips:* "... but the
       clouds ..." *Lips cease. 5 seconds.*

39. v Right.

40.   *Dissolve to M. 5 seconds.*

41. v Let us now run through it again.

42.   *Dissolve to S empty. 2 seconds. M1 in hat and greatcoat emerges from
       west shadow, advances five steps and stands facing east shadow.
       2 seconds. He advances five steps to disappear in east shadow. 2 seconds.
       He emerges in robe and skullcap from east shadow, advances five steps
       and stands facing west shadow. 2 seconds. He turns right and advances
       five steps to disappear in north shadow. 2 seconds.*

43.   *Dissolve to M. 5 seconds.*

44.   *Dissolve to W. 2 seconds.*

45.   *Dissolve to M. 2 seconds.*

46.   *Dissolve to W. 5 seconds.*

47. v Look at me. *5 seconds.*

48.   *Dissolve to M. 5 seconds.*

49.   *Dissolve to W. 2 seconds. W's lips move, uttering inaudibly:* "... clouds
       ... but the clouds ... of the sky ...," *V murmuring, synchronous with
       lips:* "... but the clouds ..." *Lips cease. 5 seconds.*

50. v Speak to me. *5 seconds.*

51.   *Dissolve to M. 5 seconds.*

52. v Right. There was of course a fourth case, or case nought, as I
       pleased to call it, by far the commonest, in the proportion say
       of nine hundred and ninety-nine to one, or nine hundred and
       ninety-eight to two, when I begged in vain, deep down into the
       dead of night, until I wearied, and ceased, and busied myself
       with something else, more ... rewarding, such as ... such as ...
       cube roots, for example, or with nothing, busied myself with
       nothing, that MINE, until the time came, with break of day, to
       issue forth again, void my little sanctum, shed robe and skull,
       resume my hat and greatcoat, and issue forth again, to walk the

roads. [*Pause.*] The back roads.

53. *Dissolve to S empty. 2 seconds. M1 in robe and skullcap emerges from
     north shadow, advances five steps and stands facing camera. 2 seconds.
     He turns left and advances five steps to disappear in east shadow.
     2 seconds. He emerges in hat and greatcoat from east shadow, advances
     five steps and stands facing west shadow. 2 seconds. He advances five
     steps to disappear in west shadow. 2 seconds.*

54. v Right.

55. *Dissolve to M. 5 seconds.*

56. *Dissolve to W. 5 seconds.*

57. v " . . . but the clouds of the sky . . . when the horizon fades . . . or a
     bird's sleepy cry . . . among the deepening shades . . ." *5 seconds.*

58. *Dissolve to M. 5 seconds.*

59. *Fade out on M.*

60. *Dark. 5 seconds.*

A PIECE OF MONOLOGUE

Curtain.

Faint diffuse light.

Speaker stands well off centre downstage audience left.

White hair, white nightgown, white socks.

Two metres to his left, same level, same height, standard lamp, skull-sized white globe, faintly lit.

Just visible extreme right, same level, white foot of pallet bed.

Ten seconds before speech begins.

Thirty seconds before end of speech lamplight begins to fail.

Lamp out. Silence. Speaker, globe, foot of pallet, barely visible in diffuse light.

Ten seconds.

Curtain.

SPEAKER Birth was the death of him. Again. Words are few. Dying too. Birth was the death of him. Ghastly grinning ever since. Up at the lid to come. In cradle and crib. At suck first fiasco. With the first totters. From mammy to nanny and back. All the way. Bandied back and forth. So ghastly grinning on. From funeral to funeral. To now. This night. Two and a half billion seconds. Again. Two and a half billion seconds. Hard to believe so few. From funeral to funeral. Funerals of ... he all but said of loved ones. Thirty thousand nights. Hard to believe so few. Born dead of night. Sun long sunk behind the larches. New needles turning green. In the room dark gaining. Till faint light from standard lamp. Wick turned low. And now. This night. Up at nightfall. Every nightfall. Faint light in room. Whence unknown. None from window. No. Next to none. No such thing as none. Gropes to window and stares out. Stands there staring out. Stock still staring out. Nothing stirring in that black vast. Gropes back in the end to where the lamp is standing. Was standing. When last went out. Loose matches in right-hand pocket. Strikes one on his buttock the way his father taught him. Takes off milk white globe and sets it down. Match goes out. Strikes a second as before. Takes off chimney. Smoke-clouded. Holds it in left hand. Match goes out. Strikes a third as before and sets it to wick. Puts back chimney. Match goes out. Puts back globe. Turns wick low. Backs away to edge of light and turns to face east. Blank wall. So nightly. Up. Socks. Nightgown. Window. Lamp. Backs away to edge of light and stands facing blank wall. Covered with pictures once. Pictures of . . . he all but said of loved ones. Unframed. Unglazed. Pinned to wall with drawing-pins. All shapes and sizes. Down one after another. Gone. Torn to shreds and scattered. Strewn all over the floor. Not at one sweep. No sudden fit of . . . no word. Ripped from the wall and torn to shreds one by one. Over the years. Years of nights. Nothing on the wall now but the pins. Not all. Some out with the wrench. Some still pinning a shred. So stands there facing blank wall. Dying on. No more no less. No. Less. Less to die. Ever less. Like light at nightfall. Stands there facing east. Blank pinpocked surface once white in shadow. Could once name them all. There was father. That grey void. There mother. That other. There together. Smiling. Wedding day. There all three. That grey blot. There alone. He alone. So on. Not now. Forgotten. All gone so long. Gone. Ripped off and torn to shreds. Scattered all over the floor.

Swept out of the way under the bed and left. Thousand
shreds under the bed with the dust and spiders. All the . . . he
all but said the loved ones. Stands there facing the wall
staring beyond. Nothing there either. Nothing stirring there
either. Nothing stirring anywhere. Nothing to be seen
anywhere. Nothing to be heard anywhere. Room once full of
sounds. Faint sounds. Whence unknown. Fewer and fainter
as time wore on. Nights wore on. None now. No. No such
thing as none. Rain some nights still slant against the panes.
Or dropping gentle on the place beneath. Even now. Lamp
smoking though wick turned low. Strange. Faint smoke
issuing through vent in globe. Low ceiling stained by night
after night of this. Dark shapeless blot on surface elsewhere
white. Once white. Stands facing wall after the various
motions described. That is up at nightfall and into gown and
socks. No. In them already. In them all night. All day. All day
and night. Up at nightfall in gown and socks and after a
moment to get his bearings gropes to window. Faint light in
room. Unutterably faint. Whence unknown. Stands stock still
staring out. Into black vast. Nothing there. Nothing stirring.
That he can see. Hear. Dwells thus as if unable to move
again. Or no will left to move again. Not enough will left to
move again. Turns in the end and gropes to where he knows
the lamp is standing. Thinks he knows. Was last standing.
When last went out. Match one as described for globe. Two
for chimney. Three for wick. Chimney and globe back on.
Turns wick low. Backs away to edge of light and turns to face
wall. East. Still as the lamp by his side. Gown and socks white
to take faint light. Once white. Hair white to take faint light.
Foot of pallet just visible edge of frame. Once white to take
faint light. Stands there staring beyond. Nothing. Empty
dark. Till first word always the same. Night after night the
same. Birth. Then slow fade up of a faint form. Out of the
dark. A window. Looking west. Sun long sunk behind the

larches. Light dying. Soon none left to die. No. No such thing
as no light. Starless moonless heaven. Dies on to dawn and
never dies. There in the dark that window. Night slowly
falling. Eyes to the small pane gaze at that first night. Turn
from it in the end to face the darkened room. There in the
end slowly a faint hand. Holding aloft a lighted spill. In the
light of spill faintly the hand and milkwhite globe. Then
second hand. In light of spill. Takes off globe and disappears.
Reappears empty. Takes off chimney. Two hands and
chimney in light of spill. Spill to wick. Chimney back on.
Hand with spill disappears. Second hand disappears.
Chimney alone in gloom. Hand reappears with globe. Globe
back on. Turns wick low. Disappears. Pale globe alone in
gloom. Glimmer of brass bedrail. Fade. Birth the death of
him. That nevoid smile. Thirty thousand nights. Stands at
edge of lamplight staring beyond. Into dark whole again.
Window gone. Hands gone. Light gone. Gone. Again and
again. Again and again gone. Till dark slowly parts again.
Grey light. Rain pelting. Umbrellas round a grave. Seen from
above. Streaming black canopies. Black ditch beneath. Rain
bubbling in the black mud. Empty for the moment. That
place beneath. Which . . . he all but said which loved one?
Thirty seconds. To add to the two and a half billion odd.
Then fade. Dark whole again. Blest dark. No. No such thing
as whole. Stands staring beyond half hearing what he's
saying. He? The words falling from his mouth. Making do
with his mouth. Lights lamp as described. Backs away to edge
of light and turns to face wall. Stares beyond into dark. Waits
for first word always the same. It gathers in his mouth. Parts
lips and thrusts tongue forward. Birth. Parts the dark. Slowly
the window. That first night. The room. The spill. The hands.
The lamp. The gleam of brass. Fade. Gone. Again and again.
Again and again gone. Mouth agape. A cry. Stifled by nasal.
Dark parts. Grey light. Rain pelting. Streaming umbrellas.

Ditch. Bubbling black mud. Coffin out of frame. Whose? Fade. Gone. Move on to other matters. Try to move on. To other matters. How far from wall? Head almost touching. As at window. Eyes glued to pane staring out. Nothing stirring. Black vast. Stands there stock still staring out as if unable to move again. Or gone the will to move again. Gone. Faint cry in his ear. Mouth agape. Closed with hiss of breath. Lips joined. Feel soft touch of lip on lip. Lip lipping lip. Then parted by cry as before. Where is he now? Back at window staring out. Eyes glued to pane. As if looking his last. Turns away at last and gropes through faint unaccountable light to unseen lamp. White gown moving through that gloom. Once white. Lights and moves to face wall as described. Head almost touching. Stands there staring beyond waiting for first word. It gathers in his mouth. Birth. Parts lips and thrusts tongue between them. Tip of tongue. Feel soft touch of tongue on lips. Of lips on tongue. Fade up in outer dark of window. Stare beyond through rift in dark to other dark. Further dark. Sun long sunk behind the larches. Nothing stirring. Nothing faintly stirring. Stock still eyes glued to pane. As if looking his last. At that first night. Of thirty thousand odd. Turn away in the end to darkened room. Where soon to be. This night to be. Spill. Hands. Lamp. Gleam of brass. Pale globe alone in gloom. Brass bedrail catching light. Thirty seconds. To swell the two and a half billion odd. Fade. Gone. Cry. Snuffed with breath of nostrils. Again and again. Again and again gone. Till whose grave? Which . . . he all but said which loved one's? He? Black ditch in pelting rain. Way out through the grey rift in dark. Seen from on high. Streaming canopies. Bubbling black mud. Coffin on its way. Loved one . . . he all but said loved one on his way. Her way. Thirty seconds. Fade. Gone. Stands there staring beyond. Into dark whole again. No. No such thing as whole. Head almost touching wall. White hair catching light.

White gown. White socks. White foot of pallet edge of frame
stage left. Once white. Least . . . give and head rests on wall.
But no. Stock still head haught staring beyond. Nothing
stirring. Faintly stirring. Thirty thousand nights of ghosts
beyond. Beyond that black beyond. Ghost light. Ghost nights.
Ghost rooms. Ghost graves. Ghost . . . he all but said ghost
loved ones. Waiting on the rip word. Stands there staring
beyond at that black veil lips quivering to half-heard words.
Treating of other matters. Trying to treat of other matters.
Till half hears there are no other matters. Never were other
matters. Never two matters. Never but the one matter. The
dead and gone. The dying and the going. From the word go.
The word begone. Such as the light going now. Beginning to
go. In the room. Where else? Unnoticed by him staring
beyond. The globe alone. Not the other. The unaccountable.
From nowhere. On all sides nowhere. Unutterably faint. The
globe alone. Alone gone.

ROCKABY

NOTES
Light

Subdued on chair. Rest of stage dark.

Subdued spot on face constant throughout, unaffected by successive fades. Either wide enough to include narrow limits of rock or concentrated on face when still or at mid-rock. Then throughout speech face slightly swaying in and out of light. Opening fade-up: first spot on face alone, long pause, then light on chair.

Final fade-out: first chair, long pause with spot on face alone, head slowly sinks, come to rest, fade out spot.

W

Prematurely old. Unkempt grey hair. Huge eyes in white expressionless face. White hands holding ends of armrests.

Eyes

Now closed, now open in unblinking gaze. About equal proportions section 1, increasingly closed 2 and 3, closed for good halfway through 4.

Costume

Black lacy high-necked evening gown. Long sleeves. Jet sequins to glitter when rocking. Incongruous flimsy head-dress set askew with extravagant trimming to catch light when rocking.

Attitude

Completely still till fade-out of chair. Then in light of spot head slowly inclined.

Chair

Pale wood highly polished to gleam when rocking. Footrest. Vertical back. Rounded inward curving arms to suggest embrace.

Rock

Slight. Slow. Controlled mechanically without assistance from W.

Voice

Towards end of 4, say from "saying to herself" on, gradually softer. Lines in italics spoken by W with V. A little softer each time. W's "more" a little softer each time.

W: *Woman in chair.*

V: *Her recorded voice.*

Fade up on W in rocking-chair facing front downstage slightly off centre audience left.

Long pause.

w   More.

[*Pause. Rock and voice together.*]

v   till in the end
     the day came
     in the end came
     close of a long day
     when she said
     to herself
     whom else
     time she stopped
     time she stopped
     going to and fro
     all eyes

all sides
high and low
for another
another like herself
another creature like herself
a little like
going to and fro
all eyes
all sides
high and low
for another
till in the end
close of a long day
to herself
whom else
time she stopped
time she stopped
going to and fro
all eyes
all sides
high and low
for another
another living soul
going to and fro
all eyes like herself
all sides
high and low
for another
another like herself
a little like
going to and fro
till in the end
close of a long day
to herself

whom else
time she stopped
going to and fro
time she stopped
time she stopped
[*Together: echo of "time she stopped," coming to rest of rock, faint fade of light.*
Long pause.]

w   More.
[*Pause. Rock and voice together.*]

v   so in the end
close of a long day
went back in
in the end went back in
saying to herself
whom else
time she stopped
time she stopped
going to and fro
time she went and sat
at her window
quiet at her window
facing other windows
so in the end
close of a long day
in the end went and sat
went back in and sat
at her window
let up the blind and sat
quiet at her window
only window
facing other windows
other only windows
all eyes
all sides

high and low
for another
at her window
another like herself
a little like
another living soul
one other living soul
at her window
gone in like herself
gone back in
in the end
close of a long day
saying to herself
whom else
time she stopped
time she stopped
going to and fro
time she went and sat
at her window
quiet at her window
only window
facing other windows
other only windows
all eyes
all sides
high and low
for another
another like herself
a little like
another living soul
one other living soul
[*Together: echo of "living soul," coming to rest of rock, faint fade of light.*
Long pause.]

w   More.

[*Pause. Rock and voice together.*]

v till in the end
the day came
in the end came
close of a long day
sitting at her window
quiet at her window
only window
facing other windows
other only windows
all blinds down
never one up
hers alone up
till the day came
in the end came
close of a long day
sitting at her window
quiet at her window
all eyes
all sides
high and low
for a blind up
one blind up
no more
never mind a face
behind the pane
famished eyes
like hers
to see
be seen
no
a blind up
like hers
a little like

one blind up no more
another creature there
somewhere there
behind the pane
another living soul
one other living soul
till the day came
in the end came
close of a long day
when she said
to herself
whom else
time she stopped
time she stopped
sitting at her window
quiet at her window
only window
facing other windows
other only windows
all eyes
all sides
high and low
time she stopped
time she stopped
[*Together: echo of "time she stopped," coming to rest of rock, faint fade of
light.*
Long pause.]

W More.

[*Pause. Rock and voice together.*]

V so in the end
close of a long day
went down
in the end went down
down the steep stair

let down the blind and down
right down
into the old rocker
mother rocker
where mother rocked
all the years
all in black
best black
sat and rocked
rocked
till her end came
in the end came
off her head they said
gone off her head
but harmless
no harm in her
dead one day
no
night
dead one night
in the rocker
in her best black
head fallen
and the rocker rocking
rocking away
so in the end
close of a long day
went down
in the end went down
down the steep stair
let down the blind and down
right down
into the old rocker
those arms at last

and rocked
rocked
with closed eyes
closing eyes
she so long all eyes
famished eyes
all sides
high and low
to and fro
at her window
to see
be seen
till in the end
close of a long day
to herself
whom else
time she stopped
let down the blind and stopped
time she went down
down the steep stair
time she went right down
was her own other
own other living soul
so in the end
close of a long day
went down
let down the blind and down
right down
into the old rocker
and rocked
rocked
saying to herself
no
done with that

the rocker
those arms at last
saying to the rocker
rock her off
stop her eyes
fuck life
stop her eyes
rock her off
rock her off

[*Together: echo of "rock her off," coming to rest of rock, slow fade out.*]

OHIO IMPROMPTU

L = Listener.
R = Reader.
As alike in appearance as possible.
Light on table midstage. Rest of stage in darkness.
Plain white deal table say 8' × 4'.
Two plain armless white deal chairs.
L seated at table facing front towards end of long side audience right. Bowed
head propped on right hand. Face hidden. Left hand on table. Long black coat.
Long white hair.
R seated at table in profile centre of short side audience right. Bowed head
propped on right hand. Left hand on table. Book on table before him open at last
pages. Long black coat. Long white hair.
Black wide-brimmed hat at centre of table.
Fade up.
Ten seconds.
R turns page.
Pause.

R [reading] Little is left to tell. In a last—
    [*L knocks with left hand on table.*]
    Little is left to tell.
    [*Pause. Knock.*]

In a last attempt to obtain relief he moved from where they had been so long together to a single room on the far bank. From its single window he could see the downstream extremity of the Isle of Swans.

[*Pause.*]

Relief he had hoped would flow from unfamiliarity.

Unfamiliar room. Unfamiliar scene. Out to where nothing ever shared. Back to where nothing ever shared. From this he had once half hoped some measure of relief might flow.

[*Pause.*]

Day after day he could be seen slowly pacing the islet. Hour after hour. In his long black coat no matter what the weather and old world Latin Quarter hat. At the tip he would always pause to dwell on the receding stream. How in joyous eddies its two arms conflowed and flowed united on. Then turn and his slow steps retrace.

[*Pause.*]

In his dreams—

[*Knock.*]

Then turn and his slow steps retrace.

[*Pause. Knock.*]

In his dreams he had been warned against this change. Seen the dear face and heard the unspoken words, Stay where we were so long alone together, my shade will comfort you.

[*Pause.*]

Could he not—

[*Knock.*]

Seen the dear face and heard the unspoken words, Stay where we were so long alone together, my shade will comfort you.

[*Pause. Knock.*]

Could he not now turn back? Acknowledge his error and return to where they were once so long alone together. Alone together so much shared. No. What he had done alone could not be undone. Nothing he had ever done alone could ever be undone. By him alone.

[*Pause.*]

In this extremity his old terror of night laid hold on him again. After so long a lapse that as if never been. [*Pause. Looks closer.*] Yes, after so long a lapse that as if never been. Now with redoubled force the fearful symptoms described at length page forty paragraph four. [*Starts to turn back the pages. Checked by L's left hand. Resumes relinquished page.*] White nights now again his portion. As when his heart was young. No sleep no braving sleep till—[*turns page*]—dawn of day. [*Pause.*]

Little is left to tell. One night—

[*Knock.*]

Little is left to tell.

[*Pause. Knock.*]

One night as he sat trembling head in hands from head to foot a man appeared to him and said, I have been sent by—and here he named the dear name—to comfort you. Then drawing a worn volume from the pocket of his long black coat he sat and read till dawn. Then disappeared without a word.

[*Pause.*]

Some time later he appeared again at the same hour with the same volume and this time without preamble sat and read it through again the long night through. Then disappeared without a word.

[*Pause.*]

So from time to time unheralded he would appear to read the sad tale through again and the long night away. Then disappear without a word.

[*Pause.*]

With never a word exchanged they grew to be as one.

[*Pause.*]

Till the night came at last when having closed the book and dawn at hand he did not disappear but sat on without a word.

[*Pause.*]

Finally he said, I have had word from—and here he named the dear name—that I shall not come again. I saw the dear face and heard the unspoken words, No need to go to him again, even were it in your power.

[*Pause.*]

So the sad—

[*Knock.*]

Saw the dear face and heard the unspoken words, No need to go to him again, even were it in your power.

[*Pause. Knock.*]

So the sad tale a last time told they sat on as though turned to stone. Through the single window dawn shed no light. From the street no sound of reawakening. Or was it that buried in who knows what thoughts they paid no heed? To light of day. To sound of reawakening. What thoughts who knows. Thoughts, no, not thoughts. Profounds of mind. Buried in who knows what profounds of mind. Of mindlessness. Whither no light can reach. No sound. So sat on as though turned to stone. The sad tale a last time told.

[*Pause.*]

Nothing is left to tell.

[*Pause. R makes to close book.*

Knock. Book half closed.]

Nothing is left to tell.

[*Pause. R closes book.*

Knock.

Silence. Five seconds.

Simultaneously they lower their right hands to table, raise their heads and look at each other. Unblinking. Expressionless:

Ten seconds.

Fade out.]

QUAD

A piece for four players, light and percussion.

The players (1, 2, 3, 4) pace the given area, each following his particular course.

Area: square. Length of side: 6 paces.

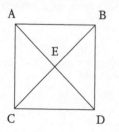

Course 1: AC, CB, BA, AD, DB, BC, CD, DA
Course 2: BA, AD, DB, BC, CD, DA, AC, CB
Course 3: CD, DA, AC, CB, BA, AD, DB, BC
Course 4: DB, BC, CD, DA, AC, CB, BA, AD

1 enters at A, completes his course and is joined by 3. Together they complete their courses and are joined by 4. Together all three complete their courses and are joined by 2. Together all four complete their courses. Exit 1. 2, 3 and 4 continue and complete their courses. Exit 3. 2 and 4 continue and complete their courses. Exit 4. End of 1st series. 2 continues,

opening 2nd series, completes his course and is joined by 1. Etc. Unbroken movement.

1st series (as above): 1, 13, 134, 1342, 342, 42

2nd series: 2, 21, 214, 2143, 143, 43

3rd series: 3, 32, 321, 3214, 214, 14

4th series: 4, 43, 432, 4321, 321, 21

Four possible solos all given.

Six possible duos all given (two twice).

Four possible trios all given twice.

Without interruption begin repeat and fade out on 1 pacing alone.

Light (2)

Dim on area from above fading out into dark.

Four sources of differently coloured light clustered together.

Each player has his particular light, to be turned on when he enters, kept on while he paces, turned off when he exits.

Say 1 white, 2 yellow, 3 blue, 4 red. Then

1st series: white, white + blue, white + blue + red, white + blue + red + yellow, blue + red + yellow, red + yellow.

2nd series: yellow, yellow + white, yellow + white + red etc.

All possible light combinations given.

Percussion

Four types of percussion, say drum, gong, triangle, wood block.

Each player has his particular percussion, to sound when he enters, continue while he paces, cease when he exits.

Say 1 drum, 2 gong, 3 triangle, 4 wood block. Then

1st series: drum, drum + triangle, drum + triangle + wood block etc. Same system as for light.

All possible percussion combinations given.

Percussion intermittent in all combinations to allow footsteps alone to be heard at intervals.

Pianissimo throughout.

Percussionists barely visible in shadow on raised podium at back of set.

Footsteps

Each player has his particular sound.

Costumes

Gowns reaching to ground, cowls hiding faces.

Each player has his particular colour corresponding to his light. 1 white, 2 yellow, 3 blue, 4 red.

All possible costume combinations given.

Players

As alike in build as possible. Short and slight for preference.

Some ballet training desirable. Adolescents a possibility. Sex indifferent.

Camera

Raised frontal. Fixed. Both players and percussionists in frame.

Time (3)

On basis of one pace per second and allowing for time lost at angles and centre approximately 25 minutes.

Problem (4)

Negotiation of E without rupture of rhythm when three or four players cross paths at this point. Or, if ruptures accepted, how best exploit?

1. This original scenario (*Quad I*) was followed in the Stuttgart production by a variation (*Quad II*). (5)

2. Abandoned as impracticable. Constant neutral light throughout.

3. Overestimated. *Quad I*, fast tempo. 15' approx. *Quad II*, slow tempo, series 1 only, 5' approx.

4. E supposed a danger zone. Hence deviation. Manoeuvre established at outset by first solo at first diagonal (CB). E.g. series 1:

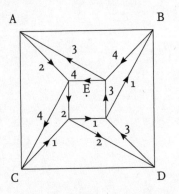

5. No colour, all four in identical white gowns, no percussion, footsteps only sound, slow tempo, series 1 only.

CATASTROPHE

For Václav Havel

Director (D).
His *female assistant* (A).
Protagonist (P).
Luke, in charge of the lighting, offstage (L).

Rehearsal. Final touches to the last scene. Bare stage. A and L have just set the lighting. D has just arrived.

D in an armchair downstairs audience left. Fur coat. Fur toque to match. Age and physique unimportant.

A standing beside him. White overall. Bare head. Pencil on ear. Age and physique unimportant.

P midstage standing on a black block 18 inches high. Black wide-brimmed hat. Black dressing-gown to ankles. Barefoot. Head bowed. Hands in pockets. Age and physique unimportant.

D and A contemplate P. Long pause.

A   [*finally*] Like the look of him?

D   So so. [*Pause.*] Why the plinth?

A   To let the stalls see the feet.
    [*Pause.*]

D   Why the hat?

A   To help hide the face.
    [*Pause.*]

D   Why the gown?

A   To have him all black.
    [*Pause.*]

D   What has he on underneath? [*A moves towards P.*] Say it.

[*A halts.*]

A   His night attire.

D   Colour?

A   Ash.

[*D takes out a cigar.*]

D   Light. [*A returns, lights the cigar, stands still. D smokes.*] How's the skull?

A   You've seen it.

D   I forget. [*A moves towards P.*] Say it.

[*A halts.*]

A   Moulting. A few tufts.

D   Colour?

A   Ash.

[*Pause.*]

D   Why hands in pockets?

A   To help have him all black.

D   They mustn't.

A   I make a note. [*She takes out a pad, takes pencil, notes.*] Hands exposed.

[*She puts back pad and pencil.*]

D   How are they? [*A at a loss. Irritably.*] The hands, how are the hands?

A   You've seen them.

D   I forget.

A   Crippled. Fibrous degeneration.

D   Clawlike?

A   If you like.

D   Two claws?

A   Unless he clench his fists.

D   He mustn't.

A   I make a note. [*She takes out pad, takes pencil, notes.*] Hands limp.

[*She puts back pad and pencil.*]

D   Light. [*A returns, relights the cigar, stands still. D smokes.*] Good. Now let's have a look. [*A at a loss. Irritably.*] Get going. Lose that gown. [*He consults his chronometer.*] Step on it, I have a caucus.

[*A goes to P, takes off the gown. P submits, inert. A steps back, the gown over her arm. P in old grey pyjamas, head bowed, fists clenched. Pause.*]

A   Like him better without? [*Pause.*] He's shivering.

D   Not all that. Hat.

[*A advances, takes off hat, steps back, hat in hand. Pause.*]

A   Like that cranium?

D   Needs whitening.

A   I make a note. [*She takes out pad, takes pencil, notes.*] Whiten cranium. [*She puts back pad and pencil.*]

D   The hands. [*A at a loss. Irritably.*] The fists. Get going. [*A advances, unclenches fists, steps back.*] And whiten.

A   I make a note. [*She takes out pad, takes pencil, notes.*] Whiten hands. [*She puts back pad and pencil. They contemplate P.*]

D   [*finally*] Something wrong. [*Distraught.*] What is it?

A   [*timidly*] What if we were . . . were to . . . join them?

D   No harm trying. [*A advances, joins the hands, steps back.*] Higher. [*A advances, raises waist-high the joined hands, steps back.*] A touch more. [*A advances, raises breast-high the joined hands.*] Stop! [*A steps back.*] Better. It's coming. Light.

[*A returns, relights cigar, stands still. D smokes.*]

A   He's shivering.

D   Bless his heart.

[*Pause.*]

A   [*timidly*] What about a little . . . a little . . . gag?

D   For God's sake! This craze for explicitation! Every i dotted to death! Little gag! For God's sake!

A   Sure he won't utter?

D   Not a squeak. [*He consults his chronometer.*] Just time. I'll go and see how it looks from the house.

[*Exit D, not to appear again. A subsides in the armchair, springs to her feet no sooner seated, takes out a rag, wipes vigorously back and seat of chair, discards rag, sits again. Pause.*]

D   [*off, plaintive*] I can't see the toes. [*Irritably.*] I'm sitting in the front row of the stalls and can't see the toes.

A   [*rising*] I make a note. [*She takes out a pad, takes pencil, notes.*] Raise pedestal.

D   There's a trace of face.

A   I make a note.
    [*She takes out pad, takes pencil, makes to note.*]

D   Down the head. [*A at a loss. Irritably.*] Get going. Down his head. [*A puts back pad and pencil, goes to P, bows his head further, steps back.*] A shade more. [*A advances, bows the head further.*] Stop! [*A steps back.*] Fine. It's coming. [*Pause.*] Could do with more nudity.

A   I make a note.
    [*She takes out pad, makes to take her pencil.*]

D   Get going! Get going! [*A puts back the pad, goes to P, stands irresolute.*] Bare the neck. [*A undoes top buttons, parts the flaps, steps back.*] The legs. The shins. [*A advances, rolls up to below knee one trouser-leg, steps back.*] The other. [*Same for other leg, steps back.*] Higher. The knees. [*A advances, rolls up to above knees both trouser-legs, steps back.*] And whiten.

A   I make a note. [*She takes out pad, takes pencil, notes.*] Whiten all flesh.

D   It's coming. Is Luke around?

A   [*calling*] Luke! [*Pause. Louder.*] Luke!

L   [*off, distant*] I hear you. [*Pause. Nearer.*] What's the trouble now?

A   Luke's around.

D   Blackout stage.

L   What?
    [*A transmits in technical terms. Fade-out of general light. Light on P alone. A in shadow.*]

D   Just the head.

L   What?
    [*A transmits in technical terms. Fade-out of light on P's body. Light on head alone. Long pause.*]

D   Lovely.
    [*Pause.*]

A   [*timidly*] What if he were to . . . were to . . . raise his head . . . an instant . . . show his face . . . just an instant.

D   For God's sake! What next? Raise his head? Where do you think we are? In Patagonia? Raise his head? For God's sake! [*Pause.*] Good. There's our catastrophe. In the bag. Once more and I'm off.

A   [*to L*] Once more and he's off.

    [*Fade-up of light on P's body. Pause. Fade-up of general light.*]

D   Stop! [*Pause.*] Now . . . let 'em have it. [*Fade-out of general light. Pause.
    Fade-out of light on body. Light on head alone. Long pause.*] Terrific! He'll
    have them on their feet. I can hear it from here.

    [*Pause. Distant storm of applause. P raises his head, fixes the audience. The
    applause falters, dies.*

    Long pause.

    Fade-out of light on face.]

NACHT UND TRÄUME

Elements.
Evening light.
Dreamer (A).
His dreamt self (B).
Dreamt hands R (right) and L (left).
Last 7 bars of Schubert's lied "Nacht und Träume."

1. Fade up on a dark empty room lit only by evening light from a window set high in back wall.

   Left foreground, faintly lit, a man seated at a table. Right profile, head bowed, grey hair, hands resting on table.

   Clearly visible only head and hands and section of table on which they rest.

2. Softly hummed, male voice, last 7 bars of Schubert's lied "Nacht und Träume."

3. Fade out evening light.

4. Softly sung, with words, last 3 bars of lied, beginning "Holde Träume . . ."

5. Fade down A as he bows his head further to rest on hands. Thus minimally lit he remains just visible throughout dream as first viewed.

6. A dreams. Fade up on B on an invisible podium about 4 feet above floor level, middle ground, well right of centre. He is seated at a table in the same posture as A dreaming, bowed head resting on hands, but left profile, faintly lit by kinder light than A's.

7. From dark beyond and above B's head L appears and rests gently on it.

8. B raises his head, L withdraws and disappears.

9. From same dark R appears with a cup, conveys it gently to B's lips. B drinks, R disappears.

10. R reappears with a cloth, wipes gently B's brow, disappears with cloth.

11. B raises his head further to gaze up at invisible face.

12. B raises his right hand, still gazing up, and holds it raised palm upward.

13. R reappears and rests gently on B's right hand, B still gazing up.

14. B transfers gaze to joined hands.

15. B raises his left hand and rests it on joined hands.

16. Together hands sink to table and on them B's head.

17. L reappears and rests gently on B's head.

18. Fade out dream.

19. Fade up A and evening light.

20. A raises head to its opening position.

21. Lied as before (2).

22. Fade out evening light.

23. Close of lied as before (4).

24. Fade down A as before (5).

25. A dreams. Fade up on B as before (6).

26. Move in slowly to close-up of B, losing A.

27. Dream as before (7–16) in close-up and slower motion.

28. Withdraw slowly to opening viewpoint, recovering A.

29. Fade out dream.

30. Fade out A.

WHAT WHERE

Bam
Bem
Bim
Bom
Voice of Bam (V)

NOTE

Players as alike as possible.

Same long grey gown.

Same long grey hair.

V *in the shape of a small megaphone at head level.*

Playing area (P) rectangle 3 m × 2 m, dimly lit, surrounded by shadow, stage right as seen from house. Downstage left, dimly lit, surrounded by shadow, V.

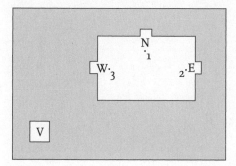

General dark.
Light on V.
Pause.

   v We are the last five.
      In the present as were we still.
      It is spring.
      Time passes.
      First without words.
      I switch on.

[*Light on P.*

Bam at 3 head haught, Bom at 1 head bowed.

Pause.]

Not good.

I switch off.

[*Light off P.*]

I start again.

We are the last five.

It is spring.

Time passes.

First without words.

I switch on.

[*Light on P.*

Bam alone at 3 head haught.

Pause.]

Good.

I am alone.

It is spring.

Time passes.

First without words.

In the end Bom appears.

Reappears.

[*Bom enters at N, halts at 1 head bowed.*

Pause.

Bim enters at E, halts at 2 head haught.

Pause.

Bim exits at E followed by Bom.

Pause.

Bim enters at E, halts at 2 head bowed.

Pause.

Bem enters at N, halts at 1 head haught.

Pause.

Bem exits at N followed by Bim.

Pause.

Bem enters at N, halts at 1 head bowed.

Pause.

Bam exits at W followed by Bem.

Pause.

Bam enters at W, halts at 3 head bowed.

Pause.]

Good.

I switch off.

[*Light off P.*]

I start again.

We are the last five.

It is spring.

Time passes.

I switch on.

[*Light on P.*

Bam alone at 3 head haught.

Pause.]

Good.

I am alone.

It is spring.

Time passes.

Now with words.

In the end Bom appears.

Reappears.

[*Bom enters at N, halts at 1 head bowed.*]

BAM   Well?

BOM   [*Head bowed throughout.*] Nothing.

BAM   He didn't say anything?

BOM   No.

BAM   You gave him the works?

BOM   Yes.

BAM   And he didn't say anything?

BOM   No.

BAM   He wept?

BOM Yes.

BAM Screamed?

BOM Yes.

BAM Begged for mercy?

BOM Yes.

BAM But didn't say anything?

BOM No.

  V Not good.

     I start again.

BAM Well?

BOM Nothing.

BAM He didn't say it?

  V Good.

BOM No.

BAM You gave him the works?

BOM Yes.

BAM And he didn't say it?

BOM No.

BAM He wept?

BOM Yes.

BAM Screamed?

BOM Yes.

BAM Begged for mercy?

BOM Yes.

BAM But didn't say it?

BOM No.

BAM Then why stop?

BOM He passed out.

BAM And you didn't revive him?

BOM I tried.

BAM Well?

BOM I couldn't.

     [*Pause.*]

BAM It's a lie. [*Pause.*] He said it to you.

[*Pause.*] Confess he said it to you. [*Pause.*] You'll be given the works until you confess.

v   Good.

In the end Bim appears.

[*Bim enters at E, halts at 2 head haught.*]

BAM   [*to Bim*] Are you free?

BIM   Yes.

BAM   Take him away and give him the works until he confesses.

BIM   What must he confess?

BAM   That he said it to him.

BIM   Is that all?

BAM   Yes.

v   Not good.

I start again.

BAM   Take him away and give him the works until he confesses.

BIM   What must he confess?

BAM   That he said it to him.

BIM   Is that all?

BAM   And what.

v   Good.

BIM   Is that all?

BAM   Yes.

BIM   Then stop?

BAM   Yes.

BIM   Good. [*To Bom.*] Come.

[*Bim exits at E followed by Bom.*]

v   Good.

I am alone.

It is summer.

Time passes.

In the end Bim appears.

Reappears.

[*Bim enters at E, halts at 2 head bowed.*]

BAM   Well?

BIM   [*Head bowed throughout.*] Nothing.
BAM   He didn't say it?
BIM   No.
BAM   You gave him the works?
BIM   Yes.
BAM   And he didn't say it?
BIM   No.
  V   Not good.
      I start again.
BAM   Well?
BIM   Nothing.
BAM   He didn't say where?
  V   Good.
BIM   Where?
  V   Ah!
BAM   Where.
BIM   No.
BAM   You gave him the works?
BIM   Yes.
BAM   And he didn't say where?
BIM   No.
BAM   He wept?
BIM   Yes.
BAM   Screamed?
BIM   Yes.
BAM   Begged for mercy?
BIM   Yes.
BAM   But didn't say where?
BIM   No.
BAM   Then why stop?
BIM   He passed out.
BAM   And you didn't revive him?
BIM   I tried.
BAM   Well?

BIM   I couldn't.
       [*Pause.*]
BAM   It's a lie. [*Pause.*] He said where to you. [*Pause.*] Confess he said
       where to you. [*Pause.*] You'll be given the works until you confess.
  V   Good.
       In the end Bem appears.
       [*Bem enters at N, halts at 1 head haught.*]
BAM   [*to Bem*] Are you free?
BEM   Yes.
BAM   Take him away and give him the works until he confesses.
BEM   What must he confess?
BAM   That he said where to him.
BEM   Is that all?
BAM   Yes.
  V   Not good.
       I start again.
BAM   Take him away and give him the works until he confesses.
BEM   What must he confess?
BAM   That he said where to him.
BEM   Is that all?
BAM   And where.
  V   Good.
BEM   Is that all?
BAM   Yes.
BEM   Then stop?
BAM   Yes.
BEM   Good. [*to Bim*] Come.
       [*Bem exits at N followed by Bim.*]
  V   Good.
       I am alone.
       It is autumn.
       Time passes.
       In the end Bem appears.
       Reappears.

[*Bem enters at N, halts at 1 head bowed.*]

BAM   Well?

BEM   [*Head bowed throughout.*] Nothing.

BAM   He didn't say where?

BEM   No.

V   So on.

BAM   It's a lie. [*Pause.*] He said where to you. [*Pause.*] Confess he said
       where to you. [*Pause.*] You'll be given the works until you confess.

BEM   What must I confess?

BAM   That he said where to you.

BEM   Is that all?

BAM   And where.

BEM   Is that all?

BAM   Yes.

BEM   Then stop?

BAM   Yes. Come.

       [*Bam exits at W followed by Bem.*]

V   Good.

       It is winter.

       Time passes.

       In the end I appear.

       Reappear.

       [*Bam enters at W, halts at 3 head bowed.*]

V   Good.

       I am alone.

       In the present as were I still.

       It is winter.

       Without journey.

       Time passes.

       That is all.

       Make sense who may.

       I switch off.

       [*Light off P.*

       Pause.

       Light off V.]

NOTES

All That Fall. Written in English, 1956. First broadcast by the BBC Third Programme, January 13, 1957. First American broadcast, by National Public Radio, took place on Beckett's eightieth birthday, April 13, 1986. First publication by Grove in *Krapp's Last Tape and Other Dramatic Pieces*, 1960.

Act Without Words I. Written in French, 1956. (*Acte sans paroles I*). First performed with *Fin de partie* (*Endgame*) at the Royal Court Theatre, London, April 3, 1957, with music by John Beckett (a cousin). Published in *Fin de partie suivi de Acte sans paroles*. First publication by Grove in *Endgame, Followed by Act Without Words*.

Act Without Words II. Written in French, 1958 (*Acte sans paroles II*). First performed at the Institute of Contemporary Arts, London, January 25, 1960. First publication by Grove in *Krapp's Last Tape and Other Dramatic Pieces*. In France, it appeared in *Comédie et actes divers* (Minuit, 1966).

Krapp's Last Tape. Written in English, 1958. First British performance at the Royal Court Theatre, London, October 28, 1958. Published in *The Evergreen Review*, 1958. First American performance at the Provincetown Playhouse, New York, January 14, 1960 (part of a double bill with Edward Albee's *The Zoo Story*). First publication by Grove in *Krapp's Last Tape and Other Dramatic Pieces*.

Rough for Theatre I. Written in French in the late fifties or early sixties (*Fragment de théâtre*). First publication by Grove in *Ends and Odds*, 1977.

Rough for Theatre II. Written in French in the late fifties or early sixties (*Fragment de théâtre*). First publication by Grove in *Ends and Odds*.

Embers. Written in English, 1957. First broadcast by the BBC Third Programme, June 24, 1959. Appeared in *The Evergreen Review*, 1959. First publication by Grove in *Krapp's Last Tape and Other Dramatic Pieces*.

Rough for Radio I. Written in French, 1961 (*Esquisse radiophonique*). Appeared as "Sketch for Radio Play" in *Stereo Headphones*, 1976. First publication by Grove in *Ends and Odds*.

Rough for Radio II. Written in French some time in the early sixties (*Pochade radiophonique*). First broadcast, in Beckett's English translation, by the BBC on April 13, 1976 (the author's seventieth birthday). First publication by Grove in *Ends and Odds*.

Words and Music. Written in English, 1961. First broadcast by the BBC on December 7, 1962, with music composed by John Beckett. Appeared in *The Evergreen Review*, 1962. First publication by Grove in *Cascando and Other Short Dramatic Pieces*, 1969.

Cascando. Written in French, with the subtitle "Invention radiophonique pour musique et voix," early sixties. First broadcast on France Culture, April 3, 1963, with music composed by Marcel Mihalovici. Beckett's translation was published in *The Evergreen Review*, 1963. First British broadcast on the BBC Third Programme, October 6, 1964. First publication by Grove in *Cascando and Other Short Dramatic Pieces*.

Play. Written in English, 1962–63. The world premiere was in German (*Spiel*) at the Ulmer Theater, Ulm-Donau, June 14, 1963. First American performance at the Cherry Lane Theater, New York, January 4, 1964. Published in *The Evergreen Review*, 1964. First publication by Grove in *Cascando and Other Short Dramatic Pieces*.

Film. Written in English, 1963. Beckett's only screenplay, which was shot in New York in the summer of 1964 and led to his only visit to the United States. Directed by Alan Schneider; starring Buster Keaton. Shown at the Venice and New York Film Festivals, 1965. First Grove edition (with illustrations, production shots, and an essay by Alan Schneider), 1969. Also in *Cascando and Other Short Dramatic Pieces*.

The Old Tune. Beckett's English adaptation of *La Manivelle*, a play for radio by Robert Pinget. First broadcast by the BBC Third Programme, August 23, 1960. Published in *The Evergreen Review*, 1961. A stage version was first performed at the Royal Playhouse, New York, March 23, 1961. First publication by Grove in *Collected Shorter Plays*, 1984.

Come and Go. Written in English, 1965. The world premiere was in German (*Kommen und Gehen*) at the Schiller-Theater, Berlin, January 14, 1966. First English-language performance at the Peacock Theatre, Dublin, February 28, 1968. First American performance at the Theater for the New City, New York, October 23, 1975. First publication by Grove in *Cascando and Other Short Dramatic Pieces*.

Eh Joe. Written in English, spring 1965. Beckett's first work for television and also his directorial debut. First broadcast in German (*He, Joe*) by Süddeutscher Rundfunk, April 13, 1966 (the author's sixtieth birthday). The first English-language production was broadcast by BBC 2, July 4, 1966. First publication by Grove in *Cascando and Other Short Dramatic Pieces*.

Breath. Written in English, composition date unknown. First performed (in a version altered without Beckett's permission) at the Eden Theater, New York, June 16, 1969, as a curtain-raiser to Jacques Levy and Kenneth Tynan's review *Oh! Calcutta!* (the title is a pun on the French "O quel cul t'as," "Oh what an ass you have"). First publication by Grove in *First Love and Other Shorts*, 1974.

Not I. Written in English, spring 1972. First performed at the Repertory Theater of Lincoln Center, New York, November 22, 1972, as part of a Samuel Beckett Festival. First publication by Grove in *Ends and Odds*.

That Time. Written in English between June 1974 and August 1975. First performed at the Royal Court Theatre, London, May 20, 1976. First American production at the Arena Stage, Kreeger Theater, Washington, D.C., December 3 of the same year. First publication by Grove in *I Can't Go On, I'll Go On*, edited by Richard Seaver, 1976. Later included in *Ends and Odds*.

Footfalls. Written in English, 1975. First performed with *That Time* at the Royal Court Theatre, London, May 20, 1976. First American performance as above. First publication by Grove in *Ends and Odds*.

Ghost Trio. Written in English, 1975. First televised on BBC 2, April 17, 1977. First publication by Grove in *Ends and Odds*.

... but the clouds ... Written in English, October–November 1976. First televised on BBC 2, April 17, 1977. First publication by Grove in the expanded edition of *Ends and Odds*, 1981.

A Piece of Monologue. Written in English, 1977–79, for the American actor David Warrilow. It premiered at the Annex of La Mama, ETC, New York, December 14, 1979. The text appeared in *The Kenyon Review* that same year. First publication by Grove in *Rockaby and Other Short Pieces*, 1981.

Rockaby. Written in English, 1980. First performed at the Center for Theatre Research (SUNY Buffalo), April 8, 1981, as part of the university's Beckett Festival. First publication by Grove in *Rockaby and Other Short Pieces.*

Ohio Impromptu. Written in English, 1981, for a symposium at Ohio State University in honor of Beckett's seventy-fifth birthday. First performed in the Drake Union, Stadium 2 Theater, May 9, 1981. First publication by Grove in *Rockaby and Other Short Pieces.*

Quad. Written in English, 1981. A work for television, first broadcast in Germany (*Quadrat 1 + 2*) by Süddeutscher Rundfunk, October 8, 1981, directed by Beckett. First publication by Grove in *Collected Shorter Plays.*

Catastrophe. Written in French, 1982, in support of imprisoned playwright Václav Havel, who later became president of the Czech Republic. First performed in French at the Avignon Festival, July 12, 1982. First American production opened at the Harold Clurman Theater, New York, June 15, 1983. Beckett's English translation appeared in *The New Yorker*, January 1983. First publication by Grove in *Three Plays*, 1984.

Nacht und Träume. Written in English, 1982 (*Night and Dreams*). A work for television, first broadcast in Germany by Süddeutscher Rundfunk, May 19, 1983. First publication by Grove in *Collected Shorter Plays.*

What Where. Written in French, 1983 (*Quoi où*). Beckett's English version premiered with *Catastrophe* and *Ohio Impromptu* at the Harold Clurman Theater, New York, June 15, 1983. First publication by Grove in *Three Plays.*